SPACE AND STORAGE

Other Publications:

THE KODAK LIBRARY OF CREATIVE PHOTOGRAPHY
GREAT MEALS IN MINUTES
THE CIVIL WAR
PLANET EARTH
COLLECTOR'S LIBRARY OF THE CIVIL WAR
LIBRARY OF HEALTH
CLASSICS OF THE OLD WEST
THE EPIC OF FLIGHT
THE GOOD COOK
THE SEAFARERS
WORLD WAR II
THE OLD WEST
LIFE LIBRARY OF PHOTOGRAPHY (revised)
LIFE SCIENCE LIBRARY (revised)

For information on and a full description of any of the
Time-Life Books series listed above, please write:
Reader Information
Time-Life Books
541 North Fairbanks Court
Chicago, Illinois 60611

This volume is part of a series offering homeowners
detailed instructions on repairs, construction
and improvements they can undertake themselves.

HOME REPAIR
AND IMPROVEMENT

SPACE AND STORAGE

BY THE EDITORS OF
TIME-LIFE BOOKS

TIME-LIFE BOOKS
ALEXANDRIA, VIRGINIA

Time-Life Books Inc.
is a wholly owned subsidiary of
TIME INCORPORATED

Founder	Henry R. Luce 1898-1967

Editor-in-Chief	Henry Anatole Grunwald
President	J. Richard Munro
Chairman of the Board	Ralph P. Davidson
Executive Vice President	Clifford J. Grum
Editorial Director	Ralph Graves
Group Vice President, Books	Joan D. Manley

TIME-LIFE BOOKS INC.

Editor	George Constable
Executive Editor	George Daniels
Director of Design	Louis Klein
Board of Editors	Dale M. Brown, Thomas A. Lewis, Robert G. Mason, Ellen Phillips, Gerry Schremp, Gerald Simons, Rosalind Stubenberg, Kit van Tulleken, Henry Woodhead
Director of Administration	David L. Harrison
Director of Research	Carolyn L. Sackett
Director of Photography	John Conrad Weiser
President	Reginald K. Brack Jr.
Senior Vice President	William Henry
Vice Presidents	George Artandi, Stephen L. Bair, Robert A. Ellis, Juanita T. James, Christopher T. Linen, James L. Mercer, Joanne A. Pello, Paul R. Stewart

HOME REPAIR AND IMPROVEMENT

Editorial Staff for Space and Storage

Editor	William Frankel
Picture Editors	Adrian G. Allen, Kaye Neil Noble
Designer	Herbert Quarmby
Associate Designer	Robert McKee
Text Editors	Don Earnest, Anne Horan, Robert Tschirky
Staff Writers	Sally French, Kumait Jawdat, Ruth Kelton, Michael Luftman, Don Nelson
Researchers	Tom Lashnits, Brian McGinn, Scot Terrell, Henry Wiencek
Copy Coordinator	Ricki Tarlow
Picture Coordinator	Barbara S. Simon
Art Associates	Faye Eng, Kaye Sherry Hirsh, Richard Salcer
Editorial Assistant	Karen Z. Barnard

Editorial Operations

Design	Anne B. Landry (art coordinator); James J. Cox (quality control)
Research	Phyllis K. Wise (assistant director), Louise D. Forstall
Copy Room	Diane Ullius (director), Celia Beattie
Production	Gordon E. Buck, Peter Inchauteguiz

Correspondents: Elisabeth Kraemer (Bonn); Margot Hapgood, Dorothy Bacon (London); Miriam Hsia, Susan Jonas, Lucy T. Voulgaris (New York); Maria Vincenza Aloisi, Josephine du Brusle (Paris); Ann Natanson (Rome). Valuable assistance was also given by: Lesley Coleman (London); Carolyn T. Chubet, Christina Lieberman (New York); Mimi Murphy (Rome).

THE CONSULTANTS: Miron Waskiw, the general consultant for this book, is an architect and the founder of Skiltech, a New York center that offers courses in home repair, woodworking and furniture design. An outgrowth of these courses is *Know-How,* a home-repair book of which he is co-author.

Harris Mitchell, special consultant for Canada, has been working in the field of home repair and improvement for more than two decades. His experience ranges from editing *Canadian Homes* magazine to writing a syndicated newspaper column, "You Wanted to Know," and he is the editor or author of a number of books on home improvement.

Don Boyce, a cabinetmaker specializing in custom-designed interior furniture, prepared the plans for and built the bunk bed and room divider project that begins on page 68.

Louis Potts, a practical master of carpentry and electrical work, has been engaged in construction projects for more than 35 years.

Eric Stand, a cabinetmaker who teaches classes in woodworking, prepared the plans for and built the wall storage units on page 6.

© 1977, 1976 Time-Life Books Inc. All rights reserved.
No part of this book may be reproduced in any form or by any electronic or mechanical means, including information storage and retrieval devices or systems, without prior written permission from the publisher, except that brief passages may be quoted for reviews.
Fifth printing. Revised 1984. Printed in U.S.A.
Published simultaneously in Canada.
Library of Congress catalogue card number 76-360447.
School and library distribution by Silver Burdett Company, Morristown, New Jersey.

TIME-LIFE is a trademark of Time Incorporated U.S.A.

Contents

1

Making This Book Work for You

Putting things within reach. The key to using space effectively lies in storing items where you can get at them conveniently. If you approach the problem with imagination and care you can wind up with a piece of furniture as handsome as the wall-storage unit at left. By studying the techniques in this volume and the construction plans that begin on page 84, you can confidently go about building these four modular units, each designed around the same basic shell. The special features shown here—glass display case, drop-leaf desk, drawers and shelves—and their locations and numbers can be varied according to your own needs and preferences.

Even in a comfortable and pleasant home, the day inevitably comes when the clothes, books, toys, tools and kitchen utensils accumulated over the years crowd all the shelves and closets that seemed quite adequate when you moved in. Fortunately, organizing space more efficiently and creating new storage capacity are tasks any imaginative homeowner can accomplish with time-tested, straightforward do-it-yourself techniques. The skills required are simple; they range from using tools correctly to joining pieces of wood together. The projects in this book have been carefully selected to present all the necessary working techniques in real situations and, within those situations, in their logical relationships to one another. As a result, the projects include procedures that will be valuable to the home craftsman in many additional ways.

The scope of this volume is, therefore, a great deal broader than the title alone may suggest. Absorbing its contents will, among other benefits, serve to explain thoroughly:

Every basic woodworking tool. As you proceed through the explanations of basic techniques found on the following pages, you will, with surprising speed, acquire an easy familiarity with all the traditional hand tools as well as the most useful power tools—from chisels to routers, awls to electric drills, planes to power saws.

Essential woodworking skills. For the home craftsman, nothing surpasses wood as an attractive, long-lasting, easy to work with, widely available and still reasonably inexpensive building material. Furthermore, wood is a more forgiving material than metal or plastic: small errors made in cutting or joining wood can easily be corrected or concealed. By starting with simple applications of tools, you will quickly learn the correct ways to measure, mark, cut and join wood, and how to hone your new-found skills to keen efficiency. By using a sequential approach, you will advance from the basic methods for measuring, cutting and fastening to the refinements of these and other skills that are required to build cabinets, shelves, drawers and beds. It is the basic theme of this book that a simple box is the traditional building block for all types of storage projects; that if you first learn to build boxes, you can then, by adding drawer-glide assemblies, transform those boxes into drawers; or by installing hinges and adding doors, create cabinets. By selecting the most suitable fasteners, you can hang those cabinets securely on any wall.

What you should know about wood. You will find a detailed discussion of the various commercial grades of softwoods, hardwoods and plywoods to help you choose the right material for any project; you will learn how to choose the right saw to cut it, the right glue to join it and the right sandpaper to smooth and finish it.

Methods of planning your own projects. The new skills at your command can spark the imagination. But first you must develop your ideas into workable plans, cutting diagrams for the most economical use of lumber or plywood and exact shopping lists for hardware. The chapter on job planning simplifies dealing with these often intimidating chores. In addition you will learn how to incorporate ready-made items into your own plans.

How to recognize craftsmanship. Once you yourself have learned how to make joints strong and true, to finish surfaces smoothly, to install hardware properly, there are added dividends: you will be much better equipped to judge craftsmanship—or lack of it—when you shop for commercial pieces of furniture, and you will be more competent in talking to professional carpenters and in judging their work.

Using the book within this book. Complete plans and instructions are furnished for constructing projects in bedrooms, kitchens, attics, closets, under staircases and even inside walls. However, even if you never build these specific projects, the wide variety of skills that are spelled out in the step-by-step presentations can be applied to any project that you create originally or wish to adapt from any source. The wall-storage project shown on page 6 and explained on pages 84 through 97, for example, includes directions for these diverse procedures: how to install drawer glides, continuous hinges, movable shelves, fixed shelves, glass doors, drop-leaf desk fronts, drawer pulls and plastic laminate. The more complete list at right offers a quick-reference guide to the innumerable techniques and procedures discussed throughout the book.

If you have never tried your hand at woodworking, start simply: shop for the best buys in good basic tools and begin acquiring a home tool kit appropriate to your immediate ambitions. But before you tackle even a simple woodworking project, get some pieces of scrap lumber and practice with them. Pick up your brand new handsaw and use it on the scrap. Develop the skill to make eye and arm work together to saw a straight cut with minimum effort. (The trick is never to force, let the sharp teeth of the saw do the real work.) Heft your hammer; find the place near the bottom of the handle that feels best to you. Drive nails of various penny ratings into the scrap boards. Discover the satisfaction of driving a nail home with a minimum of blows. Drill a number of pilot holes. Insert screws of appropriate size. Plane the scrap. Sand it.

When you feel comfortable with your tools, set about making the basic box; pages 12 through 16 tell you how to build it. Plan the job. Buy the materials you will need. Cut the wood. Glue and nail the joints. Sand the surfaces. And then apply the finish of your choice.

It takes only patience to develop the rudimentary skills. Your confidence will grow more quickly than you dream. And with that confidence you will be ready for the satisfaction of tackling your own space and storage problems with creative craftsmanship.

The Techniques of Woodworking

This is not just a book on how to use space wisely; it is a primer of many woodworking techniques. For instance, if you simply want to put up shelves, this book, properly utilized, will tell you how to measure, buy wood and cut it, what types of fasteners and supports to use, and how to drill correctly. Or, using other techniques in this volume, you can design a chest of drawers—making the cabinet any size you like, to hold as many drawers as you need. And so forth.

The complete index that begins on page 125 includes definitions of terms that are peculiar to woodworking as well as references to the tools, materials and different kinds of storage units described in the book. To use the index creatively in working out your own projects and designs, first list the elements you wish to incorporate in the plans; then look in the index for specific entries. For quick reference, use the list below to locate those basic techniques needed for planning and executing nearly any carpentry project in the home.

Tool Kit for All Projects

Tools used for the projects in this volume are shown at right. Buy the more specialized items only as you need them.

☐ To measure and mark you will need a level at least 24 inches long; a steel square; a combination square; a spring-loaded steel tape ruler at least 12 feet long; a scratch awl, which makes a finer and less conspicuous line than a pencil; and a center punch to make starting points in metal for drill bits.

☐ Cutting tools encompass the crosscut saw for across-the-grain work; a hacksaw for metal; a backsaw for use in a miter box; a block plane; wood chisels, and a cold chisel for use with harder materials, such as tiles and plaster. To keep tools well honed, a sharpening stone and machine oil are recommended.

☐ To hold pieces of wood tightly together while glue sets and you put in nails and screws, you will need bar clamps to span large pieces; general-purpose C clamps; hand screws with nonmarring wood jaws; and corner clamps, which ensure that joints will be square. Also useful is a woodworking vise to hold various pieces securely and thus free your hands for other work.

☐ Tools for joining and finishing include a curved-claw hammer; an assortment of screwdrivers, both standard tip and Phillips; locking-grip pliers; and an adjustable wrench. Also necessary will be a rubber mallet for striking wood chisels and tapping snug wood joints together; a set of hex wrenches for hardware installation; nail sets, with tips $1/32$ inch and $2/32$ inch in diameter, to countersink fasteners; and a putty knife for wood filler.

☐ Power tools require a substantial investment, but they pay off in speed, finer craftsmanship and muscle power saved. An electric drill is essential, preferably a ⅜-inch, variable-speed model. A circular saw makes easy work of long straight cuts. Also handy are a saber saw, sometimes called a jigsaw, for cutting around curves and in tight spots, and an orbital sander. A router is a versatile tool that makes dadoes and rabbets, and trims edges faster and straighter than a circular saw. And goggles are a necessary safety device when operating any power tool.

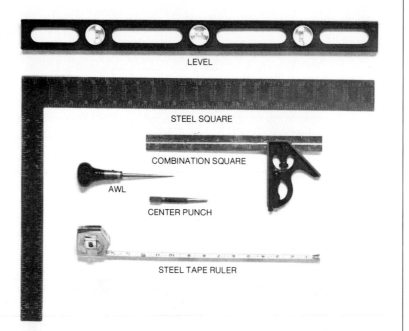

LEVEL

STEEL SQUARE

COMBINATION SQUARE

AWL

CENTER PUNCH

STEEL TAPE RULER

HACKSAW

BACKSAW

COLD CHISEL

MITER BOX

BLOCK PLANE

MACHINE OIL

CROSSCUT SAW

WOOD CHISELS

SHARPENING STONE

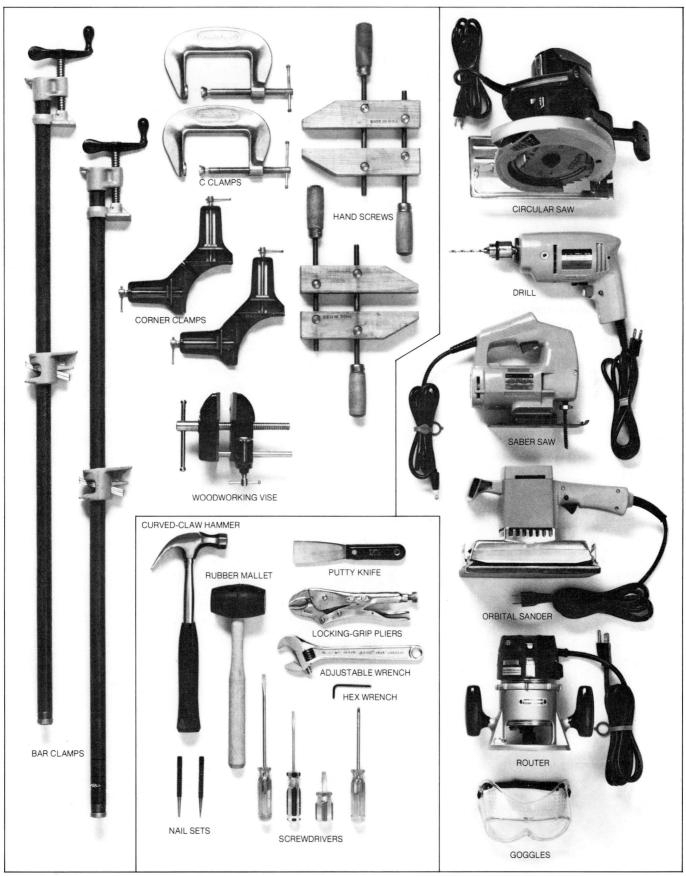

C CLAMPS

HAND SCREWS

CORNER CLAMPS

WOODWORKING VISE

BAR CLAMPS

CURVED-CLAW HAMMER

RUBBER MALLET

PUTTY KNIFE

LOCKING-GRIP PLIERS

ADJUSTABLE WRENCH

HEX WRENCH

NAIL SETS

SCREWDRIVERS

CIRCULAR SAW

DRILL

SABER SAW

ORBITAL SANDER

ROUTER

GOGGLES

Begin with the Box—A Basic Building Block

The basic building block for all storage units is the box. Place a box on its side and add horizontal dividers, and it becomes a bookshelf; add doors and it becomes a cabinet; attach tracks and it becomes a drawer.

All boxes, whatever their use, share one common element of construction: the right-angle corner. The joint most commonly used to make a right-angle corner—because it is the easiest—is the butt, which is used to illustrate the construction of a simple box on the pages immediately following. Although it is sufficient for many purposes, the butt joint is, however, the weakest. Of the many alternatives of varying complexity and strength, five joints stand out as the most useful: the rabbet, dado, miter, end lap and mid-lap; they are described on pages 17 through 23.

Many of the tools, techniques and procedures employed in making a butt joint are applicable to the other types:

□ MEASURING. The cardinal principle of good craftsmanship is to check and recheck the accuracy of your measurements. This rule, unfortunately, too often falls victim to impatience. Even before measuring, check the end of every piece of wood with a right-angle square; if the piece is not precisely squared, the subsequent measurements are bound to be inaccurate. Measurements should be rechecked after you have marked a piece of wood and before you start to cut. Then check yet again after cutting.

□ MARKING. Always scratch your measurements on wood with an awl; whereas a pencil leaves a relatively wide mark difficult to erase, marks from an awl's fine point are more precise and, if necessary, easily sanded away.

Assembling the Basic Box

1 **Measuring the wood.** To make the first side of a box with butt joints, lay a tape measure on a piece of wood parallel to an edge. Using an awl, scratch a point on the wood to indicate the length you want minus the thickness of the wood to which it is to be joined. For example, if the side of the box is to be 11 inches long and the abutting piece is ¾ inch thick, the wood should be cut to a length of 10¼ inches.

□ CUTTING. As a saw cuts, its blade chews up an amount of wood equal to the thickness of the blade. This loss, called kerf, must be taken into account both when measuring and when cutting. Always saw on the "waste" side of the mark made for cutting so that the kerf will not affect the measured area. For the same reason, when cutting several sections from one piece of wood, measure and cut each piece individually: measure and cut the first piece, and only then measure the next piece.

There are many kinds of cutting tools, some much more specialized than others for shaping joints. For example, for work with boxes built from pieces of wood less than 2 inches thick and no more than 4 inches wide—such as the box on the following pages—the rigid backsaw used in conjunction with a miter box is without peer. For larger boxes, power cutting tools *(pages 10-11)* provide greater accuracy with considerably less effort than hand saws.

□ ASSEMBLING. The wood adhesive most often used is white glue. Though only one of a wide variety of adhesives, some of which are compared on page 61, white glue is favored because it becomes transparent as it dries. Follow the instructions on the container.

When nails are combined with glue, they strengthen a box substantially. Use a finishing nail whose length is three times the thickness of the piece of wood into which it is being driven initially and—unless otherwise indicated—always hammer it in at a slight angle to increase its holding power. Blunt the point of each nail with a light hammer blow before driving it in; a blunted nail crushes the fibers of the wood instead of parting them, and is less likely to split the wood.

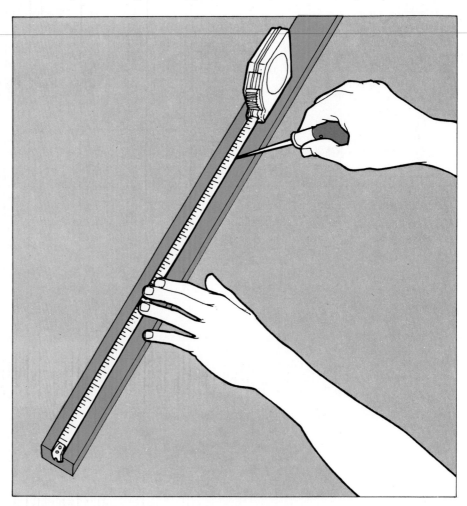

2 **Drawing a guideline.** Place the handle of a combination square flush against the edge of the wood and position it so that the ruler intersects the awl mark made in Step 1; scratch another awl line across the board through the mark.

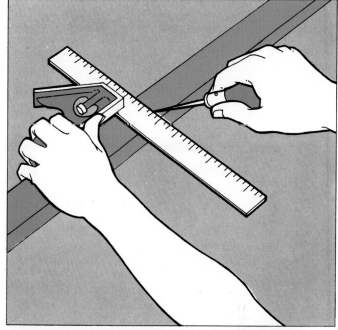

3 **Cutting the wood.** Place the wood in a miter box *(below)* and set the angle at 90°. Align the blade to cut just barely on the waste side of the awl line. Begin sawing on the backstroke and continue in long, smooth strokes, to ensure a clean cut. Check the newly cut end for squareness and smooth it down, if necessary, with medium-grade sandpaper. Measure, mark and cut the other three sides in the same manner. Compare opposing sides with each other to make sure that the measurements are exactly the same.

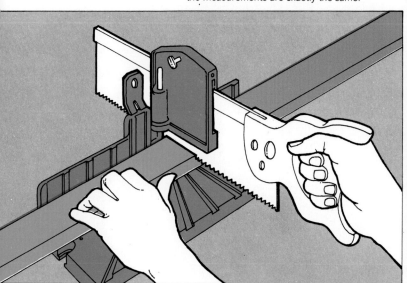

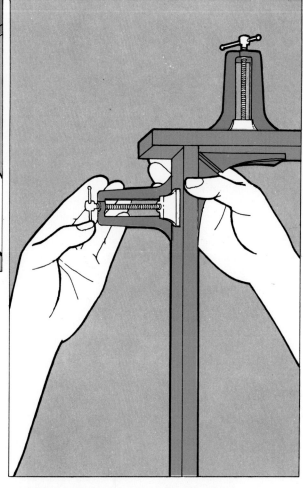

4 **Positioning the first two sides.** Place one of the pieces of wood on its edge in a corner clamp, with the end projecting at least 2 inches beyond the corner of the clamp. Tighten the clamp screw. Place the second piece in the clamp so it butts against the first piece and tighten the second clamp screw. (If the box is to be rectangular rather than square, join the sides in a consistent order: either butt the longer piece against the shorter piece, or the shorter against the longer, but make sure the order is the same for both joints. Butting the wrong piece will give the wrong dimensions.) Remove the first piece of wood from the clamp.

5 Applying glue. Spread glue on the end of the side that is still in the clamp, using just enough for an even coating. Return the first piece of wood to the clamp so that its end is flush with the outside edge of the piece already in the clamp; tighten the piece of wood in place.

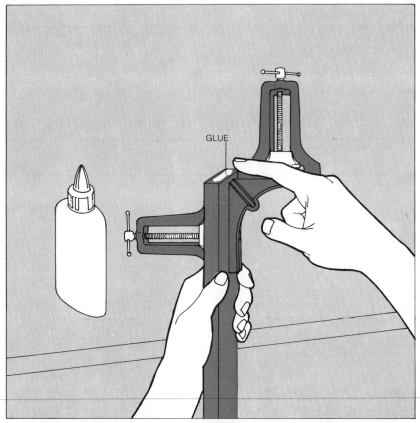

GLUE

6 Securing the joint. Blunt the point of a nail and position it at a point about one third of the way in on the top board. Holding the nail at a slight angle, drive it through the top board to secure it to the lower piece of wood (below); stop hammering before the nailhead meets the surface. Measuring from the other edge, drive in a second blunted nail at a point one third in from the end. If the board is wider than 6 inches, space the nails about 2 inches apart.

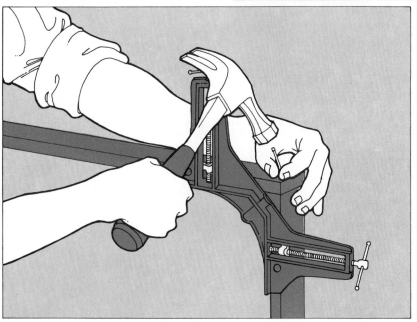

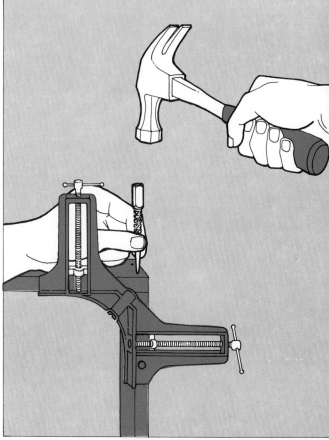

7 Finishing the joint. Using a nail set no larger than the nailhead, drive the nails to just below the surface of the wood. Wipe away any excess glue, and set the joint aside to dry. Remove the corner clamps and repeat Steps 4 through 7 to make the second joint of the box.

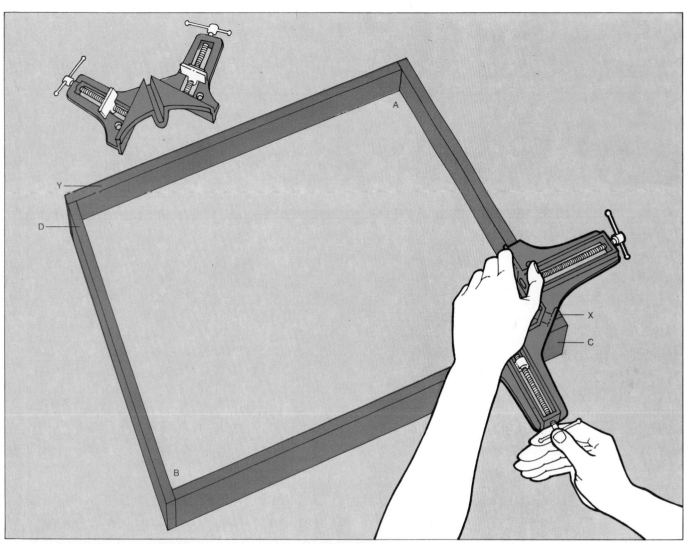

8 **Joining the four sides.** Lay the two L-shaped sections already joined at A and B on a flat surface so that the unjoined corners abut: X against C and D against Y. Place the clamps over the two new corners. Then loosen the matching screw on each clamp to free one of the sections and remove it. Apply glue to ends D and X, return the free section to its place in the clamps, tighten the clamp screws and nail the new joints in place. Set aside to dry.

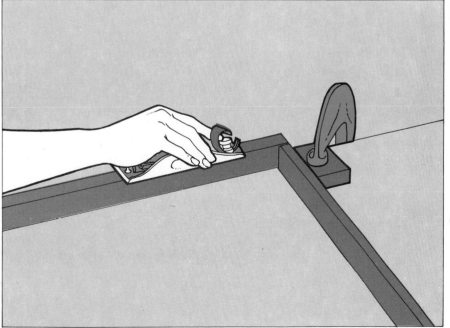

9 **Truing the joint.** To true up any minor misalignments at the corners, remove excess wood with a block plane (as shown) or a wood chisel. Brace the joint against a small block of wood held tightly with a C clamp to the top of a workbench, and begin planing or chiseling several inches away from the joint. Repeat the truing process with the other joints. Then smooth the surfaces with medium-grade sandpaper.

10 **Marking off the bottom.** Lay the sides on a large board from which the bottom will be cut; align one corner and two sides, and mark off the other two sides with an awl. If it matters which surface of the wood will show, be sure to mark the correct surface. Different kinds of saws splinter the wood on different surfaces: for a crosscut saw, mark the surface that will be visible; for a saber or a circular saw, mark the surface that will not be seen. Cut just outside the awl lines.

11 **Attaching the bottom.** Sand all four edges with medium-grade sandpaper. Spread glue along the bottom edges of the four sides and place the bottom in position. Secure the bottom with nails at 4-inch intervals and countersink the nails. Using a putty knife (*below*), fill the countersunk indentations, the spaces between the bottom and sides, and any scratches or dents with wood putty. To keep excess putty off the wood, apply enough pressure to the knife to keep the blade slightly bent while spreading the putty toward you. Set the box aside to dry.

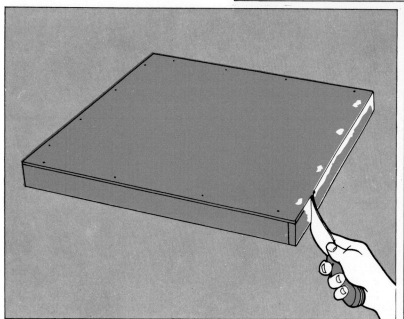

12 **Sanding the finished box.** Sand the entire surface of the box, beginning with a medium-grade sandpaper, then advancing to a fine grade. If you are sanding by hand, wrap half a sheet of sandpaper around a small block of wood and work with the grain, keeping the sandpaper flat against the surface of the box.

Strengthening the Basic Box

When storage boxes are to be pushed and pulled (as they are when used as drawers), or if they are to be hung on walls (cabinets) or loaded with heavy objects (tool chests), the corners should be strengthened. This can be done by making joints that are stronger than the butt type used for the basic box on the preceding pages; also, the box can be reinforced by bracing or framing.

The butt joint is relatively weak because the area of contact at the corners is limited to only one surface on each piece of wood. The stronger joints, however, may have many shared surfaces, which are formed by cutting the ends of two pieces of wood into various complementary shapes. The drawings at right show the areas of contact for six types of joints—those most commonly used for building storage units—and outline their strengths and weaknesses. Instructions for making each type begin overleaf.

Whichever type of joint you opt for, it can be made stronger by adding braces. Metal angle irons in the corners of small boxes, for instance, add rigidity and help prevent warping. Such braces are also useful for repairing loose joints.

For larger boxes, braces of solid wood give still greater support. Such blocks can be glued and nailed inside the corners and along the full length of the joint. Wood blocks are particularly useful for making boxes from plywood, which is made of several layers of wood pressed together. Joints made at the ends of most types of plywood are relatively weak; glue applied there seeps into the plies instead of adhering to the surface, and nails or screws separate the plies and do not hold securely. Wood blocks solve this particular reinforcing problem.

The largest—and strongest—boxes generally are constructed over a wooden frame, thereby reducing stress on the corners. Basic techniques for building frames are on page 24.

Before choosing a joining technique, consider the time you want to give to a project and how important the subtleties of craftsmanship are to you. In any case, practice on scraps of lumber before tackling a real job with expensive wood.

Types of Wood Joints

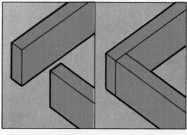

Butt. As indicated on the preceding pages, the area of contact for this joint is limited to the end of one side that butts against the surface of a second side. It is the weakest type of joint, but it is also the easiest to make; when reinforced with braces, the butt can hold together a large box if not subjected to too much weight.

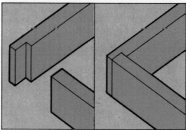

Rabbet. The shared area of contact is increased by joining one piece of wood to a notch cut out of the end of a second piece. This type of joint construction also allows nails or screws to be used on both pieces at right angles to each other, which creates a strong, locking effect.

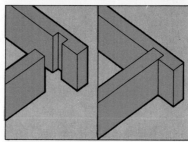

Dado. To make this joint a groove is cut into the surface of one piece of wood so that a second piece of wood can butt into it. Most drawers are constructed with dadoes, since this type of joint withstands stress from several directions.

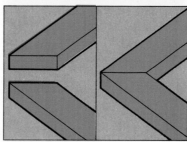

Miter. For a miter joint, the ends of two pieces of wood are cut at a 45° angle. The miter, which is only marginally stronger than the butt, is used almost exclusively for appearance: the joint successfully conceals the exposed ends of each piece of wood. It is the standard type used for picture frames and small decorative boxes.

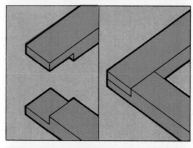

End lap. To cut this joint, half the thickness of the wood is removed from the end of each corner piece. Cutting the notches so that they fit together precisely requires care and skill, but the final result is a very strong joint that is the preferred type in building frames for boxes.

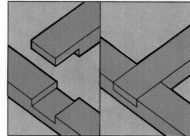

Mid-lap. A variation of the end-lap joint, this type is formed by fitting the end of one piece of wood into the middle of another, with half the thickness removed from the area shared by each piece. It is used exclusively on frames for boxes —especially large plywood boxes such as cupboards, for which the additional strength provided by the frame is essential.

The Rabbet Joint

1 Marking the wood. Hold the two pieces of wood together in a position approximating a butt joint. With the edge of the vertical piece as a guide, use an awl to scratch a line across the surface of the horizontal piece (drawing). Then use a ruler and the awl to extend the line on the wood to the desired depth of the notch for the rabbet.

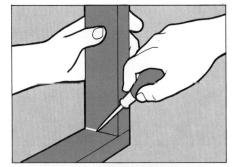

2 Starting the notch. Place the marked piece of wood flat in the miter box. Align the backsaw so that the kerf will be on the waste side of the awl line; then cut the wood to the depth of the awl line that was marked on the edge.

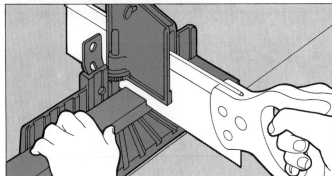

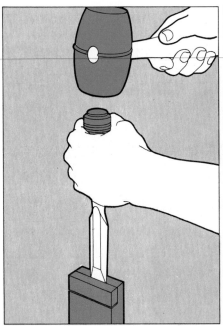

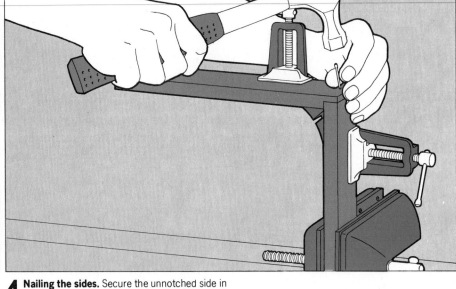

3 Chiseling out the notch. Set the piece of wood in a woodworking vise with cut end up. Position the blade of a chisel in the end, perpendicular to the saw cut and at the same depth as the cut. With the beveled face of the chisel on the same side as the cut, use a rubber mallet to hammer the chisel into the wood until the block falls away. Sand the surfaces of both ends that will be in contact, place the two in a corner clamp and check for fit. Chisel or sand if necessary. Remove one piece, apply glue and replace in the clamp.

4 Nailing the sides. Secure the unnotched side in the vise. Place a nail one third the distance from each edge of the notched piece and hammer both nails into the second piece. Loosen the clamp and countersink. To strengthen the joint further, hammer a third nail through the center of the butt piece into the notched piece, positioning the nail at a right angle to the other nails. Retighten the clamp and allow the joint to dry.

The Dado Joint

1 Marking the dado groove. Determine how far from the end of the wood you want the dado groove to be, and indicate the position with a small mark. To establish the outside edge of the groove, place the handle of a combination square flush against the side of the wood, aligning the ruler with the small mark. Make a line with the awl across the surface. To establish the inside edge, butt the second piece of wood against the first, align its outer edge with the awl mark and scratch a line along the inside edge of the butting piece (drawing). Using a ruler and the awl, extend the two lines down both edges to the desired depth of the groove.

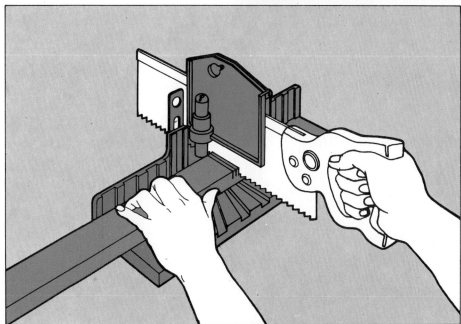

2 Cutting the groove. Place the marked piece of wood in a miter box and saw along the inside of each awl mark to the desired depth of the groove. One or two additional cuts sawed into the wood between the first two saw cuts will make it easier to chisel out the groove.

3 Chiseling out the groove. Set the cut piece of wood on its edge in a woodworking vise. Position the blade of a chisel at the edge of the wood and at the same depth as the saw cuts; hold the chisel perpendicular to the wood, with its beveled side facing the cuts. Use a rubber mallet to hammer the chisel into the wood to begin a rough groove (drawing). Reverse the wood in the vise and begin chiseling the groove from the other edge of the wood. Next turn the chisel so the beveled side faces the bottom of the groove and finish cutting out the groove. Hammer gently to prevent the wood from splitting. Then smooth the groove with sandpaper.

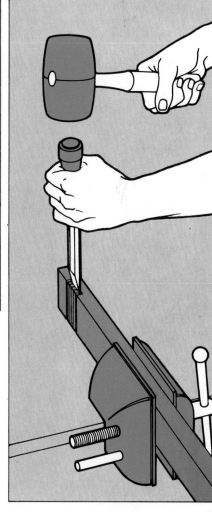

4 **Tapering the butt piece.** If the butt piece does not fit into the groove, brace its end against a block clamped to the worktable. With the chisel's beveled face down as shown, use it to taper the width of the wood slightly. Try fitting the butt piece again. Repeat until the butt piece fits snugly into the groove, each time chiseling as little as possible to avoid removing too much.

5 **Joining the sides.** Secure the butt piece perpendicularly in a woodworking vise and apply glue to all surfaces to be joined. Place the groove over the end of the butt piece, and a corner clamp on the joint. Position two blunted finishing nails on the grooved piece, one third of the way in from each edge (drawing); drive them in as far as the surface of the wood. Loosen the corner clamp and countersink the nails. Retighten the clamp.

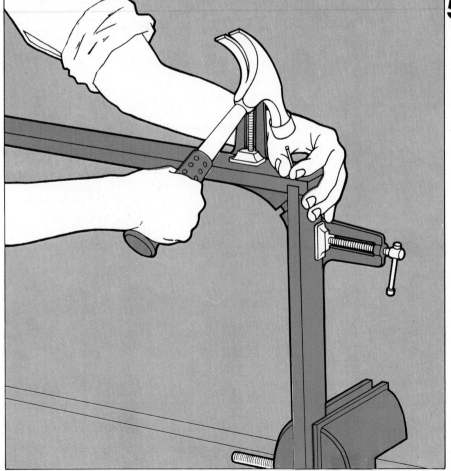

The Miter Joint

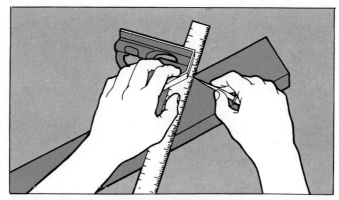

1 Marking a miter. Place a combination square slightly in from the end of the piece of wood, with its handle flush against the edge of the wood, and the ruler at a 45° angle across the surface. Use an awl to mark a line across the surface (as shown). When marking the miter at the other end, turn the square over so the angle of the second cut will be the reverse of the first.

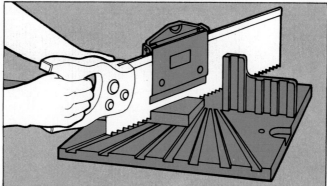

2 Cutting the miter. Adjust the miter box so that the backsaw will cut at a 45° angle. Place the marked piece of wood flat in the miter box and align it so that the backsaw kerf will be on the waste side of the awl mark. Cut all the way through the wood. Then mark and cut the second piece of wood in the same manner.

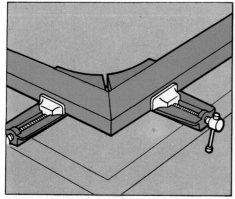

3 Checking the miter. Place the two pieces of wood in a corner clamp. If the ends do not fit snugly, remove both of the pieces from the clamp and lightly sand the rough areas. Check the fit again and repeat the procedure until the two ends fit exactly. Remove one piece of wood from the clamp, apply glue to both surfaces of the joint and return the loose piece to the clamp.

4 Nailing the joint. Place one piece of the miter joint in a woodworking vise. Drive at least one blunted finishing nail into the center of the top piece of wood, about 1 inch from the end, into the second piece (drawing); for the greatest holding power, hammer the nail straight in. Loosen the clamp and countersink the nail. Remove the joint from the vise, turn the joint around and put it back in the vise. Drive at least one finishing nail into the joint from the other side and countersink the nail. Retighten the corner clamp.

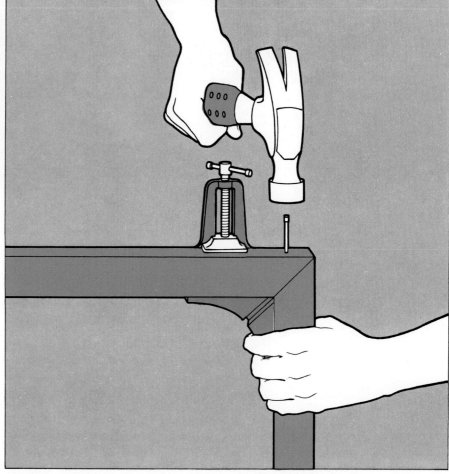

The End-Lap Joint

1 Marking the notch. Make sure the ends of both pieces of wood are squared. Lap the end of one piece over the end of the second piece so each end is flush with the outside edge of the other. With the inside edge of the top piece as a guide, use an awl to mark a line across the surface of the bottom piece (drawing); using a ruler, extend the line halfway down the edge. Turn the two pieces over, align their edges again and mark the second piece in the same manner. Place one piece of wood in a miter box and saw on the waste side of the awl mark to the depth marked on the edge. Make several more parallel cuts in the area to be notched. Then cut the second piece of wood in the same manner.

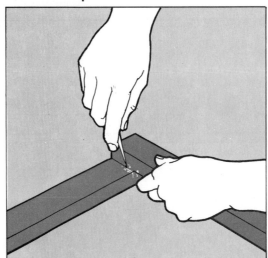

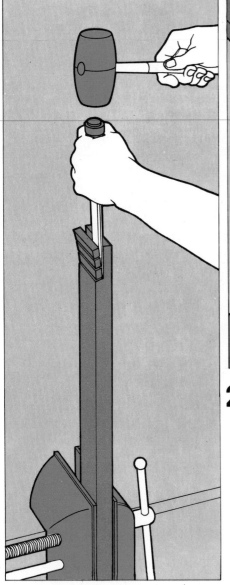

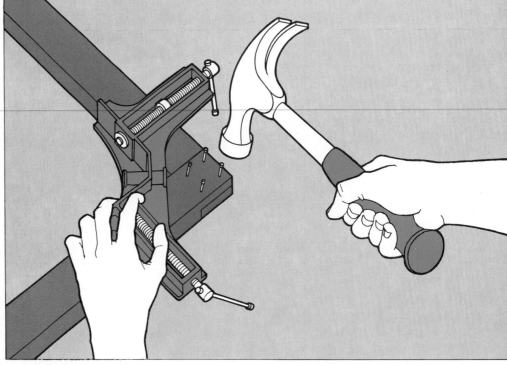

2 Chiseling out the notch. Place one of the pieces of wood in a woodworking vise with the cut end up. Position the chisel at the same depth as the cuts, with the beveled face of the chisel toward the cuts. Hammer the chisel into the wood with a rubber mallet to start the notch (as shown). Reverse the chisel so that the beveled side faces away from the cuts. Drive the chisel down until all the blocks have fallen away. Repeat with the second piece of wood. Smooth both notches with sandpaper and place the pieces in a corner clamp to check for fit; chisel or sand as necessary. Remove one piece of wood from the clamp, apply glue to all of the surfaces that are to be joined and return the pieces to the clamp.

3 Nailing the joint. Lay the clamped pieces of wood flat. Drive four blunted finishing nails, each slightly shorter than the total thickness of the joint, at a slight angle through the top piece and into the second piece; countersink the nails. To reinforce the joint, turn the wood over and drive another, longer finishing nail through the top piece and into the second piece, but this time drive the nail at a sharp angle.

Another kind of lap. This joint combines the grooving and notching techniques used in making the dado joint and the end-lap joint. As shown on page 19 in Steps 2 and 3 for the dado joint, cut and chisel a groove the desired distance from the end of a piece of wood; make the groove as wide as the piece of wood to be joined. To mark and cut the notch in the end of the second piece of wood, follow directions given in Steps 1 and 2 for the end-lap joint. Then place the two pieces of wood in a corner clamp to make sure they fit together snugly. Sand the rough areas if necessary. Remove the notched piece, apply glue to both notch and groove and replace the piece in the clamp (drawing). Secure the joint with finishing nails as described in Step 3 for the end-lap joint.

Wood. Rectangular wood blocks (*top*) are frequently used to reinforce a joint along its entire length. They also make it possible to join two thin pieces of wood; attaching a wood block to one piece of wood creates an edge to which the second piece can be joined. Triangular blocks (*middle*) occupy less space than square blocks and look neater. Attach any wood block with glue, then secure it with nails; stagger the nails as shown, so as not to split the wood. Gussets (*bottom*), triangles of thin plywood glued and nailed to the corners, add extra strength to a bottomless box, such as an unbacked bookcase.

The Mid-Lap Joint

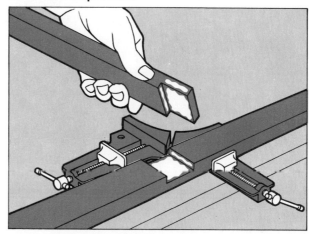

Types of Joint Braces

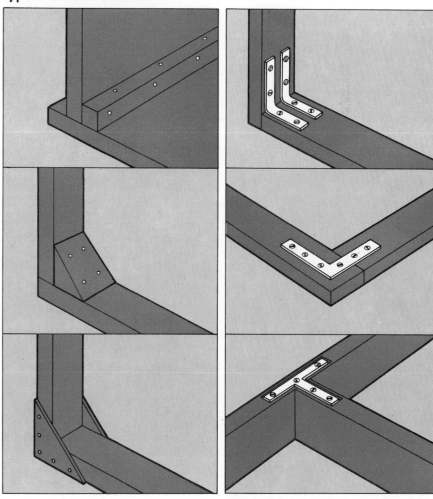

Metal. These devices can strengthen or repair a joint. The inside corner brace (*top*) and the flat corner brace (*middle*) reinforce a corner joint; the T brace (*bottom*) gives added support to the joints on a box frame. Braces can be screwed directly onto the surface of the wood or they can be mortised in (*page 35*).

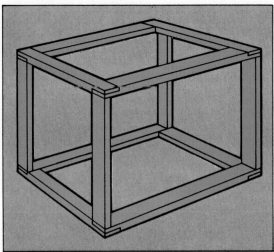

Framing for Greater Strength

Box frames. If thin pieces of lumber or plywood are to be used for a box, the box must be built around a frame. To build one, make two identical squares or rectangles, using the type of corner joint you prefer (end-lap joints are shown). Connect the two with butt joints at the four corners, using pieces of wood of equal length. For larger boxes (*below*) reinforce the top and bottom of the frame with ribs (attached here by mid-lap joints). To complete the framed box, attach the sides in the manner shown for attaching the bottom to the basic box (*page 16, Steps 10-12*).

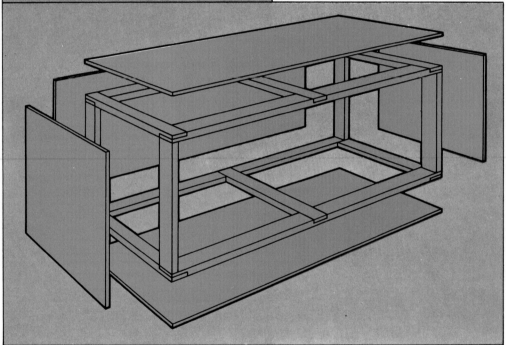

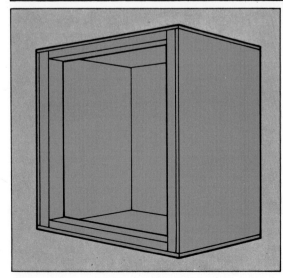

Face frames. If a door is to be put on a box made of thin lumber or plywood, a frame secured within the opening and flush with the sides of the box will supply all the surface area needed so that hinges can be securely mounted. Cut the four sides of the frame, making sure they fit precisely inside the box. Apply glue to the sides of the frame that will butt against the box. Then reinsert the frame—sides first, then top and bottom—so that its face is flush with the face of the box. Drive and countersink nails.

Correcting Mistakes

Cutting a dado—or any other kind of groove—in the wrong place or driving a nail where it is not wanted are common errors that anyone working with wood is bound to make sooner or later.

A dado groove that has been mislocated and then left empty not only looks unprofessional but it also weakens the piece of wood. However, the groove can be filled in with a wood strip that is hardly noticeable and the piece will be as strong as ever.

A nail that has been hammered all the way in at the wrong place, or one whose head has been countersunk, can be removed only by cutting away the wood with a chisel until the nail is sufficiently exposed to be grasped and pried out. The area around the nail will be marred, but the damage can be concealed by filling in the excavation with wood putty and sanding the area smooth.

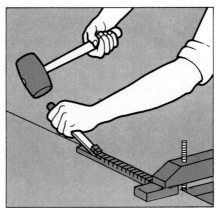

Mislocated Grooves

1 **Cutting a dado filler.** Saw a strip of matching wood as wide and as long as the dado. If the strip is thicker than the depth of the dado, remove most of the excess by making a series of parallel cuts across the underside of the strip, using a backsaw and miter box. If you are using lumber (as opposed to plywood), saw to a depth that leaves a solid strip of wood under the cuts about ⅛ inch thicker than the depth of the dado; if you are using plywood, cut the strip to the same thickness as the depth of the dado. With a wood chisel—beveled side facing down—chisel off the blocks (drawing) and sand the rough side.

2 **Fitting the strip.** Place the strip in the dado with the better surface up. The strip should fit snugly and protrude slightly above the surface. Sand the sides of the strip, if necessary, to get it into the groove. Apply glue to the dado and the strip, and clamp the strip in place. When the glue has dried, sand the top of the strip flush with the surface. Use wood putty (page 16) to fill any cracks between the strip and the sides of the grooves.

To fill an incorrect rabbet, follow the procedure in Steps 1 and 2, sanding the strip flush with both the surface and the edge of the board.

Misplaced or Damaged Nails and Screws

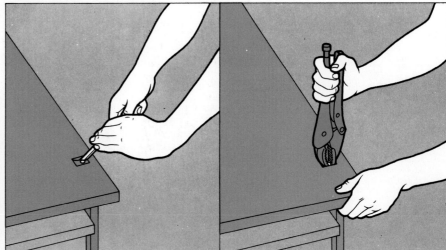

Leverage for hard-to-pull nails. A nail driven into the dense grain of a knot often bends or sticks fast in the wood, or the nailhead breaks off when you try to remove it. First place a piece of scrap wood under the hammer to avoid marring the wood surface. To get sufficient leverage, slide the claws of the hammer around the shaft of the nail and use both hands to push the head of the hammer down on its side (drawing) with only one claw touching the wood. Remove the hammer and repeat the procedure, repositioning the hammer and pushing it over in the opposite direction; the nail should then come out easily.

Getting at a sunken nail or screw. If you can reach the point of a hammered-in nail, place the concave tip of a nail set on the point and, with a hammer, tap the nail back through the board until you can grip the nailhead with the hammer's claws. If, however, it is not possible to reach the point of the nail—or if you want to remove a countersunk screw whose slot has been damaged —use a utility knife to score a shallow rectangle, ½ inch by ¾ inch, around the nail- or screwhead. With a ¼-inch-tip wood chisel, chip out the rectangle to the depth scored by the knife (drawing). Repeat scoring and chiseling until you have ex-

posed at least ¼ inch of the nail or screw. Clamp a pair of locking-grip pliers onto the head. Instead of trying to pull a nail directly up and out, however, rock the pliers forward and the nail will come out more easily. To remove a screw, turn it with the pliers instead of prying it out.

Two Power Tools That Make Joining Easier

With the help of power cutting tools, the work of making storage units becomes surprisingly easier than it is with hand tools alone. The router and circular saw, particularly, make it simple to join wood in ways that reflect true craftsmanship.

The router can be fitted with a wide variety of bits to carve almost any kind of joint on the surface or along the edge of a piece of wood. If you have not used a router before, get the feel of the tool by trying it out on scrap wood. Attach the appropriate bit for the test cut, and adjust the tool's depth scale for the desired depth of the cut. As you should with any cutting tool, direct the router away from your body to prevent injury in case it slips. There will be circumstanc-

es in which you cannot avoid working the router by pulling it toward you (particularly when dealing with large expanses of wood); in such situations always stand to one side and proceed with utmost caution. Guide the router across wood at moderate speed: pushing it too slowly scorches the wood; pushing it too fast may burn out the motor. When the test cut is completed, use a ruler to check that its depth agrees with the reading on the router's depth scale.

The circular saw, while designed primarily for standard cuts on lumber, can also shape rabbets, dadoes and a number of other joints. In addition, it can be tilted on its base to a 45° angle, providing an accurate way of cutting a miter

—the only joint not in the router's repertoire. The circular saw is particularly useful in cutting miter joints too long to be made with a backsaw and miter box. Before making a miter cut, try the saw on a piece of scrap wood.

Before using either a router or a circular saw, make sure that the tool will cut exactly where you want it to by setting up a guide—also called a jig: a straight-edged piece of wood clamped to the actual piece to be cut and along which you direct the tool. Directions on these pages explain how to set up a guide for both tools. Although they apply specifically to cutting a dado, the instructions are valid for cutting any joint that entails the use of a guide.

The Router

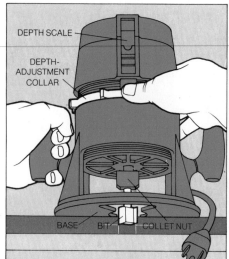

DEPTH SCALE

DEPTH-ADJUSTMENT COLLAR

BASE · BIT · COLLET NUT

1 Adjusting the depth of cut. With power off, insert the bit in the router and tighten the collet nut with the wrench supplied with the router. Hold the router upright above the piece of wood to be cut. Loosen the locking screw and turn the depth-adjustment collar until the tip of the bit just makes contact with the wood; set the depth scale to zero. Then bring the router to the edge of the wood (drawing), turn the collar until the scale registers the desired depth and tighten the locking screw. If your router does not have a depth scale, mark the desired depth on the edge of the wood and raise or lower the bit until its tip just reaches the mark.

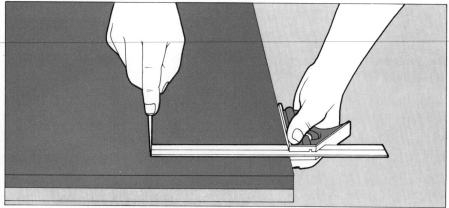

2 Marking the dado groove. Determine how far in from the end of the wood you want to make the dado groove. Place the handle of a combination square against the edge of the wood, with the rule extending across the surface. Mark the outside edge for one end of the groove with an awl (drawing). To establish the width of the groove, measure from the first mark and indicate the position for the groove's inner edge with a second awl mark. Extend the two marks down the edge of the wood. Indicate the position for the groove at the other end of the wood in the same way. Connect each pair of marks across the surface.

3 Marking the guide position. Place the router on the piece of wood so that the bit lies flush with one edge of the wood and between the two marks. Make a third mark (drawing) where the outside edge of the router base intersects the edge of the wood. Mark the far, or opposite, edge of the wood in the same manner and, using a ruler and awl, connect the two points.

4 **Setting up the guide.** Place the straight-edged piece of wood chosen for a guide along the guideline just drawn; secure the guide in place at each end with a C clamp. If the guide does not touch the line at all points, the guide's edge is not absolutely straight; substitute another.

5 **Routing the dado groove.** Place the router on the surface of the wood so that the outside edge of its base touches the guide, and the bit nearly touches the edge of the wood. Turn on the power. Ease the router forward, bringing the bit into contact with the wood. Move the router along the guide at a constant speed. At the end of the cut, lift the router clear and turn the power off. If you must make the dado groove wider, move the guide and repeat the routing process.

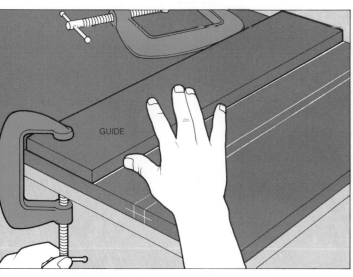

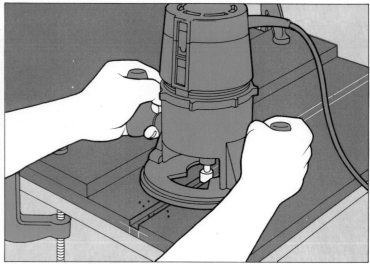

The Circular Saw as a Router

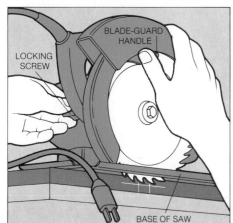

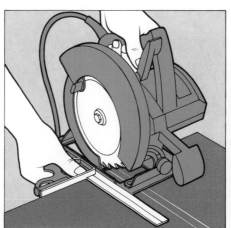

1 **Adjusting the depth of cut.** Mark the two edges of the dado groove on the surface of the wood, as in Step 2 for using the router. Then mark the desired depth of the groove on the edge of the wood. With the power off, place the circular saw on the wood so that the side of the blade is flush with the edge of the wood. Loosen the saw's locking screw with your left hand (drawing). With your right hand, lift or lower the blade until the point of the lowest tooth just touches the mark on the edge of the wood; at the same time lift the blade guard out of the way with your thumb. Once the blade is in position, tighten the locking screw.

2 **Setting up the guide.** With your left hand, hold the saw in the cutting position, just on the waste side of either line drawn across the surface of the wood; with your right hand, use a combination square to make sure the side of the saw base is at right angles to the edge of the wood (drawing). Remove the square and mark the point where the side of the saw base intersects the edge of the wood. Measure the distance between the point and the line you want to cut along, and mark that distance at the far end of the groove to be cut. Scratch a straight line between the two marks with an awl. Clamp a guide along the line.

3 **Cutting the dado groove.** Hold the circular saw on the edge of the marked piece of wood so that the side of the saw base is flush with the guide, and the blade almost touches the edge of the wood. Turn the power on and move the saw forward across the surface of the wood, keeping the side of the saw base flush with the guide. When you reach the far edge of the wood, lift the saw clear and turn the power off. Reposition the guide along the other edge of the groove, following the instructions in Step 2, and cut again. Make several cuts between the two edges of the groove until most of the wood has been removed; chisel out the remainder.

Turning Boxes into Drawers: Add Glides and Pulls

A drawer is simply a box that slides easily into and out of another larger box. To do that well, however, the box being transformed into a drawer must be built with an arrangement of joints that holds together firmly, since most drawers are heavily used and subject to a variety of stresses. The box must also be rigged with a sliding device to reduce friction and control the movement of the drawer.

A simple, sturdy drawer can be built with glue, nails and butt-jointed plywood or lumber. But unlike the basic box, the front and back pieces should be inset so that they butt against the sides —otherwise the front might pull away from the sides under frequent use. Wood blocks glued in the corners add extra strength. Stronger drawers (below) use dadoes to attach the back and the bottom to the sides, and a rabbet to attach the front so that it fits flush with the sides. Whichever method of construction is used, the wood should be at least ½ inch thick for the sides and ¼ inch thick

for the bottom; lighter wood might split.

There are many ways of equipping a drawer to slide. Hardware devices called drawer-glide assemblies are among the most commonly used because they work smoothly, are easily installed, and come in different lengths and load capacities; the extendable type (pages 29-30) allows the drawer to be pulled all the way out without falling. But these devices can be used only on cabinets constructed from wood at least ½ inch thick; thinner wood will not hold a hardware glide's mounting screws, which must be driven from the inside of the cabinet.

For such cabinets, strips of molding, attached by driving screws from the outside of the cabinet, should be used as runners (pages 30-31). The screws are then countersunk and covered. These wood runners can also be used in place of the more expensive hardware devices in cabinets made from thicker wood, in which case the runners should be installed from the inside.

The type of glide will determine the width of a drawer. The metal glide used on pages 29 and 30, for instance, is ½ inch thick, so the outside width of the drawer must be an inch less than the cabinet opening. When wood runners are used, the drawer should clear the cabinet by ⅛ inch on each side.

The finishing touch for most drawers is a false front; it can be mounted flush with the cabinet's sides (page 32), or partially overlapping the sides, or it can be fitted within the opening. A false front is mandatory on drawers with metal glides because the glides would otherwise be visible in the space between the drawer and the cabinet's sides. (If the false front fits within the opening, allow for its thickness when attaching the assemblies. Also, cut the false front ¼ inch narrower than the width of the opening to allow a ⅛-inch clearance at the sides.) A false front can be cut from finer wood than the drawer, enhancing the appearance of the project while keeping down the cost.

A Drawer with Grooved Joints

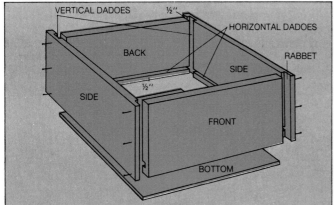

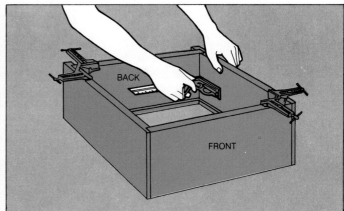

1 Routing the dadoes and rabbets. Cut the front, back, sides and bottom of the drawer. The bottom of the drawer should be cut ½ inch longer and ½ inch wider than the drawer's interior dimensions. Next, cut dadoes on all four pieces to receive the bottom; locate them at least ½ inch from the lower edge of each piece. Rout the dadoes ¼ inch deep and as wide as the thickness of the drawer bottom—also usually ¼ inch. Cut vertical dadoes ½ inch from the rear edges of the side pieces ¼ inch deep and as wide as the thickness of the back piece. The rabbets cut at the front edges of the sides should also be cut ¼ inch deep and the thickness of the front piece. Sand all of the pieces smooth.

2 Truing the drawer. Dry-fit the sides of the drawer by putting them in place without gluing or nailing. Place clamps on one front corner and one rear corner. Check the corners for trueness by setting a combination square into an unclamped rear corner (drawing). If the angle is slightly greater than 90°, the front piece of the drawer is too long; sand it down. If the angle is slightly less than 90°, the back is too long; sand it down. Next, insert the bottom in the dadoes and recheck the corners; sand the edges of the bottom piece as necessary. Disassemble the drawer.

3 **Assembling the parts.** Spread glue in the dado grooves of both the back piece and one of the sides. Fit the back and side together and insert the bottom (drawing). Nail the side to the back, spacing the nails 2 inches apart and nailing at a slight angle. With glue join the other side to the back and bottom, and nail this side to the back. Finally, attach the front, using glue and nails where it meets the sides, but only glue where it meets the bottom. Put clamps on the four corners. Wipe the excess glue off with a damp cloth and set the drawer aside to dry.

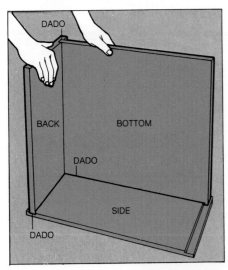

Pilot Holes for Screws

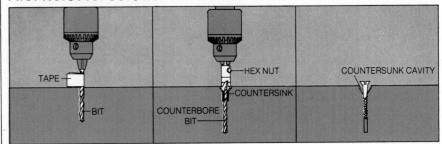

The holding power of a nail does not equal that of a screw. In addition to adding strength, screws should be used where a piece may have to be repositioned—such as a drawer-glide assembly—or where a project might be disassembled, moved and set up again.

Holes should be drilled to receive the screws. These pilot holes prevent wood from splitting and make it easier to drive the screws. To drill a pilot hole, select a bit with a diameter slightly less than the screw's diameter at a point halfway down its shaft.

Hold the screw alongside the bit with the point of the screw $1/16$ inch short of the bit's tip. Wrap a piece of tape around the bit to mark a line even with the top of the shaft of the screw and drill to that point (*above, left*).

If you want the head of a screw to be recessed into the wood, use a countersink bit after drilling the pilot hole. A simpler technique is to drill both the pilot hole and the countersunk cavity at the same time with a counterbore bit (*above, center*). Simply hold the screw alongside the counterbore bit with the point of the screw $1/16$ inch short of the tip of the bit, loosen the setscrew on the bit and adjust the collar until it is even with the top of the head of the screw; retighten the setscrew and you are ready to drill.

Installing Hardware Glides

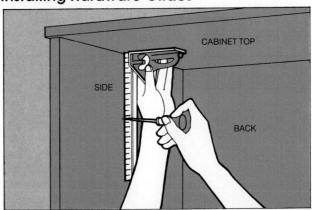

1 **Measuring the location.** Within the cabinet for which the drawer has been built, place a combination square so that its handle lies against the top of the cabinet and the ruler lies against one side (drawing). Mark with an awl a point that equals the height of the drawer plus ⅛ inch; for example, if the drawer is 4 inches high, put the awl mark 4⅛ inches below the cabinet top. Moving the square along the cabinet side toward the back, make several additional marks, each of them 4⅛ inches from the top. With a straight edge and an awl, scratch a line to connect the points. Repeat the procedure on the opposite side.

2 **Positioning the screws.** Place the bottom of the outer casing of a glide assembly along the awl line so that its front edge is flush with the front of the cabinet. (Note: Some casings are identified for specific use on the left or right side.) Pull out the glide extension far enough to expose all the screw holes in the casing; there will be two oblong holes and several round ones. Holding the casing in position, use an awl to mark the center of each oblong hole (drawing). Repeat for the other side of the cabinet. Drill pilot holes in the places marked, then attach the outer casings.

3 **Mounting the glides on the drawer.** The package containing the glide assembly will indicate the positions of the inner-glide mounting screws —generally about $1\frac{1}{16}$ inch from the bottom of the drawer. Place the handle of a combination square flush against the bottom edge of the drawer, with the ruler running up the side. Make an awl mark at $1\frac{1}{16}$ inch (or whatever the designated measurement is) and then several more marks, extending all the way from front to back. Connect the marks with an awl line. Position the inner glide so the awl line appears through the center of the screw holes and the glide is even with the front of the drawer. Mark the center of each oblong hole. Remove the glide, drill pilot holes and attach the glide (drawing). (Do not install screws in circular holes.) Repeat the procedure for the other side.

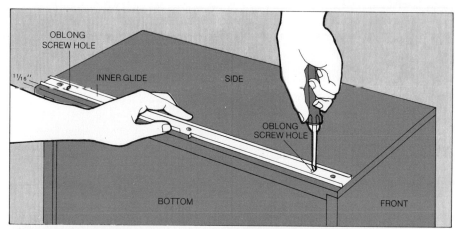

4 **Checking alignment.** Slide the inner glides of the drawer onto the front wheels of the outer casings. When the glides hit the stops in the casings, tilt the drawer up; this will enable the drawer to clear the stops and slide the rest of the way into position. The top of the drawer should clear the cabinet by $\frac{1}{8}$ inch, and the front of the drawer should be level with the front of the cabinet. Check for alignment and remove the drawer.

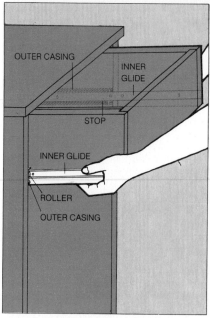

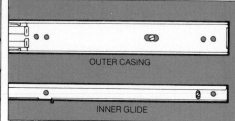

5 **Adjusting the assemblies.** If in Step 4 the drawer was not precisely aligned with the top of the cabinet, loosen the inner-glide screws and move the glide up for more clearance or down for less clearance. Tighten the screws again and put the drawer back in to recheck the clearance. If the drawer does not close flush with the front of the cabinet, loosen the outer-casing screws; pull the casing forward or backward as necessary and retighten the screws. Recheck the fit. When the adjustments are exact, remove the drawer. Mark the centers of all circular screw holes on each of the glides and casings. Drill pilot holes and install the remaining screws to fix the glides.

Wood Runners

1 **Cutting and locating the runner.** For the simplest kind of drawer runner—blocks of wood on top of which the drawer rides—begin by cutting two strips of ¾-inch molding, each one as long as the cabinet is deep. To position these runners, make initial awl marks, following the same procedures used in Step 1, page 29, for installing hardware glides. Hold one runner against a side of the cabinet and align the top edge of the runner with the awl marks. Using the top edge of the runner as a guide (drawing), scratch a line across the side of the cabinet with the awl. Repeat for the other runner on the opposite side.

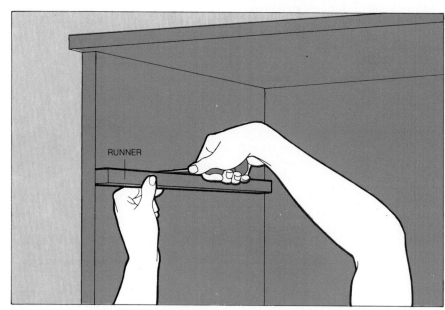

2 **Locating the screws.** Measure in 3 inches from the front edge of the cabinet. Place the handle of a combination square on the top of the cabinet with the ruler extending downward along the side (drawing). Measure a distance equal to the height of the drawer, plus the thickness of the cabinet top, plus half the height of the runner, plus ⅛ inch for clearance. If, for example, the drawer is 4 inches high, the cabinet top is 1 inch thick and the runner is ¾ inch thick, the total measurement from the top of the cabinet would be 5½ inches. Mark the measurement with an awl. Make a similar mark 3 inches in from the back of the cabinet, and a third mark halfway between the two. With a counterbore bit, drill pilot holes at the three marks through the cabinet wall. Repeat the procedure on the opposite side of the cabinet.

3 **Fastening the runner.** Hold the runner firmly inside the cabinet with its top edge along the awl line. From the outside of the cabinet, push the awl through each of the three holes in the side and make a mark on the runner. Clamp the runner to your workbench and drill pilot holes at the three marks. Spread glue on the runner, return it to the cabinet and align the three sets of holes. Fasten the runner in place from the outside. Repeat the procedure for the other runner. Fill the countersunk cavities with wood putty. Sand off excess wood putty after it has dried. Finally, coat the top edges of the runners with paste wax.

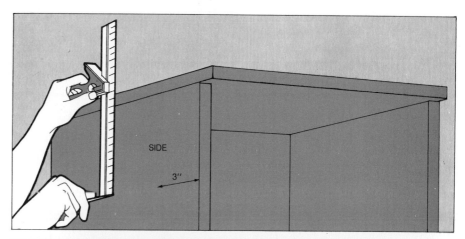

SIDE

3″

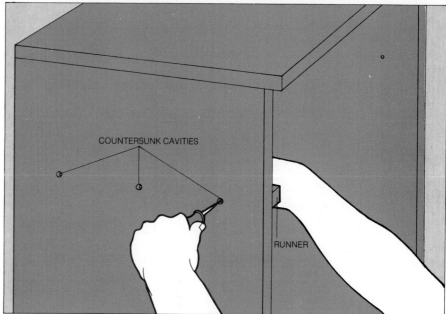

COUNTERSUNK CAVITIES

RUNNER

Channeling Drawers for Wood Runners

1 **Routing the channels.** For a steadier arrangement than platform runners, runners can be fitted into grooves cut into the sides of the drawer. In that case the drawer should be built slightly smaller to allow room for the runners. Mount the runners at a point half the height of the drawer, plus the thickness of the cabinet top, plus half the height of the runner, plus ⅛ inch for clearance. Rout grooves in the sides of the drawer ¾ inch wide and half as deep as the sides are thick. The top edge of the grooves should run along the midpoint of the drawer side (drawing). Sand the grooves with 120-grade sandpaper.

2 **Adjusting the drawer.** Slide the drawer onto the runners (drawing). If the fit is tight, sand the groove with 100-grade sandpaper until the drawer runs smooth. When the fit is correct, coat the runners and the grooves with paste wax.

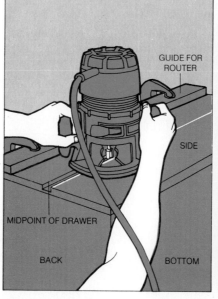

GUIDE FOR ROUTER

SIDE

MIDPOINT OF DRAWER

BACK

BOTTOM

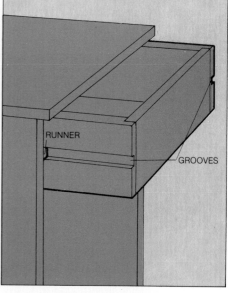

RUNNER

GROOVES

Adding False Fronts

1 Marking for a close fit. Measure the cabinet opening from the outside edge of one side to the outside edge of the other. From a piece of wood that is at least an inch wider than the drawer is high, cut a length as long as the cabinet is wide. Position this false front against the front of the drawer so there is a clearance of ⅛ inch between it and the overhanging cabinet top; the false front should be flush with the outside of the cabinet on both sides. Holding the false front in position, open the drawer partway and scratch guidelines on the back of the false front to indicate the top and the sides of the drawer (drawing, below).

DRAWER FRONT

FALSE FRONT

2 Cutting and attaching the front. Place the false front, with the drawer on top of it, on the workbench. Realign the drawer with the guidelines on the false front if necessary. Scratch another line on the back of the false front, this time to indicate the bottom edge of the drawer. Remove the drawer and cut the false front on the waste side of the line indicating the bottom edge.

Clamp the drawer and the false front together, and to the workbench. Working from the inside out (drawing, left), drill two pilot holes—the exact position is not critical—through the drawer front and just into the false front. Secure with screws long enough to go about halfway through it.

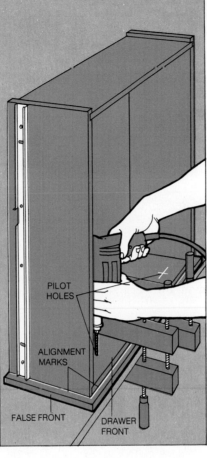

PILOT HOLES

ALIGNMENT MARKS

FALSE FRONT

DRAWER FRONT

Drawer Pulls

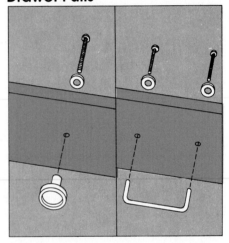

Attaching hardware. Use a single pull for a small drawer that will hold lightweight things; use two pulls for a large drawer that will hold a heavy load. Knob pulls and bar pulls (drawings) serve equally well. Placement of the pulls is largely a matter of taste and the relative size of drawer and pulls, but a good rule of thumb is to align them parallel with the unseen glides or runners; this facilitates opening and closing the drawers. A single pull should be centered. A pair generally is located 2 to 3 inches from each of the sides; for precise alignment procedure, see page 97.

Select a bit with a diameter of the same size as the pull's mounting bolt. Clamp the drawer to the workbench and drill entirely through the drawer and the false front. Then insert the mounting bolts from the inside of the drawer, and screw the bolts into the pulls.

Troubleshooting Drawers

☐ DRAWER STICKS. To find the problem area, rub chalk along the top and bottom edges of the drawer and in the grooves, if any. Open and close the drawer several times. The chalk will rub off of any high areas where the drawer is sticking. If the high area follows the grain of the wood, use a plane to smooth down the high spot. If the high area goes across the grain, sand the wood with 120-grade sandpaper. Also, remove the drawer to check for protruding nailheads and countersink them with a nail set.
☐ LOOSE BOTTOM. If the bottom is flush-mounted (overlapping), insert a wedge, such as the tip of a screwdriver, at the loose area and squeeze more

glue into the crevice. Drive extra nails into the glued area. For grooved bottoms, follow the procedure below for tightening loose joints.
☐ LOOSE JOINTS. Use a toothpick to work glue into a joint that is loose but only slightly separated. Attach a corner clamp and nail the joint. Use wood blocks or metal braces in the corner for greater strength (page 23).
☐ LOOSE PULLS. If the pull you have used is attached from the front, remove its mounting screws. Fill the screw holes with wood putty. Replace the screws immediately and allow the putty to dry before using the drawer. For better results, switch to the bolt-mounted type (above, right).

Turning Boxes into Cabinets: Install Doors

The two principal ways of enclosing boxes that will be used as cabinets are with hinged doors (illustrated below) or with sliding doors *(pages 38-39)*. While both methods have their advantages, hinged doors are considerably more versatile because they can be attached to boxes in several different ways.

The main types of hinged doors are:

☐ OVERLAPPING. This type fits over the entire cabinet front, rather than into the opening. It is the easiest door to cut and install since precise measurements are not necessary. The door also covers slight irregularities in the cabinet itself.

☐ PARTIALLY OVERLAPPING. A variation for cabinets that have face frames *(page 24)*, this door requires special hinges such as the semiconcealed hinge that is shown on page 36.

☐ INSET. Since it fits inside the cabinet opening, the inset door must be cut and hinged carefully if it is to open and close smoothly.

☐ LIPPED. This type fits both into and over the cabinet opening, creating a tight seal. The overlapping lip is usually made by cutting a rabbet *(page 18)* around the edges. But the door can also be made by gluing two panels together. Since it requires hinges shaped to accommodate the lip, buy the hinges first, then cut the door to fit them.

☐ CONTIGUOUS DOUBLE. Double doors meet at the center of a single large opening in this arrangement; they should always be used when an opening is wider than it is high, in order to avoid straining the hinges. The doors can be overlapping, inset or lipped. The center edges can be rabbeted so that they fit into each other, as shown, or they can be cut so that they just clear each other.

☐ SEPARATED DOUBLE. This type is divided by a center partition, or stile, which gives the cabinet greater rigidity.

Hinges for any of these doors can be mounted on any edge—top, bottom, left or right—depending on your preference or particular needs. Most hinges are side-mounted, but whether they are placed on the left or on the right side will be dictated for you by the location of the unit and the use to which you are putting it.

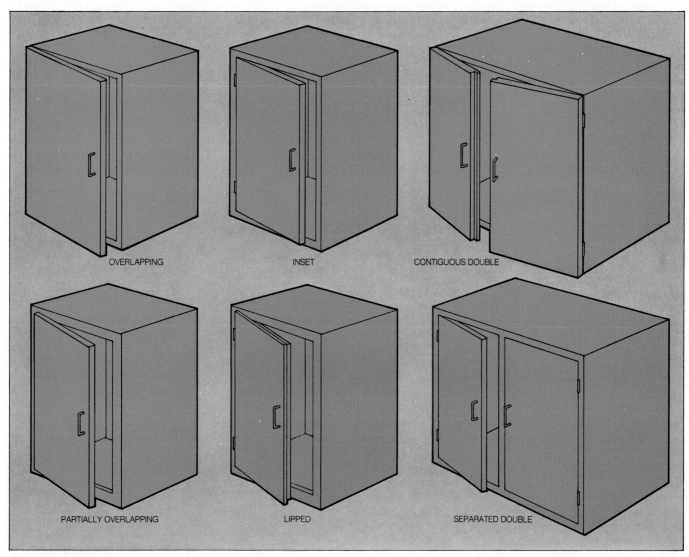

OVERLAPPING   INSET   CONTIGUOUS DOUBLE

PARTIALLY OVERLAPPING   LIPPED   SEPARATED DOUBLE

Hinges: Types and Techniques

The most widely used hinge is the simple butt type, which consists of two rectangular leaves rotating on a central pin. The butt can be installed in two ways: it can be attached to the outside of a cabinet so that it is exposed—a technique known as surface-mounting—or it can be attached so that the hinge leaves are concealed between the door and the cabinet, with only the pin portion visible when the door is closed. In the latter case, the leaves fit into shallow carved-out areas, called mortises. Once you have learned to install the butt hinge by both methods, you can use the same techniques for virtually any other type.

Butt hinges can be used only on inset doors and on overlapping doors that cover the entire cabinet front. For lipped doors and partially overlapping doors, special hinges are required. The most popular types of special hinges, and the doors they are compatible with, are described along with auxiliary hardware on pages 36 and 37.

In addition to the plain butt hinge and special hinges, there are many types of decorative hinges; nearly all are functionally the same as butt hinges and are designed to be surface-mounted.

For installation of all types except the continuous hinge *(page 91)*, there are two rules of thumb: on any door that is longer than 2 feet, install three hinges; and the total length of the hinges should be equal to one sixth the length of the hinged edge. For example, if the door is 24 inches long, use two 2-inch hinges; or if the door is 72 inches long, use three 4-inch hinges. When only two hinges are required, they are usually placed a quarter of the way from the top and bottom of the door; when three hinges are installed, one hinge is centered and the other two are placed 4 or 5 inches from the top and bottom.

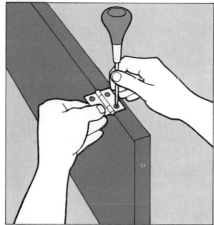

Surface-mounting Butt Hinges—Overlapping Doors

1 **Installing hinges on the door.** Align the leaf of one hinge on the side edge of the door so the pin is centered on the back edge. Mark the screw holes. Remove the hinge and drill pilot holes. Attach the hinge leaf. Repeat for the other hinge or hinges.

2 **Attaching the door to the cabinet.** Lay the cabinet on its back and fit the door over the opening. On the side of the cabinet, mark the screw holes for the unattached hinge leaves; drill pilot holes for the screws and attach the hinges to the cabinet.

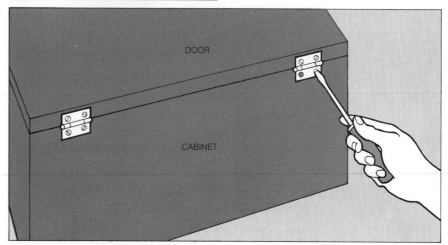

Surface-mounting Butt Hinges—Inset Door

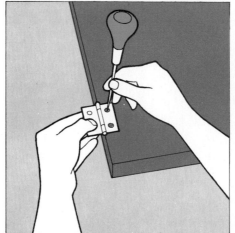 

1 **Installing hinges on the door.** Align the leaf of one hinge on the front of the door so the pin is centered on the back edge. Mark the screw holes. Then remove the hinge and drill pilot holes. Attach the hinge leaf and repeat for the other hinge or hinges.

2 **Attaching the door to the cabinet.** With the cabinet upright, set the door into the opening, and wedge it in place with slivers of wood on all sides except the hinge side, where the door should fit flush against the cabinet. Mark the screw holes for the hinge leaves on the front of the cabinet; drill pilot holes and attach the hinges.

Mortising Butt Hinges—
Overlapping Door

1 **Marking the mortise.** If your hinge has a removable pin, take it out; it is best to work with separated leaves. Place one leaf on the back of the door so that only the pin loops extend beyond the back edge of the door. Trace the outline of the leaf with an awl.

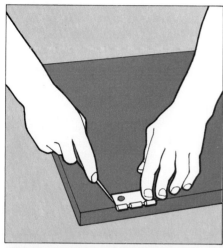

2 **Cutting the mortise.** Using a woodworking chisel and a hammer, tap around the outline to make a small cut approximately the depth of the hinge leaf. Hold the chisel perpendicular to the door with its beveled side toward the mortise area. Then hold the chisel at a low angle to the wood—with its beveled side down—and tap out a series of small shallow cuts; small even cuts make a smoother mortise than longer ones. Finish by using the chisel alone to shave the mortise to the exact depth that is needed to make the leaf fit flush with the surface.

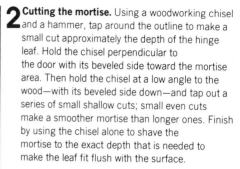

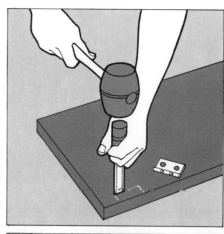

3 **Attaching the hinge.** Place the hinge leaf back in the mortise and again align it so that only the pin loops extend beyond the edge of the door. Mark the screw holes. Remove the hinge and drill pilot holes for the screws. (Be careful not to drill through the front of the door.) Attach the leaf to the door. Mortise and attach the other hinge or hinges in the same way.

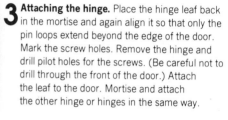

4 **Attaching the door to the cabinet.** Lay the cabinet on its back, and fit the door over the opening. Mark the ends of each attached hinge on the side of the cabinet; set the door aside. Using the marks for orientation, position the other hinge leaves on the front edge of the cabinet side and trace outlines of the leaves. Cut mortises for the hinges along the outlines. Replace the hinge pins. (If your hinges do not come apart, follow the procedure as above, but use a combination square to transfer the dimensions of the leaves to the cabinet edge.)

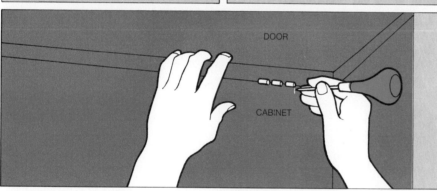

Mortising Butt Hinges—
Inset Door

1 **Installing hinges on the door.** On the side edge of the door, mortise the hinge leaves by following Steps 1 through 3 above. Be sure the pin loops extend beyond the door's front edge.

2 **Attaching the door.** With the cabinet upright, set the door into the opening; wedge it in place with thin slivers of wood at the top and bottom. Mark the ends of the hinges on the front edge of the cabinet and remove the door. Using the marks on the front of the cabinet for orientation, position the hinge leaves just inside the cabinet with the pin loops extending beyond the front edge. Trace the outlines of the leaves, and cut the mortises. (If your hinges do not come apart, use a combination square as in Step 4 for the overlapping door.)

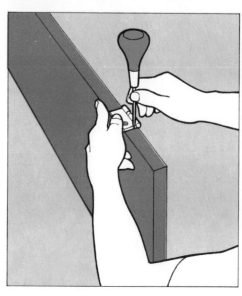

Special Hardware

Shutter hinge. This type is a useful substitute for the butt hinge on cabinets made from plywood. Since the hinge has one offset leaf, it can be screwed into the surfaces of both the door and the cabinet rather than into the edge of the plywood, which does not hold screws well. Suitable for either inset or overlapping doors, the shutter hinge must be mortised, not surface-mounted. It must be selected with care so its offset leaf matches the plywood thickness.

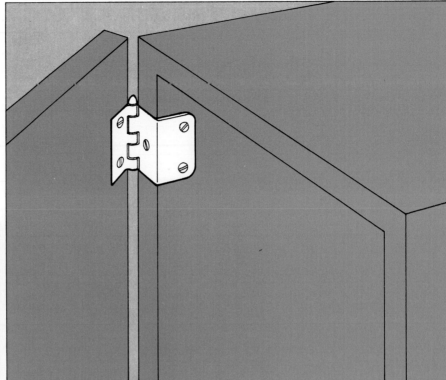

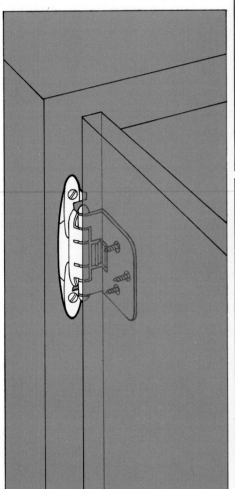

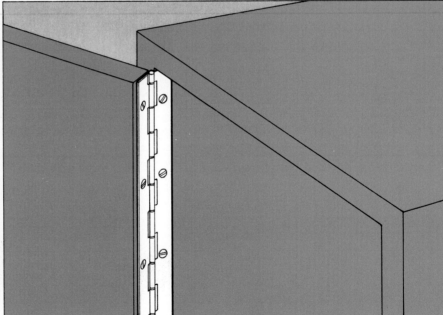

Semiconcealed hinge. When this type of hinge is installed, one leaf is visible, the other hidden. The semiconcealed hinge is used only on lipped or partially overlapping doors. The leaf that is visible is surface-mounted on the front of the cabinet. The hidden, offset leaf is mortised into the back of the door. (For lipped doors, the hidden leaf has a double offset.)

Continuous hinge. Also called a piano hinge, the continuous hinge is in effect a concealed butt hinge running the entire edge of the door. Most often used on inset doors, it eliminates the need for mortising; the door is adjusted to allow the closed hinge to fit between the door and the cabinet. Its installation (*page 91*) differs from that of standard butt hinges. Sold by the foot, it can be cut with a hacksaw to the exact length of the door. Because of the support it gives, this hinge is well suited for hanging heavy doors.

Catches and latches. To keep a door closed, a catch or latch is required. One popular type of catch *(left, below)* consists of an arrow-shaped "strike" mounted on the door, and a spring-loaded receptacle attached to the inside of the cabinet. Precise measurement is essential to make sure that these two parts are lined up. Another type of catch, which requires less precise alignment, is magnetic *(center)*. A bar latch *(right)*, which is decorative as well as useful, is attached to the outside of a cabinet with an inset door, and serves as both a catch and a knob.

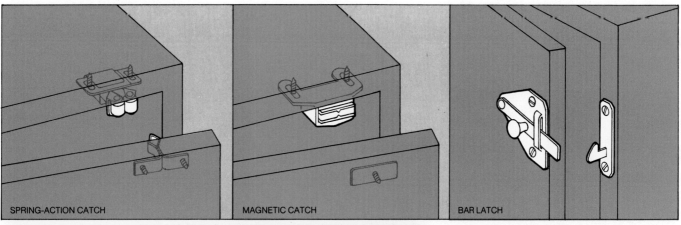

SPRING-ACTION CATCH MAGNETIC CATCH BAR LATCH

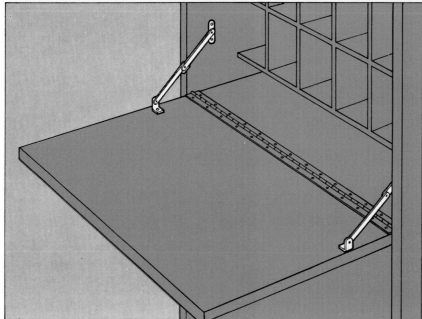

Stay supports. Used in addition to hinges, these collapsible retainers limit the degree to which a door can be opened—whether the door is the fold-down type shown or is mounted in the usual manner. When the door is closed, the stays fold up. Several types are available. All are easy to attach: they simply screw to the side of the cabinet and to the inside of the door.

Troubleshooting Doors

Whatever the cause, the symptoms are much the same on all malfunctioning hinged doors. They either are hard to open or will not stay closed. Here are the most common problems—together with their solutions—in the order that you should check them:

□ WARPED DOOR. The single solution, short of replacing the door, is to install a bar latch, if possible.

□ LOOSE HINGE SCREWS. Replace all the screws with longer ones. Or, if longer screws would go completely through the wood, cram the screw holes with wood splinters (kitchen matches or toothpicks will do); replace the same screws.

□ DOOR EDGE NOT CLEARING. To find the exact point where the door is sticking, rub chalk along the door edges. Open and close the door a couple of times. The chalk will rub off at the point where the door is sticking. Remove the door from the cabinet; plane and sand the chalked areas.

□ MISALIGNED CATCH. Remove and reposition the strike on the door. It may be necessary to fill the old screw holes with wood putty and refinish.

Tracks: An Alternative to Hinges

There are several ways, as shown at right, to put in tracks for sliding doors: by installing hardware, by routing channels and by attaching strips of molding. Hardware tracks are usually best. Not only are they easy to install but they also give assured straightness and smoothness. Of the other methods, which are more traditional in woodworking, routed tracks are preferable. Because the tracks are cut into the cabinet—rather than being nailed on like molding—they are neat and unobtrusive. However, the only way to create tracks when you do not want to use hardware or do not have a router is by attaching molding.

Since they do not have to be thick enough to hold screws, sliding doors are usually made from thinner material than their hinged counterparts. In addition, a thin door slides more easily than a door made from a thick material because it weighs less and creates less friction. But since thin material is more likely to warp, and a door that is distorted will not slide easily, the material used must be virtually warp-proof. For most cabinets, the best-quality ⅜- or ½-inch plywood (page 58) is recommended, although less expensive ¼-inch tempered hardboard can be used for utilitarian storage units.

Tracks of any kind should be installed before the cabinet is assembled. However, when you are working with unassembled pieces, be sure to anticipate the way you are going to put the cabinet together. Often, to allow space for joints, the tracks cannot run all the way to the side edges of the wood.

To ensure a perfect fit, the doors themselves, like all doors, are cut after the cabinet is assembled (opposite).

As a general rule, a cabinet with sliding doors should not be much more than 2 feet high and should be at least twice as wide as it is tall. Doors running on wooden tracks are harder to push; therefore, the length of the tracks should be limited to 4 feet. And, in order to get the doors in and out (Step 2, opposite), the tracks at the top must be deeper—by at least ¼ inch—than the lower ones.

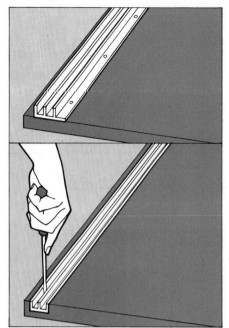

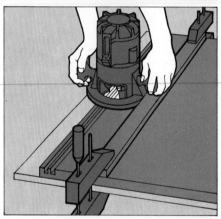

Installing Tracks

Hardware. Metal or plastic tracks always come in pairs: a shallow bottom track and a deeper top one. Available in standard lengths, they can be cut with a hacksaw to the exact measurements required. Hardware tracks may be surface-mounted (top left). Or, for better appearance, they can be sunk into channels routed in the top and bottom of the cabinet, as shown in the lower drawing. If channels are routed, the cabinet material must be at least ⅜ inch thicker than the deeper track. Both top and bottom channels should be at least ½ inch inside the front edge.

Routed. Since these tracks are cut into the cabinet itself, the cabinet material must be ¾ inch thick or more to accommodate channels at least ⁵⁄₁₆ inch deep on the bottom and the same depth plus another ¼ inch on the top. On both top and bottom pieces of the cabinet, rout the first track ½ inch inside the front edge. Rout the second track ¼ inch inside the first. Make each track ⅛ inch wider than the door thickness, and use a mortising or straight-cut bit. Guide the router with a straight piece of wood clamped to the cabinet piece. Apply paste wax to the tracks.

Molding. These tracks are usually made with three pieces of molding (left). On the bottom of the cabinet, use a length of ⅜-by-½-inch molding and position it to form tracks ½ inch deep. On the top, use ⅜-by-¾-inch molding and make the tracks ¾ inch deep. Space the molding so that each strip is separated from the other ones by the thickness of the door plus ¹⁄₁₆ inch, using the actual door material as a guide. Glue and nail the molding, making sure to clamp each piece in place before nailing. A variation (below) is to replace the outer molding with a board that is nailed to the cabinet's front edge. Whichever method is used, be sure to apply paste wax to the tracks.

Making the Doors

1 **Measuring and cutting.** To determine the height for both doors (*below*), measure from the groove of a bottom channel to the lip of the corresponding upper track; then add ¼ inch so that the doors will project into the top channel when they are installed. To determine the width (*below, right*) for the first door, measure half the length of the track. For the second door, add ½ inch to the measurement to provide a center overlap. Cut the doors, using the dimensions thus established.

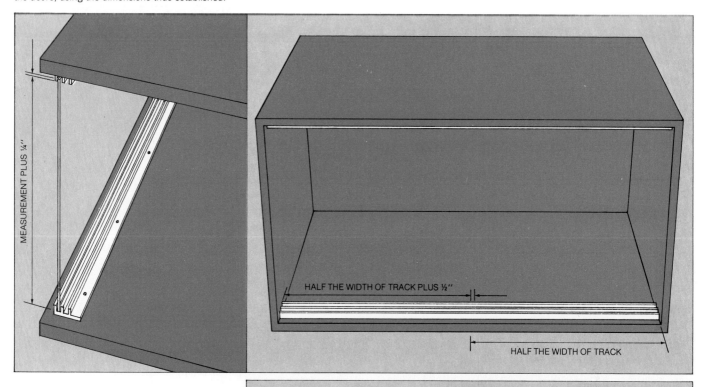

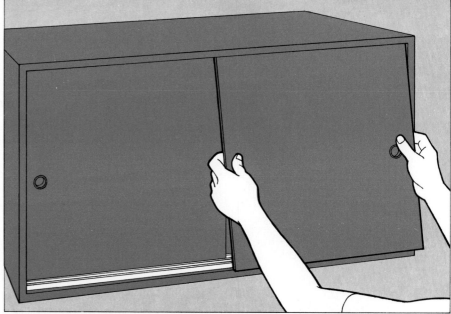

2 **Finishing and installing.** To reduce friction, sand the door edges as smooth as possible and wax the lower ones. Add recessed pulls—no deeper than the thickness of the doors—one near the left side of the left door and the other symmetrically on the right door. To do so, drill or chisel out an opening in each door to accommodate the shape of the pull. To install each door, push it all the way up into the top channel; then let it drop into the bottom one. Place the wider door in the inside channel so that both of the doors will appear to be the same width when they are closed.

The Vertical Dimension: Hanging Things on Walls

Almost any object that occupies valuable floor space—from a bookcase to a bed—can be raised out of busy home traffic patterns if it is hung on a wall. Vertical storage is usually only one layer deep, so items are easy to see and more accessible. And because wall units tend to range from waist height to arm's reach, stretching and bending are reduced to a minimum. To make efficient use of this vertical space, you need to know the kind of wall you have and the best fastener to use in attaching a particular storage unit to it.

Walls appear much the same from the outside, but interior construction varies greatly. Some walls are solid: masonry block, brick or solid concrete. Others are hollow: plaster and lathing or wallboard (both these materials are usually fastened to metal or wood support beams called studs). To identify the construction of your wall, drill a small hole in an inconspicuous spot. Note the kind of dust that the drill grinds out, then check your observations against the information in the chart on page 42.

If the wall is solid, you will need a special carbide-tipped drill bit. If the wall is hollow, you will need to know its thickness and the amount of space inside the wall to select the proper fastener.

Bend the very tip of a thin wire into a right angle and poke the wire through the test hole as far as it will go. The distance from the bent tip of the wire to the outside of the wall reveals the thickness of the wall plus the space behind it. Pull the wire until the bent end snags on the inside of the wall. The distance from the bent end of the wire to the outside of the wall is the wall thickness.

Now consider the weight the wall can bear. Some materials—for example, mortar joints between bricks or masonry blocks—cannot support weights greater than 10 pounds per square foot. But nearly everything except bric-a-brac runs well beyond that limit: for example, books average 20 pounds per square foot; a foot-high stack of 12-inch records weighs 45 pounds; two gallon cans of paint weigh 22 pounds. In any case, bathroom scales will give the weight of nearly anything you intend to hang on your wall.

If the load is to be relatively light, or if the wall is backed by wood studs (page 42), the fasteners you choose can be as simple as common nails or wood screws. But for some situations, specialized fasteners like those shown below and at right are needed.

Each type of fastener is suited to particular wall and weight combinations as outlined in the chart on page 43. Fasteners are measured in increments of inches, in penny sizes (abbreviated as "d"), in screw numbers or gauges—all of which simply indicate relative sizes.

Types of Fasteners

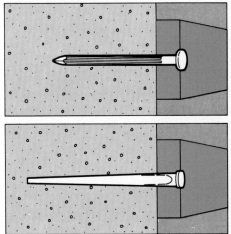

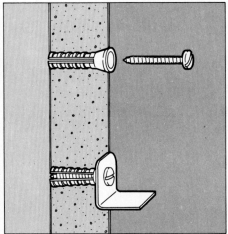

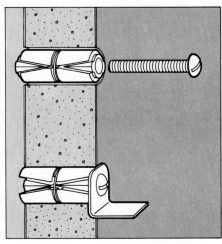

Masonry nails and cut nails. These fasteners are used in walls made of brick, or of cinder or concrete block. Masonry nails (top), which are made of hardened steel, are often finely ridged from tip to shank, and are coated with a thin layer of zinc (galvanized) to prevent rust. Cut nails (bottom) are stamped from sheet iron or steel. Their sharp, squared edges can damage soft materials such as wood; before using a cut nail to fasten a piece of wood to any kind of masonry, drill a pilot hole in the wood slightly smaller then the thickness of the nail at its widest point. Hammer the nail through the hole in the wood and into the wall.

Anchor fasteners. Anchors are sheaths that expand when matching screws are driven into them. They are multipurpose fasteners for use in solid walls or in hollow walls thick enough not to crumble when the anchors expand as the screws in them are tightened. Lead anchors (shown) and lag anchors are for heavy-duty use with wood or lag screws. Plastic anchors—for light loads—are used with self-tapping sheet-metal screws (opposite page, bottom right). To install these devices, drill a tight-fitting hole that matches the length and outside diameter of the anchor precisely. Tap in the anchor with a light hammer, and drive in the screw.

Expansion shields. Used in masonry walls to support exceptionally heavy weights, these devices vary in appearance but they all work on the same basic principle: when a bolt in the metal shield is tightened, the shield expands in the wall. In the shield above, wedges at each end are drawn toward the center as the bolt turns, forcing apart a sheath bound by wire. To use an expansion shield, bore a hole the size of the shield. Tap in the shield, thread the bolt through the object being hung, and tighten. Be sure to select a bolt that is long enough to pass through both the object you are hanging and the length of the expansion shield.

Dowels with wood screws. These homemade fasteners attach fairly heavy loads to masonry and are most useful in old or crumbling walls. To make one, cut a 2- to 3-inch strip of wooden doweling ¾ to 1 inch in diameter. Using a carbide-tipped bit in your drill, bore a hole in the wall the same length as the dowel and slightly smaller in diameter. Rub the dowel with soap, and hammer it in. Drill a pilot hole in the center of the dowel, pass a wood screw through the object you are hanging and drive the screw into the pilot hole; once inside the wall, the dowel will expand for a firm grip.

Mollies, or hollow-wall anchors. These fasteners are bolts encased in retracting sheaths. The length of the sheath shank—the smooth area near the head—must match the thickness of the wall. To install, drill a hole the diameter of the sheath. Tap the Molly into the hole (*top*). Hold the sheath in place by setting a screwdriver in one of the open wedges in the sheath head and, with another screwdriver, tighten the bolt (*center*). The sheath will retract to grip the wall. Do not overtighten. Remove the bolt, slip it through the object to be hung, and screw it back into the sheath.

Toggle bolts. Like Mollies, toggles fasten things to hollow walls, but they take greater weights. One type is the spring wing, or butterfly—a nut split into two wings joined by a spring. To attach, drill a hole the diameter of the closed butterfly. Probe with a wire to make sure there is room for the toggle to open inside the wall. Before inserting the fastener, unscrew the bolt and pass it through the object to be hung. Replace the toggle and force it and the bolt through the hole; the toggle will open to grip the inner surface of the wall. Tighten the bolt while pulling it steadily toward you.

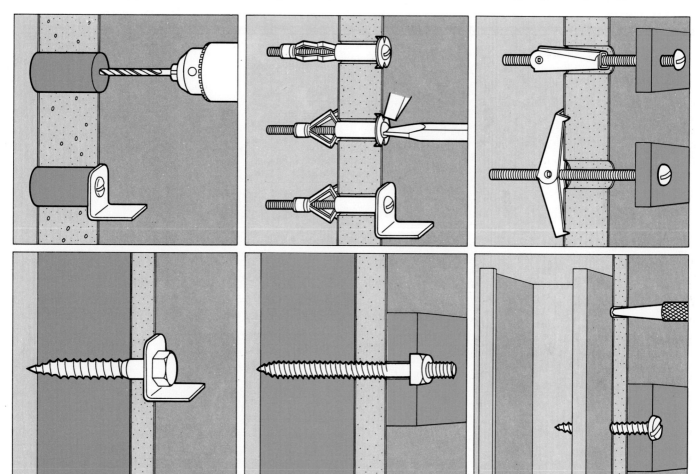

Lag bolts and screws. These devices are used for such extra-heavy jobs as hanging cabinets or bookcases on walls with wood studs, or in combination with lag anchors (*opposite, center*) in masonry. They are sold in various diameters and lengths up to 16 inches, and their square or hexagonal heads are tightened with a wrench rather than a screwdriver. To insert one of these fasteners in a wood stud, drill a pilot hole slightly smaller than the diameter of the screw through the wall into the stud. Thread the screw through the object that you are hanging—usually a heavy-duty brace or metal cleat —and drive the screw into the pilot hole.

Hanger bolts. Threaded at one end like a coarse wood screw and at the other more finely, like a machine bolt, these fasteners also are used to attach very heavy objects to wood studs. To drive one, drill a pilot hole slightly smaller than the diameter of the bolt through the wall and into the stud. Insert the wood-screw end into the pilot hole and tighten the bolt by grasping its smooth center section with locking-grip pliers. The smooth portion and the end that is machine-threaded should remain outside the wall. Drill a hole through the object that you are hanging. Then mount the object on the projecting bolt and fasten it with a nut.

Self-tapping sheet-metal screws. Used in walls that are constructed with hollow metal studs instead of wood ones, these screws have full-length threads and either slotted or Phillips heads. To drive one, drill a small hole through the wall to expose the metal stud. Make a starter point for the drill on the exposed stud by making a small dent in the metal with a center punch (*top*). In the stud, using a high-speed steel bit, drill a hole that is half the diameter of the screw. Then drill a hole in the object to be hung. Drive the screw through the object and into the stud; the screw threads will cut their own grooves in the metal.

Matching Walls and Fasteners

The chart at right shows how to identify varying types of wall construction, and the chart opposite lists the proper fastener for a particular kind of wall. To use the chart at right, drill a hole in your wall, then read down the left-hand column until you find a pattern that matches the kind of dust and the amount of resistance you encounter. The right-hand column identifies the wall construction. After determining the wall type, calculate the weight of the object to be hung. Then use the chart opposite for the correct fastener. If your wall consists of dry flaky plaster, stick a piece of transparent tape where you intend to drill; the tape will help prevent crumbling.

The weight ranges shown on the fastener chart are approximate. Fasteners in the lightest weight range (0 to 5 pounds) can usually bear an extra pound or two. In the 5-to-10-pound range, 11 to 14 pounds can be supported if the wall is cinder or concrete block or if the fastener is driven into wood or metal studs.

The best support for any heavy object is a solid wood stud (below). But if studs are not available or not conveniently located, a heavy-duty fastener will do the job even in lighter walls. An expansion shield in thick plaster, for instance, will support weights far above the 10-pound figure shown in the last column.

Determining Wall Construction

If your drill in the test hole produces...	the wall is made of...
White dust, then gray dust; moderate, then heavy resistance to the drill bit	Plaster over cinder or concrete block
Dark or brownish gray dust; continuous heavy resistance	Cinder or concrete block
Brownish gray dust; continuous very heavy resistance (drill has difficulty biting into wall surface)	Solid concrete
White dust, then red dust; moderate resistance, followed by heavy resistance as red dust appears	Plaster over brick or hollow tiles
White dust; lengthy moderate resistance (drill bit under 3″ long will not break through)	Thick plaster
White dust; little resistance, drill bit breaks through quickly	Wallboard—Sheetrock, gypsum board, plasterboard or other thin sheet material
White dust, then brown dust; moderate resistance, drill bit breaks through quickly	Plaster over lath
White dust, then brown dust, wood shavings; continuous moderate resistance	Plaster and lath over wood stud
White dust, then brown dust, metal shavings; moderate resistance followed by heavy resistance as metal shavings appear	Plaster and lath over metal stud
White dust, wood shavings; little resistance, then moderate resistance as wood shavings appear	Wallboard over wood stud
White dust, metal shavings; little resistance, then heavy resistance as metal shavings appear	Wallboard over metal stud

Locating wall studs. Most wall studs are spaced 16 inches apart, center to center. Once you find one, quick measurements on the surface of the wall will locate the rest. In very old houses, studs may be randomly spaced, but a little probing will locate them. It is sometimes possible to find a stud simply by tapping the wall, but a surer method is to drill a small, inconspicuous hole at an acute angle along the wall's surface. Feed a piece of stiff wire at least 18 inches long into the hole (drawing) until it meets resistance—a stud. Grasp the wire where it enters the wall and draw it from the hole. Hold the wire just outside the hole and at the same angle to the wall at which it entered. The edge of the stud lies behind the point where the tip of the wire meets the wall.

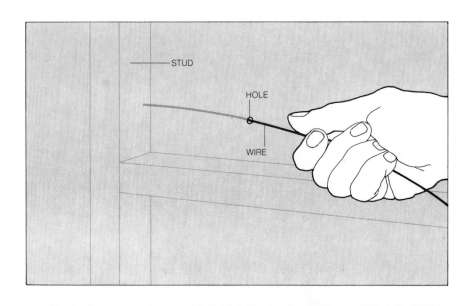

STUD
HOLE
WIRE

Selecting the Correct Fastener

Wall type	0-5 pounds per sq. ft.	5-10 pounds per sq. ft.	Over 10 pounds per sq. ft.
Cinder and concrete block (solid portions)	6d cut nail ⅞'' plastic anchor with No. 4 to No. 6 self-tapping sheet-metal screw	No. 7 to No. 9 gauge masonry nails 8d cut nail Lead anchor with No. 6 to No. 8 wood screw Dowel with No. 6 to No. 8 wood screw	Expansion shield with bolt of ¼'' diameter or larger Lag anchor with ¼''-diameter lag screw up to 6'' in length for very heavy loads
Brick	⅞'' plastic anchor with No. 4 to No. 6 self-tapping sheet-metal screw	6d or larger cut nail Lead anchor with No. 6 to No. 8 wood screw Dowel with No. 6 to No. 8 wood screw Expansion shield with ¼''-diameter bolt	Expansion shield with ¼''-diameter bolt Lead anchor with No. 10 wood screw Lag anchor with ¼''-diameter lag screw 2'' to 3'' long for very heavy loads
Mortar joints (between cinder or cement blocks or bricks)	4d finishing nail ⅞'' (or less) plastic anchor with No. 4 to No. 6 self-tapping sheet-metal screw	No. 7 to No. 9 gauge masonry nail 6d cut nail ⅞'' plastic anchor with No. 6 to No. 8 self-tapping sheet-metal screw	Not recommended: mortar joints crumble easily
Hollow tile	Toggle with ¼'' diameter bolt, long enough to pass through object being hung plus wall thickness (Note: be sure toggle can open within tile)	Toggle with ¼''-diameter bolt, long enough to pass through object being hung plus wall thickness (Note: be sure toggle can open within tile)	Toggle with ¼''-diameter bolt, long enough to pass through object being hung plus wall thickness (Note: be sure toggle can open within tile)
Thick plaster (2'' to 3'')	4d finishing nail ⅞'' plastic anchor with No. 4 to No. 8 self-tapping sheet-metal screw	Expansion shield with ¼''-diameter bolt Lead anchor with No. 6 to No. 8 wood screw	Expansion shield with ¼''-diameter bolt Lead anchor with No. 8 or larger wood screw
Cinder and concrete block (hollow sections)	4d common nail 4d finishing nail 4d cut nail	Lead anchor with No. 6 to No. 8 wood screw Expansion shield with ¼''-diameter bolt Toggle with ¼''-diameter bolt, long enough to pass through object being hung plus wall thickness	Lead anchor with No. 8 or larger wood screw Expansion shield with bolt of ¼'' diameter or larger Toggle with bolt of ¼'' diameter or larger, long enough to pass through object being hung plus wall thickness
Wallboard (Sheetrock, gypsum board, plasterboard); lath and plaster	4d to 8d finishing nail ⅞'' plastic anchor with No. 4 to No. 8 self-tapping sheet-metal screw	Molly in a size to match wall thickness Toggle with bolt of ¼'' to ³/₁₆'' diameter, long enough to pass through object being hung plus thickness	Molly in a size to match wall thickness Toggle with bolt of ¼'' diameter or larger, long enough to pass through object being hung plus wall thickness (Caution: wallboard and thin plaster may collapse under heavy weights)
Wood stud behind wallboard or plaster	2d to 4d finishing nail 6d common nail No. 6 wood screw long enough to be driven at least 1'' into wood	4d to 8d finishing nail 10d common nail No. 6 to No. 8 wood screw long enough to be driven at least 1'' into wood	No. 8 wood screw long enough to be driven at least ½'' into wood 8d common nail Lag or hanger bolt of ¼'' diameter, long enough to be driven at least 1½'' into wood
Metal stud behind wallboard or plaster	No. 4 or larger self-tapping sheet-metal screw	No. 6 or larger self-tapping sheet-metal screw	No. 8 or larger self-tapping sheet-metal screw

Hanging Shelves and Cabinets

Once you have determined the wall type and selected the appropriate fastener for hanging a shelf or cabinet securely *(charts, pages 42-43)*, make sure it will be perfectly level. Supports should usually be spaced from 20 to 32 inches apart, depending on the load. If supports are more than 32 inches apart, most wood shelving will sag under its own weight. Nor should the ends of a shelf extend more than 8 inches beyond the outside supports; the ends might bow and the shelf would lose stability.

If your wall is hollow, it is probably backed by wood or metal studs. Locate the studs according to the instructions on page 42; and, if possible, attach the supports to them. Since most studs are about 16 inches apart, a support attached to every other stud will work for most loads.

In leveling a shelf or cabinet, do not rely on visual judgment; use a level *(Step 4)*. Wall, ceiling and floor lines are seldom straight, even in new homes.

The most common methods for hanging shelves use braces that are attached directly to the wall, or brackets that fit into upright standards installed on the wall. Braces are usually used to put up a single, stationary shelf. Heavy angle irons, like the one shown below, or braces made from molded metal can be used to support heavy weights. But whether braces are decorative or utilitarian, all are attached to walls in much the same way.

Standards are most often used to support several shelves on removable brackets. Most standards are attached as described in the instructions on page 46. Brackets differ, however; the most widely used brackets, with instructions for installing them, are on page 47.

Shelves are also installed in closets and corners, across windows or in hallways, where they can be supported at the sides instead of—or in addition to—the back. For this kind of installation, use the specialized mountings shown on page 48.

Heavy objects can be supported firmly —and later removed easily, if desired— with the aid of mitered cleats: wood strips cut lengthwise from 1-by-4 lumber at a 45° angle, and fastened to the wall and to the back of the cabinet being attached to the wall. Directions for making these cleats are on pages 48 and 49.

Wall storage devices are not, of course, limited to shelves and cabinets. One way to put vertical space to work is to use perforated hardboard, or pegboard. This composition board comes in thicknesses of ⅛ inch for light loads, and ¼ inch for heavier jobs. Holes punched at 1-inch intervals over its surface vary from under ¼ inch in the ⅛-inch-thick board to about $3/_{16}$ inch in the ¼-inch board. Pegboard can be attached to a wall by inserting fasteners through the holes. To maintain space behind the board for insertion of pegboard hooks, frame the back of the pegboard with ½-inch molding or insert a cylindrical rubber spacer between the pegboard and the wall. Tool departments and hardware stores carry hooks, clamps and other support devices in sizes appropriate to the thickness of the board (⅛ inch, ¼ inch).

With imagination, you can use pegboard in many ways, or create your own storage devices from objects you have at home. Big, bulky equipment can be lifted onto braces installed to be used as hooks. Dowels will support snow tires in a garage, or plants on a porch. Even wood soft-drink cases make splendid compartmental storage for small items.

Putting up a Shelf

1 **Leveling the first brace.** Decide where you want your shelf. Place the first brace against the wall. Hold a level vertically against the brace and the wall. Adjust the position of the brace until the air bubbles in the end vials of the level are centered. With an awl, scratch circles through the screw holes. Remove the brace and drill pilot holes. Center the drill bit precisely; even a small error can throw off the alignment. Attach the brace with the appropriate fastener *(chart, page 43)*.

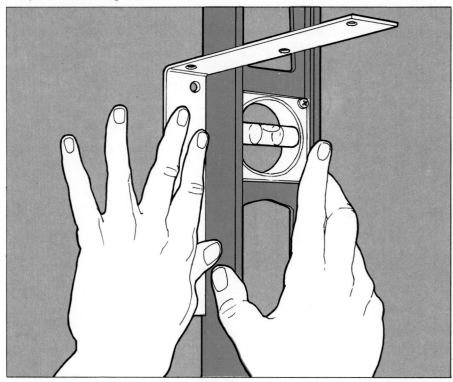

2 **Positioning the other braces.** If the shelf is short enough to require only two braces, decide on the amount of overhang you want at each end. Measure in that amount from each end and mark the shelf lightly on its underside. If the shelf will need more than two braces, mark the positions of the braces at each end in the same manner. Then measure the distance between the position of these braces and divide this measurement by the number of additional braces you intend to use plus one. The resulting figure will provide an equal distance from brace to brace.

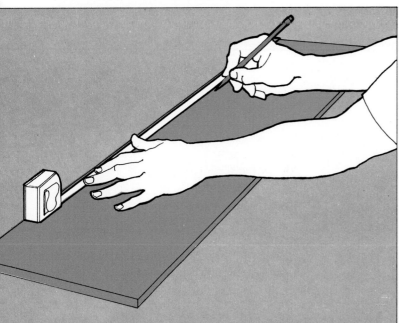

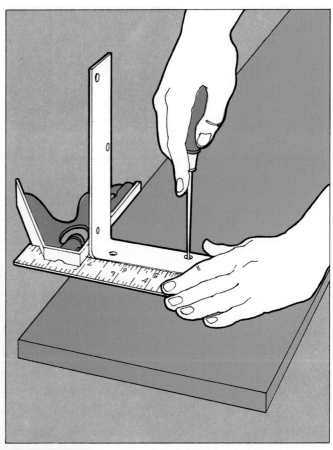

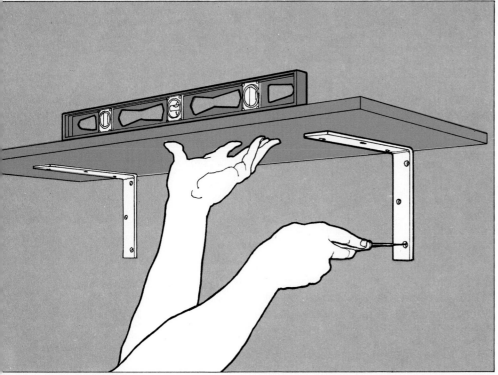

3 **Setting the second brace.** Set the second brace at one of the marked positions on the shelf (except where the brace already attached to the wall is to align). Square the brace against the back edge of the shelf by fitting it against a combination square as shown. Mark the screw holes, drill pilot holes and attach the brace to the shelf with wood screws. Attach all other braces (if any) in the same way, centering them carefully on the positions marked on the underside of the shelf.

4 **Leveling the shelf.** Rest the shelf, its braces attached, on the brace already fastened to the wall. Make sure the brace is centered on the mark made for it on the shelf. Put a carpenter's level on the shelf and adjust the shelf position until the middle bubble in the level is centered. With an awl, scratch the wall through the screw holes in the braces. Remove the shelf and drill all pilot or anchor holes in the wall. Replace the shelf and fasten the braces to the wall. Drill pilot holes in the shelf through the holes in the brace that was first fastened to the wall. Drive in wood screws.

Hanging a Shelf on Standards

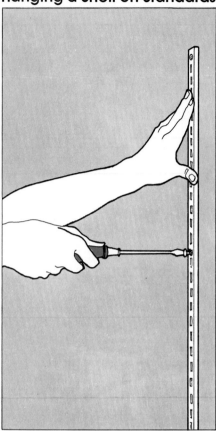

2 Attaching the standard. Align the standard vertically with a level. Mark the positions of the other fastener holes and, if necessary, swing the standard aside when you drill the pilot or anchor hole. Make sure that the drill bit is centered precisely. Attach the remaining fasteners.

3 Hanging the shelf. Insert one shelf bracket in the first standard. Fit a bracket into the corresponding holes of a second standard. Place the second standard against the wall, centering it on the mark made for it, and set the shelf, with a level on it, on top of the brackets. Adjust the shelf until the bubble in the level is centered. Mark the top and bottom of the second standard on the wall; remove the shelf and attach the second standard as described in Steps 1 and 2. If the shelf is to be supported by more than two standards, repeat Steps 1 to 3 for each.

1 Positioning the first standard. Mark the location of the shelves lightly on the wall. Determine the location of the end standards, then of the middle ones, if any, as described in Step 2, page 45, but mark the positions on the wall, not on the shelves. Place a standard against the wall on the spot marked for an end standard. (Check to make sure the standard is top end up; some standards are made to be oriented in one way only.) Mark one fastener hole—the center one if there are more than two—and drive in an appropriate fastener. Do not tighten, so you can swing aside the standard to insert the remaining fasteners.

Types of Standards and Brackets

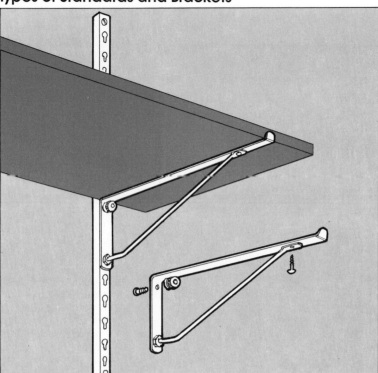

Keyhole. Because of their triangular design, brackets of this type can support very heavy weights. Slip the bolts that come with the brackets into the holes in the standards. Press the bolts down and tighten the bracket nuts.

Tracked. This slotted metal standard is fitted with sliding inserts equipped with a bolt and flat nut. To attach a bracket, press an insert into the track of the standard. The top of the insert must be at shelf level minus the thickness of the bracket. Tighten the bolt with a hex wrench *(inset)* until the nut grips the standard. Slip the spade pin at the end of the bracket sidewise into the standard slot and turn the bracket till it fits into the groove on the face of the insert. (These standards will also hold lamps with spade-pin attachments similar to those on the brackets.)

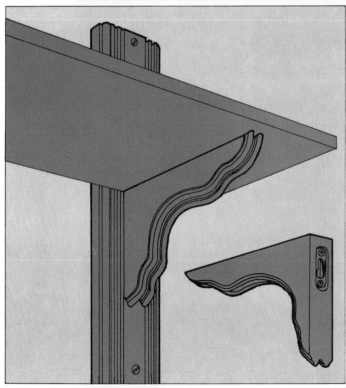

Carved wood. These decorative brackets are hooked over screws driven into their standards. To attach them, partially drive a screw into the standard at the level on the wall where you want to hang the shelf. Then fit the small, metal-lined hole on the bracket's inner surface *(inset)* over the projecting screwhead.

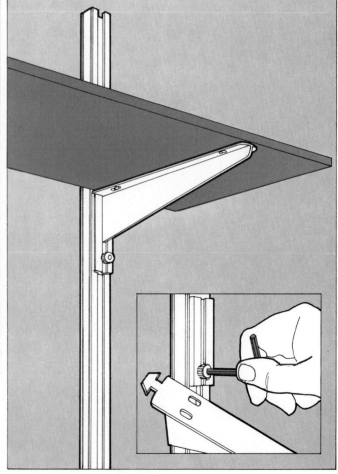

Supporting Shelves from the Side

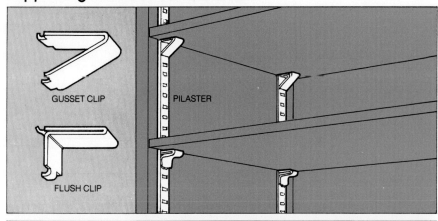

GUSSET CLIP

FLUSH CLIP

PILASTER

Pilasters and clips. Slotted metal tracks, or pilasters, can be screwed or nailed to the side of a bookcase or wall, or dadoed in for a neat, flush fit. Squeeze the clips into the slots of the metal tracks with a pair of pliers. The gusset clip *(top)* can support more weight than the flush clip *(bottom)* because it has a triangular shape.

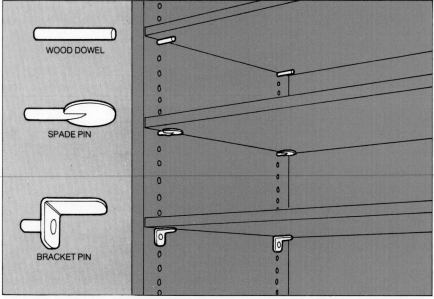

WOOD DOWEL

SPADE PIN

BRACKET PIN

Pins. These supports fit into holes drilled to match their diameter. Wood dowels *(top)* can be fashioned as described on page 41. The load to be carried by the shelf will determine the diameter and length of the dowel. Metal spade pins *(center)* and bracket pins *(bottom)* offer a flat surface for greater stability. When marking hole positions before drilling, use a level and straight edge to ensure evenness. You need not drill a row of holes on the side pieces if you do not plan to make frequent shelf adjustments.

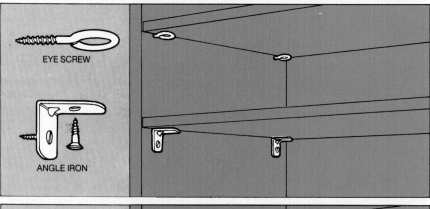

EYE SCREW

ANGLE IRON

Eye screws and angle irons. A light load can be supported by eye screws *(top)*, which are easily driven into wood. They can also be used in masonry with the help of a lead anchor *(page 40)*. A small angle iron *(bottom)* can be installed in most walls relatively unobtrusively and will take 5-to-10-pound loads. Neither support is elegant, but both may serve well in a garage or basement.

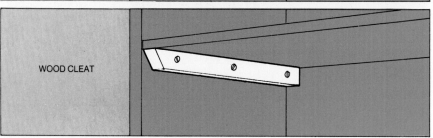

WOOD CLEAT

Wood cleats. For the strongest side support, cut strips of ¾-inch molding about ½ inch shorter than the depth of the shelf. Saw off the front edges at a 45° angle before you attach the cleats to the sides of the wall or storage unit. If great strength is required, attach a third cleat beneath the back of the shelf and then set the shelf on the cleats. For extra stability in an installation that will be permanent, you can drive small finishing nails at an angle through the shelf into the cleats.

Hanging a Large Unit on Mitered Cleats

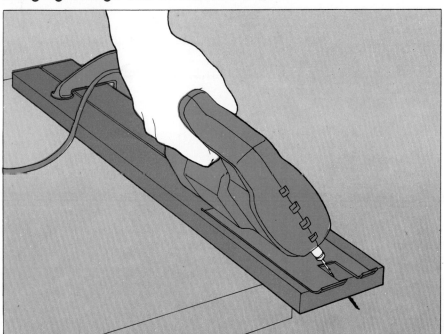

1 Cutting the cleats. Using C clamps, fix a piece of 1-by-4 lumber, slightly shorter than the width of the back of the unit, to your worktable. With a crosscut saw, or a circular or saber saw set to cut at a 45° angle, cut the lumber lengthwise into two cleats, as shown. A perfect cut is not necessary, since the cleats will fit together precisely along their sawed faces. But make sure to angle the saw blade away from the table while you work and remove and replace the C clamps as you cut down the length of the board.

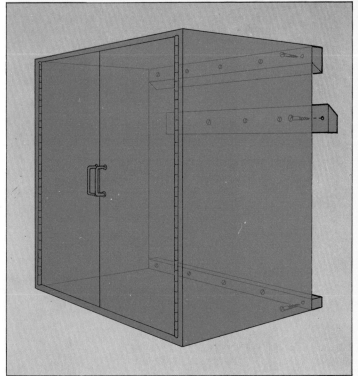

2 Attaching the cleats. Fasten one of the cleats to the wall, with its sawed edge up, as shown here. Then attach the other cleat, with its cut edge down, to the upper edge of the back of the unit by driving wood screws from the inside of the unit at least ½ inch into the cleat. In order to prevent the unit from wobbling or tilting after you have hung it on the wall, attach a strip of ¾-inch molding, also slightly shorter than the width of the back, to the bottom of the unit.

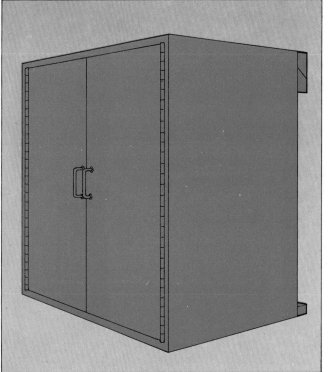

3 Hanging the cabinet. Ease the unit onto the wall cleat, so that the two matching faces of the 1-by-4 board meet. When you construct a cabinet or other storage item to be hung this way, you can hide the cleats by constructing the top and sides to extend about ¾ inch beyond the back.

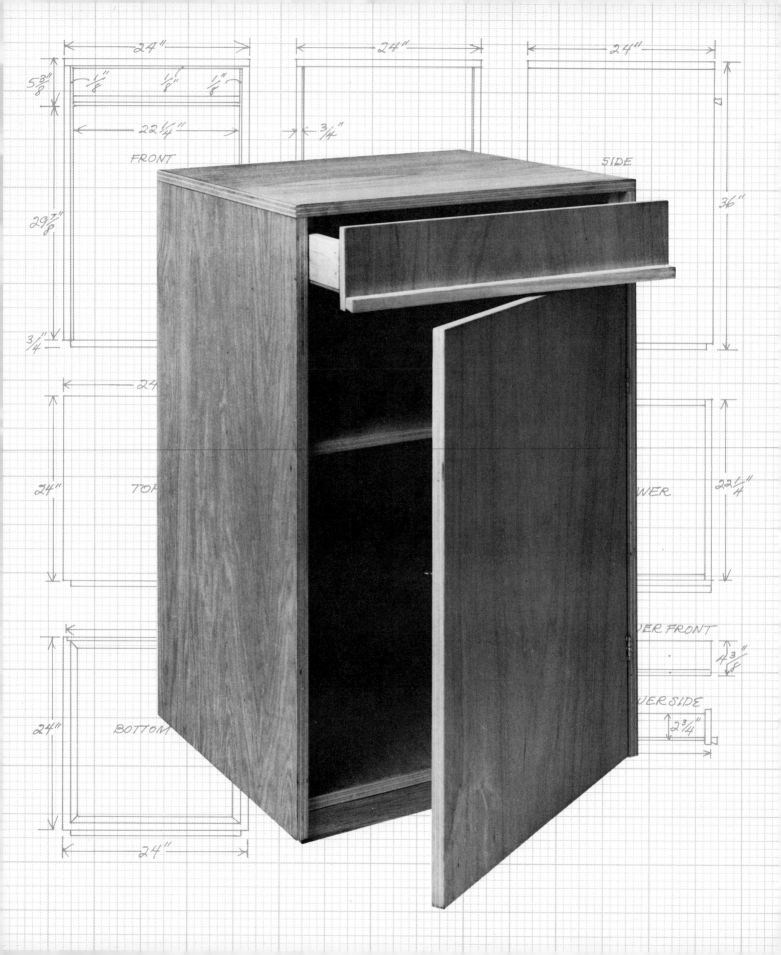

24″

5 3/8″ 1/8″ 1/8″ 1/8″

22 1/4″

FRONT

3/4″

SIDE

29 7/8″

36″

3/4″

24″

TOP

24″ WER 22 1/4″

24″

24″ BOTTOM

ER FRONT 1 3/8″

ER SIDE 2 3/4″

24″

2

Planning a Project Step by Step

From start to finish: The set of working drawings *(background, left)* provides the take-off point for construction of this general-purpose storage cabinet. Sturdily built, it can be used in a kitchen, family room or workshop—depending on the finishing materials chosen. As designed, it has a drawer and an adjustable shelf, but the cabinet can be easily modified to include additional shelves or drawers, by substituting hardware for the wooden pull or by adding decorative veneer strips to the exposed plywood edges.

Before actually starting to build any project three basic questions must be answered: What are the dimensions of the project? How will its parts be joined together? What materials can best be used in its construction? The answers to these questions, taken one at a time and in logical sequence—as they are in the chapter that follows—are indispensable to accomplishing your goal with both maximum efficiency and economy.

One of the simplest projects in this book, building the general-purpose cabinet shown opposite, is used to demonstrate this basic planning process. The cabinet is an example of a project conceived from scratch—one that starts as an idea and is carried to full realization—but the same process can be used when you decide to modify plans that already exist, including the instructions provided for the particular projects in this book.

Whether you are altering existing designs or working out your own, step-by-step planning demands, first of all, a complete set of working drawings *(pages 54-57)*. These flat two-dimensional representations of the project—from the side, front, top, bottom and back—show the size of each component part. The drawings are indeed similar to an architect's blueprints in their function; but the prospect of making them should not be inhibiting. They really are not that difficult to do and one does not have to be a professional draftsman to produce effective results.

The sole purpose of the plans is to provide yourself with all the essential information you will need before you go to the workbench. If you are a neophyte at working with wood, it's best to start with graph paper, which is inexpensive, readily available and provides a built-in scale. Once you have done a few projects, even small ones, you may then find that you can draw plans freehand on plain paper —as long as you are careful to record all of the measurements precisely, all of the parts, all of the joints, all of the clearances; in short, all of the interrelationships of the various pieces, taking into account the amount of space available, the location of adjacent walls and items of furniture.

Obviously, once you have completed the working drawings, you will have answered the first two of the three essential questions: What dimensions? How do the pieces fit? And the third question —What materials?—will have begun to answer itself. From the working drawings you can now compile an efficient shopping list, itemizing all the materials you will need. Furthermore, you can do so in the special language of lumberyards and hardware stores *(pages 58-61)*, thereby assuring that you will get everything in the sizes and grades and types you require.

The First Step:
Using Design Norms to Determine Dimensions

When you start planning a project, you will already have a general idea of the size you want the structure to be and how it will fit into the room. But before you can make actual construction plans, you will have to pin down precisely the basic dimensions of the unit: height, width and depth.

Fortunately, you do not have to work out these dimensions in the abstract: There are established norms for the critical dimensions of most pieces of home furniture. The norms are based on average measurements for adult men and women; the ones to keep foremost in mind when planning storage projects are shown below. In the case of storage units, these dimensions take into consideration the maximal size of things that are typically stored in them. Bear in mind, however, that children's proportions vary greatly according to age; if you are building something for a child, use the same points of reference that you would use for adults, but scale to size and remember to allow for growth, since the average child grows 2 inches every year between the ages of five and 16.

The utility cabinet shown on page 50, which is planned and built on the following pages, was designed using two standard dimensions for counter cabinets. Its height, 36 inches, places the work area at a level where most individuals will find it convenient to use while standing; it is a few inches lower than the average measurements from the floor to the elbow of both men and women (right). The cabinet's depth, 24 inches, keeps everything in or on it within reach;

the measurement is a good half foot less than that of the average outstretched arm. At the same time, because the dimensions of the cabinet are standard, the unit will fit uniformly side by side with most kitchen cabinets and built-in appliances, which have been designed with the same norms in mind.

Other factors, of course, will also help you determine the final size: available space, appearance and desired storage capacity. Even the economical use of wood (page 60) should be considered.

Finally, to avoid the classic dilemma of the man who builds a boat in the basement only to discover he will have to tear down the house to get it out, make sure your storage unit is not too large to be moved from your work area to its eventual location. Check not only doorways but also the amount of room you will need for turning in halls. For large projects, plan to make the final assembly in the room where the unit will be used.

Using human norms. The average dimensions illustrated at right are derived from research by the U.S. armed services, public health agencies and various universities. If you are building something for which some or all of the dimensions are optional, use the data in the drawings as a starting point, but also take measurements of yourself and your family to be sure that the project will be conveniently proportioned for those who will be using it most frequently.

Norms for Adult Men and Women

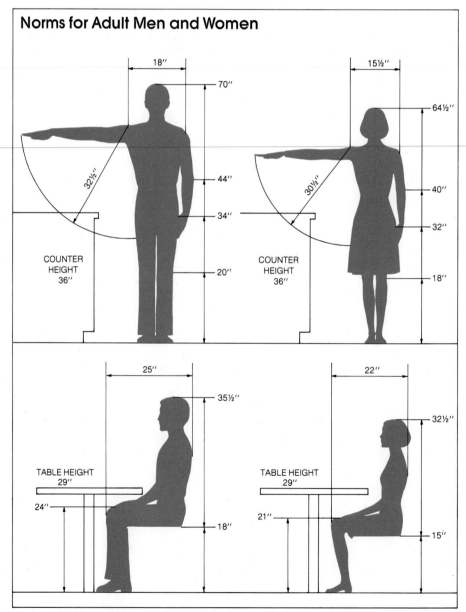

Using norms for stored items. Many of the common household items listed at right are, of course, available in a wide range of sizes. But for initial planning purposes, the chart will provide a good approximation of the amount of space required to store these representative items. You should list the specific items to be stored and take their pertinent measurements before determining the exact inside dimensions of a project. The abbreviations used in the chart—H, W, D and L—stand for height, width, depth and length.

Sizes of Common Household Items (in inches)

Kitchen
Frying pan, 10″ to 20″ L (with handle) × 5″ to 12½″ diameter
Pressure cooker, 15″ L (with handle) × 7½″ diameter
Roasting pan, 7½″ to 9″ H × 17″ to 20″ L
Mixing bowls, 3″ to 4½″ H × 6″ to 11″ diameter
Saucepan, 3″ to 7″ H × 8″ to 16″ L (with handle)

Closet
Garment bag, 57″ H × 8″ to 24″ W × 21″ D
Coat, 50″ H × 22″ W
Suit (pants folded), 38″ H × 20″ W
Slacks (hung full length), 44″ H × 16″ W
Skirt, 35″ H × 13″ W

Attic
Footlocker, 13″ H × 30″ W × 17″ D
Suitcase, 20″ H × 26″ W × 6¾″ D
Hatbox, 12″ to 14″ diameter
Shoe box, 4″ to 6″ H × 7″ to 14″ W × 13″ D

Basement
Toolbox, 5″ to 9″ H × 11″ to 22″ L
Miter box, 4¾″ H × 15¾″ W × 3⅝″ D
Broom, 48″ to 60″ H × 8″ to 10″ W
Rake, 64″ H × 24″ W
Skis, 48″ to 84″ H × 3½″ W
Golf bag, 35″ H × 8″ W

Using norms for furniture. Norms are useful guidelines in establishing the proportions of any piece of home furniture you build. Height measurement is the most critical dimension for all the pieces listed, except for drawers and beds. The height of all the other pieces listed should not vary from the norms more than an inch or two so that the furniture will be comfortable for most people to use. Dimensions for depth and width are less critical and can be changed according to the amount of space available for the piece and the amount of storage room needed inside it.

Standard Dimensions of Common Home Furniture (in inches)

Item	Height (above floor)	Width (side to side)	Depth (front to back, or head to foot)
Bed, double	20	54	75
Bed, twin	20	39	75
Bed, king-size	20	72-76	80-84
Bed, queen-size	20	60	80-84
Bookcase	84 (maximum)	optional	12-18
Cabinet, counter	36	15-42	24
Cabinet, wall	87 (maximum)	optional	13
Chest-of-drawers	41-56	32-40	18-22
Desk	29	60	30
Dining table	29	optional	optional
Drawer	–	optional	16-24
Dresser	29-34	35-80	20
Dressing table	26-30	36-50	15-22
Kitchen stove	36″	19½-40	24¼-27½
Night table	25	optional	20
Sewing table	26	optional	17 (minimum)
Straight chair	18 (seat), 31 (back)	20	22
Typing table	26	optional	17 (minimum)
Workbench	32	optional	26

Step Two:
Preparing the Working Drawings for Your Project

Like a good road map, a set of working drawings enables you to arrive at your destination by the best and quickest route. Preparing the plans is easy; with them, you can make all the main decisions in advance, such as the type of joints that will hold a cabinet together, the positions of shelves, the exact sizes of drawers and doors, and the way the doors will open and close.

The number of drawings needed depends on the complexity of the structure you are building. For most units, the basic set of plans consists of flat, two-dimensional views of the outside from every vantage point: front, back, top, bottom and sides. In addition, any box within the basic box—such as a drawer or bin—requires its own external plans; for them, views of the object from top, front and side will suffice.

The easiest way to make a basic set of drawings is to start with graph paper, letting each square on the grid represent 1 inch. Draw the outside dimensions of each view of the cabinet (black lines, opposite). Within those lines, add all appropriate measurements (lines in color). Fractions of an inch can be approximated, so long as the precise dimensions are written on the plan. Another set of drawings, cutaways like the ones shown on pages 56 and 57, are needed for interior parts or for those that are too small to be drawn accurately on the external views. These drawings, called sections, focus on such details as the way pieces go together at the joints and the way drawers, doors and other moving parts fit into the structure. They should be drawn larger —a scale of four graph squares to the inch is recommended.

To work out the measurements on both the exterior and sectional drawings, you need to decide which of the two general types of wood—lumber or plywood—you will be using for each part of the cabinet. Choosing the exact grade and finish of the wood can be left for later (pages 58-59), but the width and thickness of the wood must be shown on your drawings (chart, right).

Since commonly available lumber is not wide enough to be used for the large pieces of a storage unit, these parts are nearly always made from plywood. This material is usually sold in 4-by-8-foot sheets in thicknesses measuring ¼, ⅜, ½, ⅝ and ¾ inch. For the large pieces that bear the most structural stress—the top, bottom, sides and shelves—you will most often need a ¾-inch thickness. For less critical large members—the back and the drawer bottoms—thinner plywood, usually ¼ inch, can be used.

Plywood measurements are easy to calculate, because the listed thickness is the actual thickness. But the problem is more complex when lumber is used, since its actual size and its nominal size usually differ. Lumber is used mostly for smaller, interior parts. On the utility cabinet, for example, the drawer sides, base sections, runners and pull, and the blocks reinforcing the joints are made of lumber.

Ready-made plans, including the ones shown later in this book, are easily adapted to your own particular requirements by revising the measurements in the working drawings to conform to your needs. But remember, if you change the scale of a project drastically, you may have to change the size of wood, or even add a frame (page 24).

Lumber:
Nominal versus Actual Size

For the parts of a project that require lumber—rather than plywood—you will nearly always be using one of the softwoods (pine, spruce, fir) since they are more commonly available and much less expensive than hardwoods (oak, walnut, mahogany). However, the designations by inches for most sizes of softwood are not their actual measurements. By long-standing custom—now codified by lumber associations—the dimensions cited for the thickness and width of a piece of softwood refer to the size of the rough-cut lumber before it is dried and trimmed to make it smooth and square. As a result, the real size of the piece of lumber you buy is smaller than the nominal size as shown in the chart at right.

For example, the boards used for the four sides of the drawer in the utility cabinet are designated as 1-by-3-inch lumber, but the wood actually measures ¾ by 2½ inches. In preparing your working drawings, be sure to use only the actual size of the lumber.

This rule does not apply to lumber smaller than the nominal 1 by 2. These smaller pieces are considered molding and are sold in exact inch sizes. For example, the wood blocks used to reinforce the joints on the utility cabinet and the runners for the drawers call for ¾-inch-square molding—its actual size.

Hardwood is also sold in exact inch sizes, but the widths vary from board to board. Only the thicknesses are standardized; the most common thicknesses in inches are $3/16$, $5/16$, $7/16$, $9/16$, $13/16$ and $1 1/16$.

Nominal lumber sizes	Actual sizes (in inches)
1 × 2	¾ × 1½
1 × 3	¾ × 2½
1 × 4	¾ × 3½
1 × 6	¾ × 5½
1 × 8	¾ × 7¼
1 × 10	¾ × 9¼
1 × 12	¾ × 11¼
2 × 2	1½ × 1½
2 × 3	1½ × 2½
2 × 4	1½ × 3½
2 × 6	1½ × 5½
2 × 8	1½ × 7¼
2 × 10	1½ × 9¼
2 × 12	1½ × 11¼

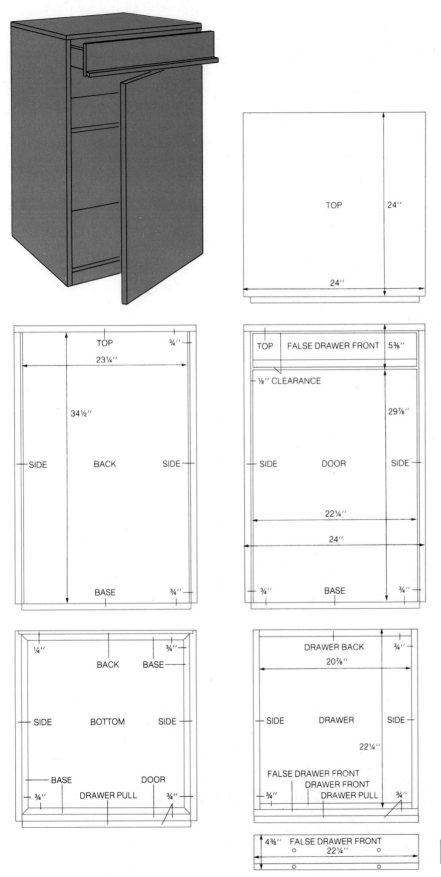

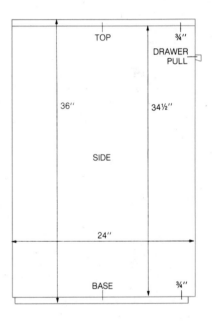

Sizing the parts. For the utility cabinet at far left, the set of two-dimensional views shown at left and below helps you figure out the exact size of the exterior component parts. The colored lines on the exterior views show how the size of a structure's parts is determined by the clearance required for doors and drawers, and by allowances for wood thickness. For example, the sizes of the door and false drawer front are calculated by first drawing lines representing the ¾-inch thickness of the cabinet's plywood sides and top, and then drawing lines indicating the ⅛-inch clearance that will be necessary in order to allow the door to open and shut without binding.

Diagraming the Sections

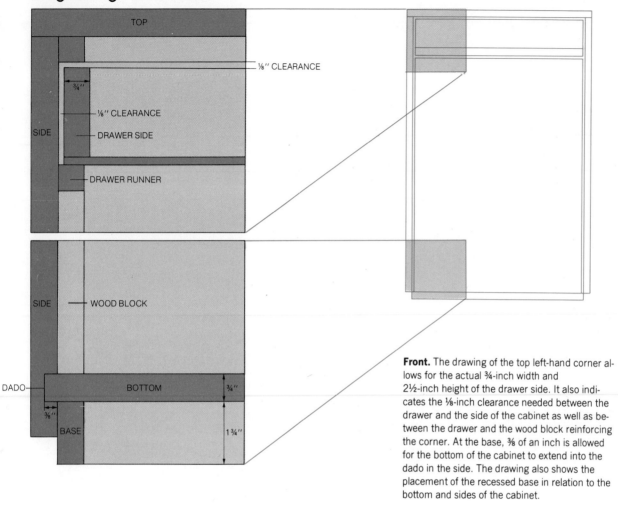

- TOP
- 1/8'' CLEARANCE
- 3/4''
- 1/8'' CLEARANCE
- SIDE
- DRAWER SIDE
- DRAWER RUNNER
- SIDE
- WOOD BLOCK
- DADO
- BOTTOM
- 3/4''
- 3/8''
- BASE
- 1 3/4''

Front. The drawing of the top left-hand corner allows for the actual ¾-inch width and 2½-inch height of the drawer side. It also indicates the ⅛-inch clearance needed between the drawer and the side of the cabinet as well as between the drawer and the wood block reinforcing the corner. At the base, ⅜ of an inch is allowed for the bottom of the cabinet to extend into the dado in the side. The drawing also shows the placement of the recessed base in relation to the bottom and sides of the cabinet.

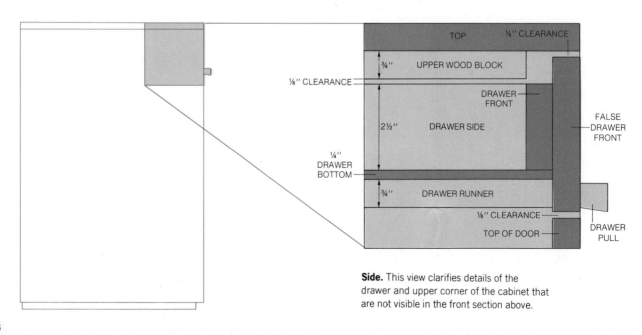

- TOP
- 1/8'' CLEARANCE
- 3/4''
- UPPER WOOD BLOCK
- 1/8'' CLEARANCE
- DRAWER FRONT
- 2½''
- DRAWER SIDE
- FALSE DRAWER FRONT
- ¼'' DRAWER BOTTOM
- 3/4''
- DRAWER RUNNER
- 1/8'' CLEARANCE
- TOP OF DOOR
- DRAWER PULL

Side. This view clarifies details of the drawer and upper corner of the cabinet that are not visible in the front section above.

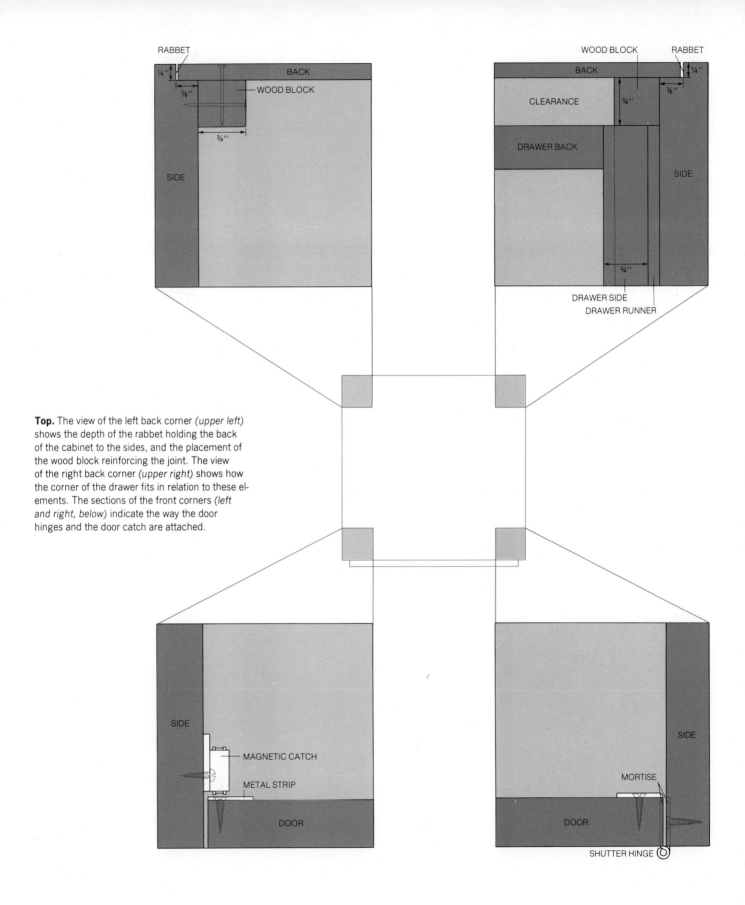

RABBET

WOOD BLOCK   RABBET

¼″

BACK

⅜″

WOOD BLOCK

¾″

SIDE

BACK

WOOD BLOCK

¼″

⅜″

CLEARANCE

¾″

DRAWER BACK

SIDE

¾″

DRAWER SIDE

DRAWER RUNNER

Top. The view of the left back corner *(upper left)* shows the depth of the rabbet holding the back of the cabinet to the sides, and the placement of the wood block reinforcing the joint. The view of the right back corner *(upper right)* shows how the corner of the drawer fits in relation to these elements. The sections of the front corners *(left and right, below)* indicate the way the door hinges and the door catch are attached.

SIDE

MAGNETIC CATCH

METAL STRIP

DOOR

SIDE

MORTISE

DOOR

SHUTTER HINGE

Step Three: Buying the Materials You Need

Once the working drawings for a project are complete, prepare a shopping list of materials. The sample list on page 60 has been compiled for the utility cabinet shown in the drawings on the preceding pages. The specifications are drawn from the charts here and on the facing page, which are a guide to the sizes and grades of plywood and lumber in the U.S. (Canadian designations are different.)

Most plywood is a sandwich of thin sheets of wood, called plies or veneers. The layers, whose grains run at right angles to each other, are glued together under pressure at high temperatures. The result is a strong wood that is more warp resistant than lumber and can be used in large expanses.

Plywood is graded primarily by appearance, reflecting the number of defects in the surface plies. These outer veneers can be either softwood (cut from evergreen trees) or hardwood (cut from deciduous trees like birch, oak and walnut). Each type has its own grading system (chart, below), and every sheet has its grade stamped on an edge or a back ply.

Plywood with the highest-grade surfaces on both front and back is marked N-N if it is softwood, A-A or Premium if it is hardwood. These higher grades are necessary only if a natural finish will be used and both surfaces will be seen on the finished project. If the back ply will be hidden, it is more economical to use A-D grade softwood plywood, or hardwood plywood with a Good-grade front and a Utility-grade back. If you plan to paint your project, you can even buy inexpensive B-B softwood plywood or Sound-grade hardwood plywood.

Softwood plywood, the most popular type, always is made of thin plies between the outer plies. To get it, specify veneer core. Hardwood plywood, however, is also sold with other materials sandwiched between the outer veneers. Solid lumber, for example, is often used because its solid edges hold nails and screws well. Another inner material is particle board—a slab of wood chips that are glued together under pressure. When ordering hardwood plywood, be sure to specify the core you want—either lumber, particle board or veneer.

Plywood is also classified as interior or exterior grade, depending on the moisture resistance of the glue used to bond the plies together. Interior grades resist only normal indoor dampness. The more expensive exterior grades are needed for outdoor projects or in high-moisture areas such as bathrooms.

Like plywood, lumber of both softwood and hardwood has its own grading system (charts, opposite). The more commonly used softwoods are called boards if they are nominally an inch thick and are graded for appearance. Softwood nominally 2 inches thick is called dimension lumber; it is graded for strength.

Softwood comes from the mills in standard even-numbered lengths from 6 to 20 feet. When ordering it, specify lumber that is smooth on four sides (usually abbreviated S4S). Also note that you want kiln-dried (Kd) wood; though more expensive than air-dried (Ad), it is less prone to warping and shrinking.

Hardwood is usually sold with smooth surfaces on two or three sides (S2S or S3S) and lengths are not standardized. For cabinet work, it should be kiln-dried.

Many yards now price lumber by the running foot. However, traditionally it is priced by a unit of measurement called a board foot: a square foot of lumber nominally 1 inch thick. To find the board feet in any piece of lumber, multiply its nominal thickness in inches by its nominal width in inches. Then multiply the total by its actual length in feet and divide the result by 12. For example, the 8-foot length of 1-by-3 lumber used for the utility cabinet equals 2 board feet.

Whether you are buying lumber or plywood, be sure to inspect it for damage before accepting it from the lumberyard. Plywood should be checked for nicks and gouges in the surface veneers and at edges and corners; examine lumber for similar damage as well as for warping.

Plywood Surface Grades

Type of Surface	Grade	Description
Softwood	N	No knots or blemishes. Suitable for natural finish.
	A	Smooth surface with neat repairs of blemishes. Suitable for natural finish or paint.
	B	Solid surface with large repair plugs and tight knots. Takes paint well but not natural finishes.
	C	Unplugged knotholes as large as 1½ inches. Takes paint poorly. Used where not visible.
	D	Knots and holes as large as 3 inches. Almost unpaintable. Used where not visible.
Hardwood	A or Premium	No knots or blemishes. Surface ply has well-matched grain and color. Suitable for natural finish.
	1 or Good	Best of the regular grades. Surface ply has fairly well-matched grain. Suitable for natural finish.
	2 or Sound	Smooth surface with some tight knots. Takes paint well.
	3 or Utility	Rough surface with small splits and knotholes as large as 1 inch. Takes paint poorly. Not normally available with lumber core or particle-board core.
	4 or Backing	Very rough surface with splits as large as 1 inch, knotholes as large as 3 inches. Not suitable for painting. Not normally available with lumber core or particle-board core.

Softwood Lumber Grades

Type	Grade	Category	Description
Boards	Select or Clear	A	No knots or splits. Suitable for natural finish.
		B	A few tiny blemishes. Suitable for natural finish.
		C	A few small, tight knots. Suitable for natural finish or paint.
		D	More numerous small knots than C. Takes paint well.
	Common	No. 1	Larger tight knots. Takes paint well.
		No. 2	More numerous, larger knots than No. 1, some loose. Takes paint adequately.
		No. 3	Has splits and knotholes. Does not take paint well.
		No. 4	Large waste areas with numerous splits and knotholes. Almost unpaintable.
		No. 5	Coarsest defects; unpaintable. Not suitable for storage projects.
Dimension Lumber	Light Framing	Construction	For high-stress areas.
		Standard	For medium- to high-stress areas.
		Utility	For low-stress areas only.
		Economy	Substandard wood. Not for use in storage projects.

Hardwood Lumber Grades

Grade	Category	Description
Firsts and Seconds		No knots or splits on front or back surfaces. Suitable for natural finishes.
Selects		No knots or splits on front surface, small defects on back. Suitable for natural finish.
Commons	No. 1	Some knots and splits on both surfaces. Takes paint well.
	No. 2	Numerous knots and splits. Takes paint adequately.
	Sound Wormy	Numerous large knots and splits. Does not take paint well.
	No. 3A	Unusable for storage projects.
	No. 3B	Unusable for storage projects.

Shopping List for the Cabinet

1 sheet A-A hardwood plywood, ¾″ × 4′ × 8′	4 shelf-bracket clips
1 sheet A-B softwood plywood, ¼″ × 4′ × 8′	1¼ pound finishing nails, 1″
2 lengths select A softwood molding, ¾″ × ¾″ × 8′, S4S, Kd.	¼ pound finishing nails, 1¼″
1 length select A softwood board, 1″ × 2″ × 8′, S4S, Kd.	½ pound finishing nails, 1½″
1 length select A softwood board, 1″ × 3″ × 8′, S4S, Kd.	¼ pound common nails, 1″
2 shutter hinges	2 dozen No. 6 flathead screws, 1¼″
1 magnetic catch	1 dozen No. 6 flathead screws, 1″
1 door pull	4 ounces white glue

A Plan for Cutting Wood Efficiently

To determine how much lumber or plywood is required for a project, you will need to make a "cutting diagram," like the example at right for the utility cabinet. In this diagram, every piece of the structure to be made from plywood is drawn on a piece of paper that is scaled to the dimensions of a plywood sheet, which is usually 4 by 8 feet.

To make a cutting plan, start with a piece of graph paper trimmed to a scale of 4 by 8 feet (page 54). Then, using the same scale, cut pieces from another sheet of graph paper to represent each piece of plywood needed for your project. Arrange the pieces on the 4-by-8 graph paper so that the pieces fit into the most efficient pattern—that is, with the least possible waste. At the same time, arrange the pieces so that when you actually saw the wood, the first cuts can be made in straight lines along the entire length of the sheet. Indicate the cuts as Cut No. 1, Cut No. 2, and so forth, as shown on the diagram. A further consideration is grain: arrange the pieces so that when the plywood is cut, the grain will create the effect you want.

When all the pieces are properly arranged, trace their shapes onto the sheet of paper, allowing an extra ⅛ inch along each cut for the saw kerf. To be doubly sure of allowing for kerfs, remeasure each cut before sawing the next one.

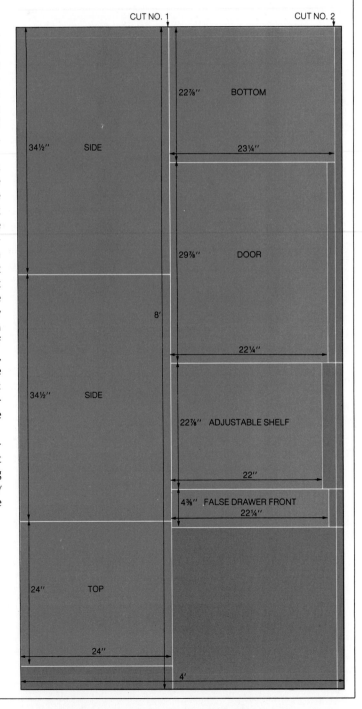

Materials for Fastening and Finishing

The shopping list for a project is not complete unless it includes the appropriate kinds of nails, screws and glues for fastening the pieces together, as well as the wood filler and abrasive paper needed to give the project a professional, finished look.

Screws have somewhat more holding power than nails and are necessary where strength is crucial. They also are used to attach parts of a structure you may later want to disassemble. Nails, when used with glue, are generally quite sufficient, however, for parts that will be permanently attached. There is a simple formula for selecting the right length: a nail or screw should be long enough so that two thirds of its shank will penetrate into the second of two pieces of wood being joined. Screws also come in various diameters, indicated by numbers from 0 to 24. The screws most frequently used in woodworking range from No. 5 (⅛ inch in diameter) to No. 14 (¼ inch); these wood screws have flat heads that can be countersunk and concealed (page 29).

Of the many types of nails sold, only two kinds are needed for most storage construction: common nails and finishing nails. Common nails have large heads for greater holding power and are used only in places where they will not be seen. Finishing nails have small heads that can be countersunk and concealed (page 16, Step 7); they should be used on exterior parts where an unblemished surface is desired.

Glue strengthens stress-bearing joints and, used in combination with nails or screws, can form a joint so strong that the pieces of wood will break before the joint itself will separate. Whenever you use glue, remember to wipe off any excess immediately; otherwise the glue will clog the wood's pores when it dries, and the wood will not take a stain. Four types of adhesives are commonly used for woodworking:

□ WHITE GLUE is the most useful all-purpose adhesive for light construction, but it should not be used on projects that will be exposed to moisture, high temperature or great stress. Wood that is being joined with white glue must remain in a clamp until the glue dries, which will take about 30 minutes.

□ ALIPHATIC RESIN GLUE has a stronger and more moisture-resistant bond than white glue. It must be used at temperatures above 50° F. The wood should be clamped for about 30 minutes. A common brand is Titebond.

□ PLASTIC RESIN GLUE is the strongest of the common wood adhesives. It is highly moisture resistant—though not completely waterproof. Sold in powdered form, this glue must be mixed with water and used at temperatures above 70° F. It is slow setting and the joint should be clamped for four to six hours. Plastic resin glue is sold under such brand names as Craftsman, Weldwood and Wilhold.

□ CONTACT CEMENT is a very strong adhesive that bonds so quickly it must be used with great care. It is ideal for mounting sheets of plastic laminate on wood (page 94). It is also useful for attaching strips of veneer to the edges of plywood. Since this adhesive bonds immediately when two pieces are pressed together, clamping is not necessary, but the parts to be joined must be very carefully aligned before being placed together. Check the label before you work with this adhesive. Most brands are quite flammable and the fumes can be harmful if inhaled. For safety's sake, work in a well-ventilated area, away from flames or heat.

After the project has been constructed, a wood-filler compound is needed to conceal surface flaws and cracks at the joints, as well as the depressions left by countersunk nails and screws. Most cabinetmakers prefer a type known as wood putty. Available only as a powder that is mixed with water immediately before it is used, this wood filler absorbs paint and stain like real wood. And unlike other fillers, including most plastic-based types, it will not shrink or loosen with time.

Before you apply a finish to a project, prepare all surfaces by sanding. The abrasive papers that are suitable for preparing the projects in this book are listed in the chart below. They are available with four kinds of grit: flint and garnet, which are inexpensive but not very durable, and aluminum oxide and silicon carbide, which are more costly but last much longer. The choice is yours. Most abrasive papers are rated by grit numbers, ranging from coarse to extra-fine, although an older system of grade numbers—also listed in the chart —is sometimes used.

Types of Abrasive Paper

	Grit No.	Grade No.	Typical Use
Coarse	40	1½	Shaping and trimming wood to fit at joints.
Medium coarse	60 80	½ 1/0	Removing small scratches and rough spots on wood.
Medium	100 120	2/0 3/0	First sanding of lumber and plywood edges.
Fine	150 180	4/0 5/0	Intermediate sanding of lumber and plywood edges.
Very fine	220 240	6/0 7/0	Sanding of lumber and softwood-surfaced plywood before applying paint or other finish.
Extra fine	280	8/0	Final sanding of hardwood-surfaced plywood before applying paint or other finish.

The Last Step: Cutting and Assembling

Once you have planned a project and bought the materials for it, you are ready to begin the job of actually building it: cutting the parts and putting them together. The procedures on this and the following pages explain how to cut and assemble the utility cabinet that is used as an example throughout this chapter.

For this project, the sheet of ¾-inch plywood should be cut first, according to the plan on page 60. This one sheet will provide the top, bottom, sides, shelf, door and false drawer front. After making these initial cuts, use masking tape as labels for the parts. You will then need to make cuts for the joints, as shown at right, on the sides, bottom and shelf.

Cut the other cabinet parts from the lumber you have purchased only as you need them, measuring the exact space each one will occupy—thus ensuring that the dimensions originally provided correspond to your actual cabinet. Even fractional variations in wood thickness and in cutting can change the size of the piece you need for a proper fit.

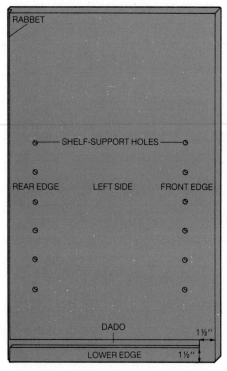

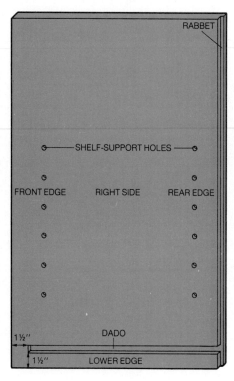

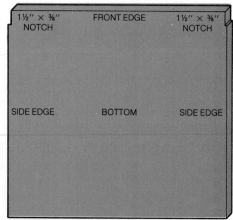

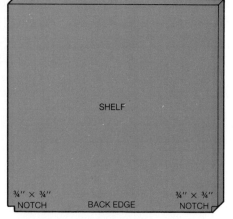

Preparing the sides. Along the rear edge of each cabinet side, cut rabbets into which the back of the cabinet will fit. Each rabbet should measure ⅜ inch deep and ¼ inch wide. Next, cut dadoes on both sides to hold the cabinet bottom; locate each dado 1½ inches above the lower edge. Each dado should run from the rabbet to 1½ inches from the front edge and be ¾ inch wide and ⅜ inch deep. Then drill two rows of holes on each side for shelf supports. Locate one row 3¼ inches from the front edge, the other 2½ inches from the rabbet in the rear edge. Drill the first hole in each row 7 inches above the dado; drill five more at 3-inch intervals above the first holes.

Notching the bottom and shelf. The front corners of the bottom of the cabinet must be notched in order to fit beyond the ends of the dadoes on the sides. Cut each notch so that it measures ⅜ inch in from each side edge and 1½ inches in from each front edge. The back corners of the shelf must also be notched so that the shelf will fit around the wood blocks at the rear of the cabinet. Cut each notch ¾ inch square.

Putting the Pieces Together

1 Attaching the wood blocks. Cut two pieces of ¾-inch-square molding, each piece 32⅝ inches long, which will be used as wood blocks to join the sides of the cabinet to the back.

At 4-inch intervals along each block, hammer 1½-inch nails through the wood until their tips just protrude. Spread white glue along the side of the blocks from which the nails protrude. Align each block along each rabbet between the dado and the top edge. Hammer the nails in. Then cut, glue and nail 22½-inch-long wood blocks along the top edge of each side, butting them against the wood blocks previously attached.

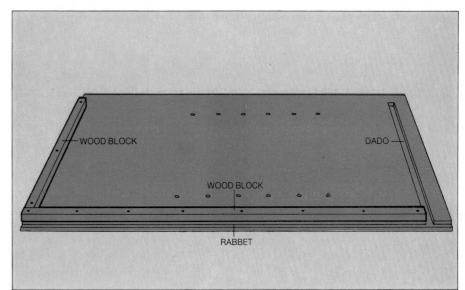

2 Installing drawer runners. Cut two 22½-inch pieces of ¾-inch-square molding for the drawer runners. Using a combination square (drawing), position a runner on one of the cabinet sides 2⅞ inches below the upper wood block and parallel to it. Hold the runner firmly in place and use it as a ruler. Mark a line the full length of the runner 2⅞ inches from the upper wood block along the side of the cabinet. Repeat on the second cabinet side. Glue and nail each runner along the awl line, making sure that its rear edge is butted against the rear wood block.

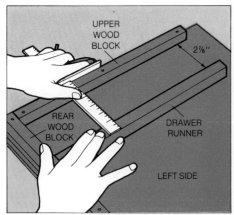

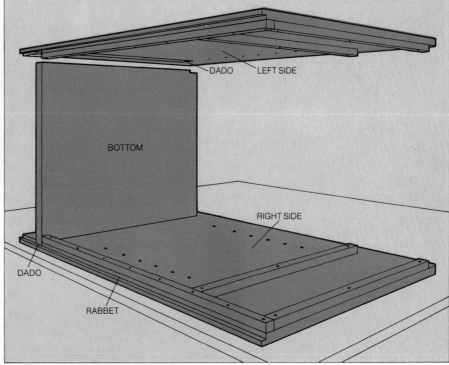

3 Gluing the bottom to the sides. Place one cabinet side on a flat surface and spread white glue inside the dado. Also spread glue along the surfaces of the bottom edge that will fit inside the dado. Tap the bottom edge into the dado, making sure the rabbet is left clear. Apply glue to the other bottom edge and to its matching side. Tap the pieces together. Turn the construction upright and proceed to the next step without waiting for the glue to dry.

4 **Installing the top.** Use corner clamps to hold the top to the sides. The top will be attached by screwing it to the upper wood blocks that are nailed to the sides. To locate the centers of the wood blocks on the top of the cabinet, scratch an awl line 1⅛ inches in from each side edge, using a combination square as a guide (drawing). To indicate the positions for the screws, make cross marks on each line at points 2 inches in from the front and back edges and at 4-inch intervals in between. Then drill pilot holes for 1¼-inch No. 6 wood screws at each cross mark. Countersink the screws.

5 **Attaching the top wood block.** To join the back of the cabinet to the top, cut a 21¼-inch length of ¾-inch-square molding. With the cabinet turned upside down, glue and nail the block to the cabinet top, positioning it ¼ inch in from the rear edge of the top so that it squares with the wood blocks on the cabinet sides, as shown.

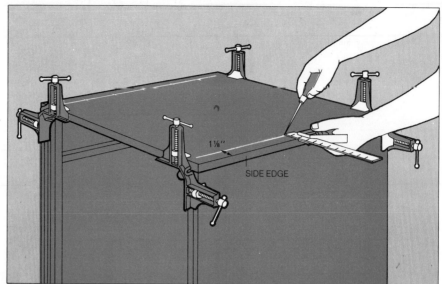

1⅛"

SIDE EDGE

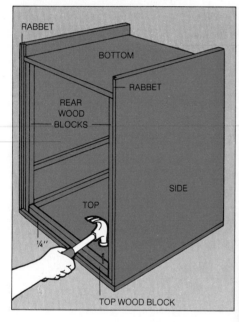

RABBET

BOTTOM

RABBET

REAR WOOD BLOCKS

SIDE

TOP

¼"

TOP WOOD BLOCK

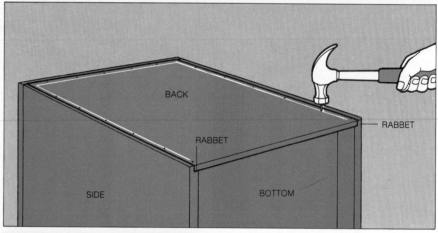

BACK

RABBET

SIDE

BOTTOM

RABBET

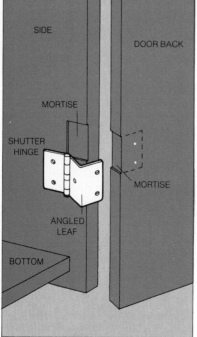

SIDE

DOOR BACK

MORTISE

SHUTTER HINGE

MORTISE

ANGLED LEAF

BOTTOM

6 **Attaching the back.** For the back of the cabinet cut a piece of ¼-inch plywood measuring 34½ by 23¼ inches. Place the cabinet face down and position the back so that it fits into the rabbets on the sides and butts against the top of the cabinet. Using a combination square in the same way as in Step 4, mark awl lines on the back of the cabinet 1⅛ inches in from the top and side edges of the cabinet, locating the centers of both the top and the side wood blocks. Then nail the back to the blocks, using 1-inch common nails spaced at 4-inch intervals.

7 **Hanging the door.** Using shutter hinges (*page 36*), attach the door according to the instructions for mortising hinges on an inset door (*page 35*). Decide whether the cabinet's final location will make a left- or right-hand opening more efficient, and locate the hinges accordingly. In either case, the hinges should be positioned 7½ inches from the top and bottom edges of the door. Attach the angled leaf of each hinge to the door as shown; it is not necessary to cut a mortise for the leaf part that will be attached to the back of the door. After hanging the door, install a catch (*page 37*) and a door pull.

8 **Building the drawer.** Cut two 22½-inch lengths of 1-by-3-inch lumber for the sides of the drawer and two 20⅞-inch lengths for its front and back. Then cut a piece of ¼-inch plywood measuring 22¼ by 22½ inches for the drawer bottom. Assemble the drawer by the method described on page 28, but do not attach the false front at this time. Use 1½-inch finishing nails to join the four sides together and 1-inch finishing nails to attach the bottom to the sides.

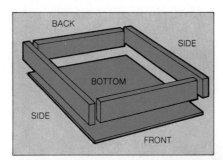

9 **Attaching the drawer pull.** To install the wood pull shown for this project, cut a 22¼-inch piece of ¾-inch-square molding. Using a wood clamp, align the pull on the outer face of the false drawer front ¼ inch from the bottom edge. Turn the false front upside down and clamp the entire assembly in a woodworking vise (drawing). Measure down ⅝ inch on the back surface of the false front to locate the center line of the drawer pull. Scratch cross marks for the screws along the center line, locating them 2 inches in from the side edges and at 4-inch intervals in between. Drill pilot holes at the marks and attach the pull with 1¼-inch wood screws.

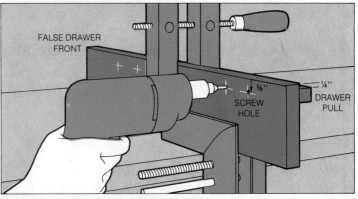

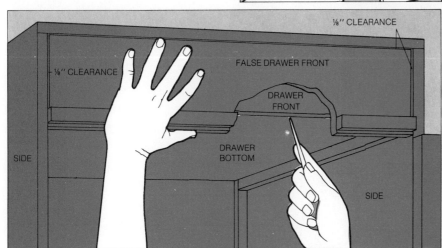

10 **Attaching the false drawer front.** With the cabinet door open, slide the drawer into the cabinet and position the false front on it so there is a ⅛-inch clearance around the false front on both sides and at the top. Mark an awl line on the back of the false front, using the bottom of the drawer as a guide (drawing).

Remove the false front and the drawer from the cabinet. Align the bottom of the drawer along the awl line and clamp the false front to the drawer. With the awl, mark positions for two screws on the inside surface of the drawer front; locate each of the screws 1½ inches below the top edge of the drawer front and 2 inches in from the sides. Then drill pilot holes for 1¼-inch wood screws and screw the pieces together.

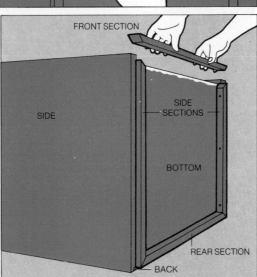

11 **Assembling the base.** Cut two 22½-inch lengths of 1-by-2-inch lumber for the front and back sections of the recessed base and two 23-inch lengths for the side sections. Miter the ends of each section, following the instructions on page 21. Place the cabinet on its back. Fit the back section into the recess at the bottom of the cabinet, and glue it in place; nails are not necessary for this one section of the base. Glue and nail the side sections to the sides of the cabinet in the same manner used for installing the wood blocks in Step 1; use 1-inch common nails. Finally, glue and nail the front section to the bottom of the cabinet, nailing from the inside of the cabinet, using 1½-inch finishing nails.

To prepare the cabinet for a stain, varnish, paint or other finish, fill in all of the nail and screw holes, and sand all surfaces (*page 16*)

16⅝"

3"/8

16"

16⅝"

79⅛"

52¾"

3"

41"

41"

3

More Room: Up, In and Under

Multipurpose divider. The bunk bed/room divider at left is designed to bring order—and privacy —to the confusion that often arises when two children and their possessions occupy the same room. To ease such a situation, this project takes full advantage of floor-to-ceiling space. With a bunk and identical storage and work facilities on each side, the unit not only partitions the room to create a separate living area for each child, but also provides more room to play in. Complete instructions for building the bunk section and the sections for work and storage start on page 68.

The bunk bed/room divider on the opposite page concentrates sleeping and storage units in the normally wasted vertical space in the center of a relatively small room, thus creating additional living space without requiring a permanent and costly alteration to your house. The divider is built using the basic techniques detailed in earlier chapters—plus some special tricks of the cabinetmaker's craft. The same is true of the other space-making projects that follow. Look around your home with an eye to those areas where the floor space is cramped or inadequate, and where a room's vertical potential could be exploited to get things off the floor. Many of these objects might be placed in a modular wall-storage unit like the one described on pages 84 through 97.

The bunk bed/room divider and the wall-storage unit combine the functions of several pieces of furniture that otherwise would be scattered about the room, thus occupying less space and reducing clutter. In addition, they enhance the attractiveness of a children's bedroom or a living room by providing display areas for pieces of sculpture, books, plants, or odds and ends. And because both projects are built in separate sections, the arrangements and relationships of the sections can be varied, or you can construct only those components that you need.

Another way to gain more room for living is to use existing storage areas more efficiently. A long, sliding-door closet, for example, can be redesigned to contain drawers and a slide-out shelf unit without sacrificing any of its clothes-hanging capacity *(page 114)*. Kitchen cabinets can be fitted with roll-out bins *(page 102)* that not only hold more but also make the contents more accessible. Other roll-out bins, installed in the often overlooked or poorly used wedge of space under the cellar stairs *(page 112),* may be an efficient solution to the problem of where to store seasonal items, like skis or fishing tackle. Or if you have an attic with an unfinished floor and expanses hard to reach from a trap door, simple platforms that roll on casters *(page 110)* can be pulled to you for easy loading and unloading.

In most houses storage space also exists between the studs in hollow interior walls. By opening up such walls *(page 98)*, you can make room for a recessed laundry hamper or shallow shelves to hold books, canned goods or other small objects.

You can construct all of the projects to the shapes and dimensions specified in this chapter by following the instructions provided. On the other hand, you can modify as necessary any of these project designs to meet your particular requirements—or even create new plans—by referring to the techniques that are outlined in the chapter about job planning *(pages 50-65)*.

Building a Bunk Bed and Room Divider

The combination of bunk beds and storage units illustrated on page 66 (and shown here in exploded views) offers an imaginative solution to the space problem created when two youngsters share one room. Built to reach the standard 8-foot ceiling, with the bunks opening on opposite sides, the project functions as a room partition that not only occupies less floor space than two single beds but also gives each child his own private living and storage area. For mobility and ease in handling, each of the five components of the project is constructed separately. The sections may be arranged as shown in the photograph or in various other combinations.

When assembled, the bunk-bed section of the room divider is 8 feet high, 42½ inches wide and 78⅜ inches long. The bunks are designed to hold standard 39-by-75-inch mattresses. Three drawers on each side are sized to accept drawer-glide assemblies ½ inch thick; be sure to buy assemblies of this thickness.

The bookshelf-closet section (opposite page, bottom) is one of two identical units, each 79⅞ inches high, 42½ inches deep and 18 inches long; each contains a 2-foot-deep closet on one side and five bookshelves plus a drop-leaf desk on the other. The bookshelves—except for the

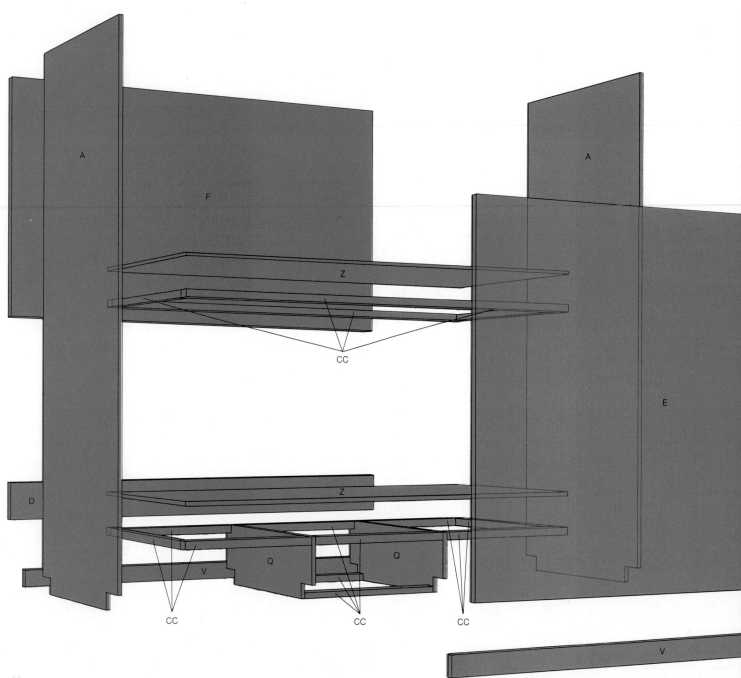

one to which the desk is hinged—are adjustable. The cabinet *(below, right),* also one of two identical units, sits on top of the bookshelf-closet section. Each cabinet is 16 inches high, 42½ inches deep and 18 inches wide; and each is divided into two compartments, one open and the other with a door.

If you build this project to reach an 8-foot-high ceiling, thus partitioning the room, be sure there is ample ventilation, heat and light on both sides. However, if you do not want it to reach the ceiling

or if the ceiling is less than 8 feet high, you can decrease the height by eliminating the cabinet units and lowering the bunk-bed section by 16 inches. You may also wish to make other modifications, such as reducing the width of the bunk beds to accommodate special-size mattresses, which would then call for corresponding alterations in the dimensions of the bookshelf-closet sections. Since any changes from the dimensions given will affect your specifications, prepare a new set of cutting diagrams and working

drawings by following the job-planning procedures on pages 54-57 and 60.

All major parts of the bunk bed/room divider shown here are made of ¾-inch A-2-grade birch plywood, which can be finished with satin oil to bring out the natural beauty of the wood.

If you prefer to paint the unit, you can economize by buying hardwood plywood with a less perfect surface (see the chart of plywood grades on page 58). Do not use plywood thinner than ¾ inch; it lacks the structural strength needed.

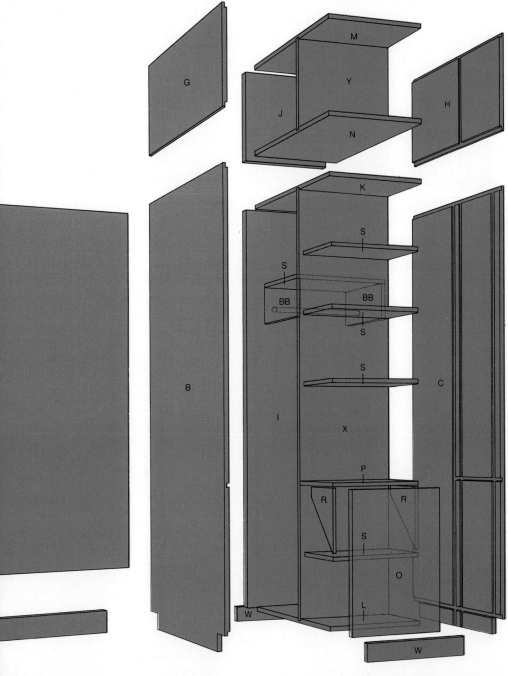

Key to the parts. The bunk-bed/room-divider parts shown in the exploded views on these pages are identified in the key below. The pieces are lettered in an order that approximates the cutting sequence *(page 70)*. Study the key and drawings carefully to familiarize yourself with the positions that the parts will occupy in the finished project. Then, as you cut the parts, stick a piece of masking tape to each and write on the tape the letter-designation of the part and, where appropriate, the side that will be more visible when finished, and an arrow indicating "top."

A| bunk-bed ends (2 pieces)
B| left bookshelf-closet sides (2 pieces)
C| right bookshelf-closet sides (2 pieces)
D| lower-bunk side
E| lower-bunk wall
F| upper-bunk wall
G| left cabinet sides (2 pieces)
H| right cabinet sides (2 pieces)
I| closet doors (2 pieces)
J| cabinet doors (2 pieces)
K| bookshelf-closet tops (2 pieces)
L| bookshelf-closet bottoms (2 pieces)
M| cabinet tops (2 pieces)
N| cabinet bottoms (2 pieces)
O| desks (2 pieces)
P| fixed shelves for desks (2 pieces)
Q| drawer support panels (2 pieces)
R| desk braces (4 pieces)
S| adjustable shelves (10 pieces)
T| drawer backs and fronts (12 pieces)
U| drawer sides (12 pieces)
V| base plates for bunk-bed unit (2 pieces)
W| base plates for bookshelf-closet (4 pieces)
X| closet backs (2 pieces)
Y| cabinet partitions (2 pieces)
Z| bunk bottoms (2 pieces)
AA| drawer bottoms (6 pieces)
BB| closet-bar supports (4 pieces)
CC| bunk-bottom supports (14 pieces in 3 sizes)

Shopping List

2 sheets A-2 hardwood lumber-core plywood, ¾'' × 4' × 8'

12 sheets A-2 hardwood veneer-core plywood, ¾'' × 4' × 8'

1 sheet A-2 hardwood veneer-core plywood, ⅜'' × 4' × 8'

1 sheet A-B softwood veneer-core plywood, ¼'' × 4' × 8'

5 lengths softwood 2 × 2s, each 10'

2 dowels, 1'' × 16½''

1 dowel, 1'' × 10''

60 feet softwood molding, ¾'' × ¾''

25 rolls veneer tape, 1'' × 8'

2 hardwood boards, 5' × 5'' × ¾''

4 hardwood boards, 18'' × 3¼'' × ¾''

6 pairs full-extension drawer-glide assemblies, 20''

8 strips metal shelf pilasters, ⅝'' × ³⁄₁₆'' × 51⅜''

8 strips metal shelf pilasters, ⅝'' × ³⁄₁₆'' × 23¼''

½ pound pilaster nails

32 pilaster clips

10 pivot hinges for ¾'' overlay doors

2 magnetic catches, 1¼''

2 heavy-duty magnetic catches, 3⅛''

2 continuous hinges, 1½'' × 15⅞''

4 continuous hinges, 1½'' × 10''

72 No. 6 slotted-head wood screws, ⅝''

10 drawer and closet pulls

200 No. 10 Phillips-head wood screws, 1¼''

80 No. 10 Phillips-head wood screws, 2''

60 No. 10 oval-head wood screws, 1½''

60 No. 10 countersunk washers

1 pound finishing nails, 1½''

1 gallon aliphatic resin glue

2 quarts contact cement

10 inexpensive paintbrushes, 1''

1 pint lacquer thinner

½ pound powdered wood putty

24 sheets No. 120-grit abrasive paper

2 gallons satin finishing oil

Cutting Diagrams

Sawing the plywood. Measure and saw one cut at a time; otherwise the kerf lost in cutting will affect later measurements. So that the circular saw will have the firm support of the rest of the plywood sheet, the first cuts in the sheet should be those for the long narrow pieces extending along the sheet's 8-foot dimension. When all the cutting is done, there should be 92 plywood pieces, identified according to the key on the preceding page. Scrap, indicated by a darker shade, is useful for making guides, straightedges and spacers. Handle the plywood sheets with care so that the factory edges remain perfect. If an edge does become damaged, rearrange the cutting diagram to leave the scrap pieces on the edge.

(Cutting of the 2-by-2s to requisite lengths is done during assembly as the pieces are needed.)

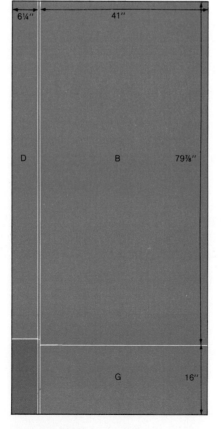

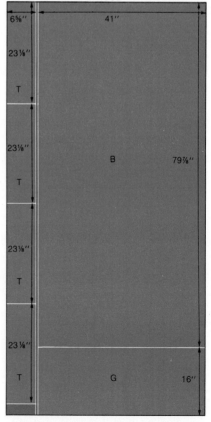

¾″ VENEER-CORE PLYWOOD

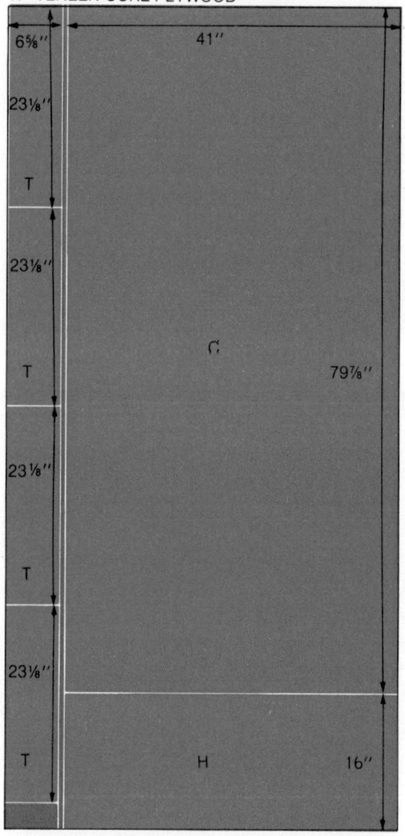
6⅝″
41″
23⅛″
T
23⅛″
G
T
79⅞″
23⅛″
T
23⅛″
T
H
16″

¾″ VENEER-CORE PLYWOOD

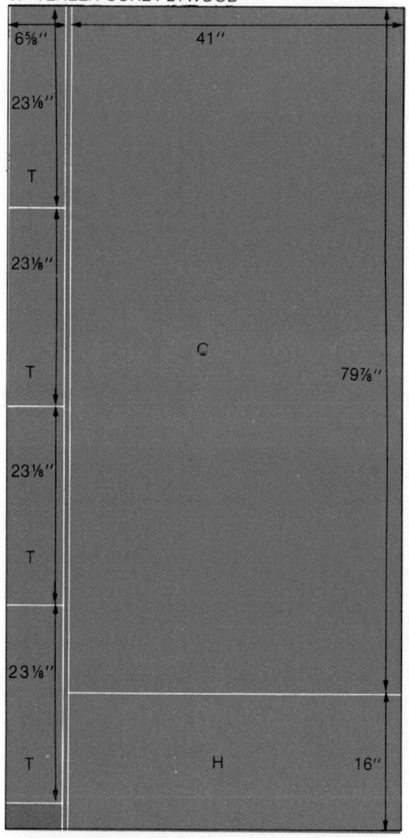
6⅝″
41″
23⅛″
T
23⅛″
C
T
79⅞″
23⅛″
T
23⅛″
T
H
16″

¾″ VENEER-CORE PLYWOOD

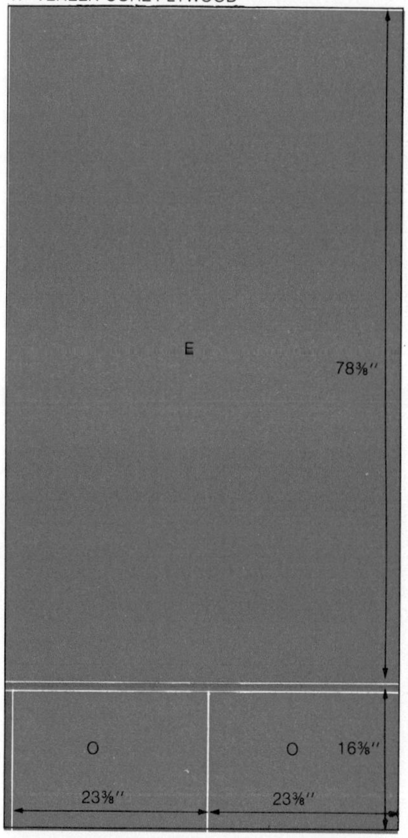
E
78⅜″
O
O
16⅜″
23⅜″
23⅜″

¾″ VENEER-CORE PLYWOOD

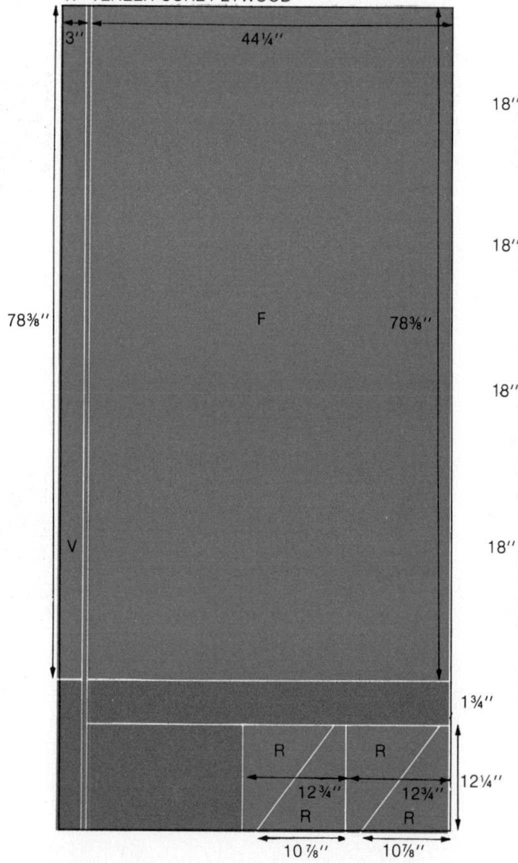
3″
44¼″
78⅜″
F
78⅜″
V
1¾″
R
R
12¾″
12¾″
12¼″
R
R
10⅞″
10⅞″

¾″ VENEER-CORE PLYWOOD

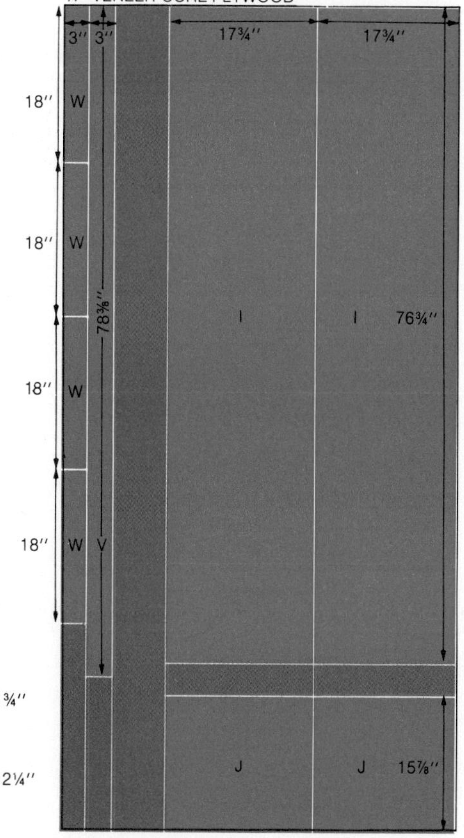
3″
3″
17¾″
17¾″
18″
W
18″
W
78¾″
I
I
76¾″
18″
W
18″
W
V
J
J
15⅞″

¾″ VENEER-CORE PLYWOOD

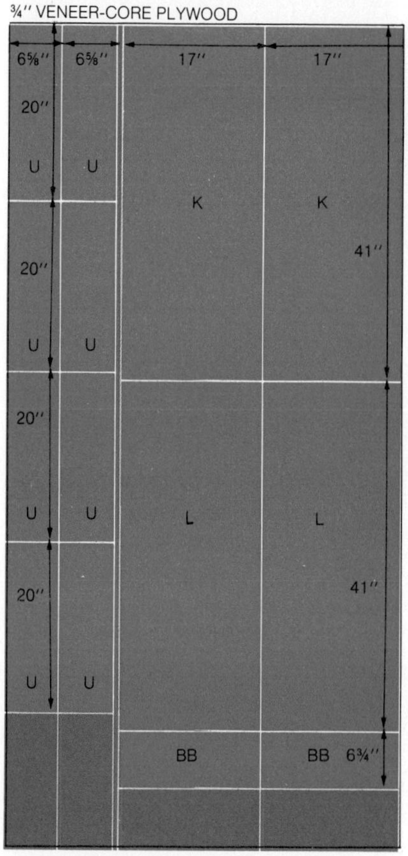
6⅝″
6⅝″
17″
17″
20″
U
U
K
K
20″
41″
U
U
20″
U
U
L
L
20″
41″
U
U
BB
BB
6¾″

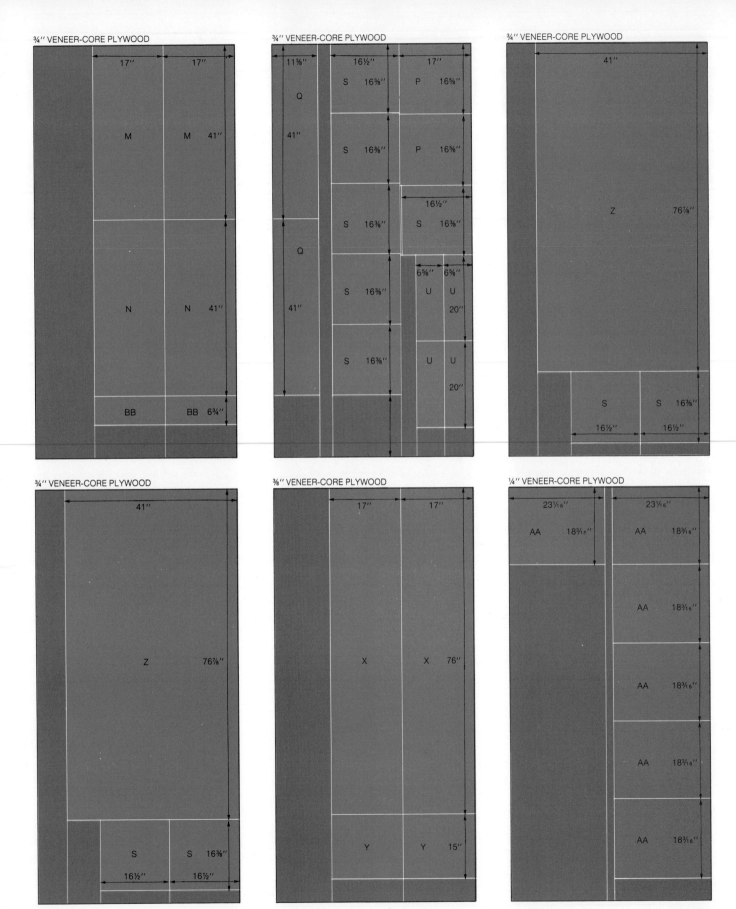

¾" VENEER-CORE PLYWOOD

17"   17"

M   M   41"

N   N   41"

BB   BB   6¾"

¾" VENEER-CORE PLYWOOD

11⅜"   16½"   17"

Q   S   16⅜"   P   16⅝"

S   16⅜"   P   16⅝"

41"

16½"

S   16⅜"   S   16⅜"

Q

6⅝"   6⅝"

S   16⅜"   U   U

20"

41"

U   U

S   16⅜"

20"

¾" VENEER-CORE PLYWOOD

41"

Z   76⅞"

S   S   16⅜"

16½"   16½"

¾" VENEER-CORE PLYWOOD

41"

Z   76⅞"

S   S   16⅜"

16½"   16½"

⅜" VENEER-CORE PLYWOOD

17"   17"

X   X   76"

Y   Y   15"

¼" VENEER-CORE PLYWOOD

23 1/16"   23 1/16"

AA   18 3/16"   AA   18 3/16"

AA   18 3/16"

AA   18 3/16"

AA   18 3/16"

AA   18 3/16"

Routing the Rabbets and Dadoes

The chart at the lower right details all the notches and grooves required in the bookshelf-closet and the cabinet.

A router is essential for speed, precision and straightness in making the great number of grooves required. If you do not own a router, rent one; with it you will be able to cut out the grooves with assembly-line efficiency—including those in drawer fronts, backs and sides, and in the sides of the bunk-bed ladder *(page 75)*. To minimize the number of times the router bit must be changed, the pieces should be grouped and the grooves cut in the numerical order shown on the chart and on the diagrams at the right.

Pieces that are to receive the same groove should be stacked on a steady work surface at least as wide and as long as the largest pieces. If you need more room, extend the work surface by using two sawhorses adjusted to the height of the work surface. After the first piece has been routed, slide it aside and rout the piece under it, and so on, down to the last piece in the stack.

Note that the bookshelf-closet sides (B and C) and the cabinet sides (G and H) will face each other, and that the grooves routed in them must therefore be made accordingly.

Setting up a router guide for some of the grooves may be done according to the instructions on pages 26 and 27. But two homemade T squares *(page 74)* are needed to set up guides for making some dadoes; a T square also speeds the work of making identical grooves on a number of pieces, and lessens the danger of error. As a further safeguard against mistakes, before routing any piece of wood make a test groove on a scrap of plywood and check its depth and width on the $1/32$-inch scale of a combination square. Rabbets and dadoes cut in plywood will have slightly splintered edges; sand the rough edges lightly by hand.

After the rabbets and dadoes have all been routed, assemble the ladder and the six drawers; these parts will then be ready when you are putting together the bunk-bed section.

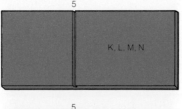

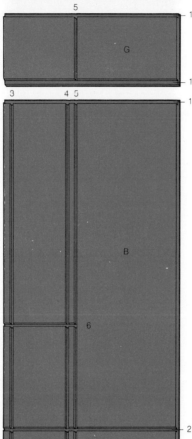

Routing diagrams. The numbers for the dadoes and rabbets in the diagrams *(left and below)* correspond to the numbers in the chart at the bottom of the page. When calculating where to set guides for the router *(pages 26-27)*, measure from the edge of the plywood that is closer to the edge of the planned groove.

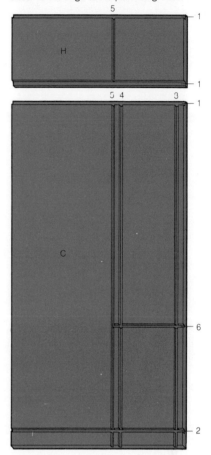

Data for the Routing Diagrams

Groove	Bit (width of groove)	Depth of groove	Distance from edge of piece to near edge of groove
1| Rabbet at top of B and C; top and bottom of G and H	¾''	¼''	None
2| Dado at bottom of B and C	¾''	¼''	3''
3| Dado for front bookshelf pilaster on B and C	⅝''*	³⁄₁₆''*	1⅜''
4| Dado for rear bookshelf pilaster on B and C	⅝''*	³⁄₁₆''*	14⅝''
5| Dado for closet back on B, C, K and L; for cabinet partition on G, H, M and N	⅜''	³⁄₁₆''	16⅝''
6| Dado for fixed shelf on B and C	¾''	¼''	27¼''

*Bit and depth of groove depend on width and thickness of shelf pilaster used.

Making and Using T Squares

1 **Positioning the router guides.** By following the method on pages 26 and 27, you can position the guide for dadoes No. 2 and 3 with a combination square. But since the combination square does not reach far enough for dadoes No. 4 and 5, you will have to make two T-square jigs (drawing) from straight-edged scraps of plywood.

Determine the length of the vertical pieces of the T squares by totaling the following measurements: the width of the scrap selected for the crosspiece, plus the distance from the edge of the piece of wood to be routed to the near edge of the intended dado, plus the width of the dado itself, plus the distance from the edge of the router base to the router bit. The length of the crosspieces is not critical. Be sure to square the bottom corners of the vertical pieces. Use a combination square to check that the pieces intersect at right angles; secure the pieces with nails.

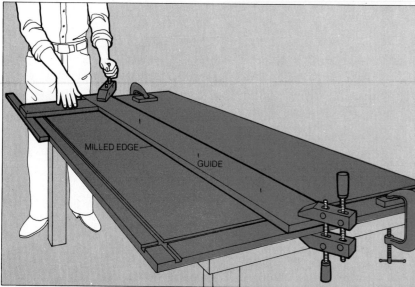

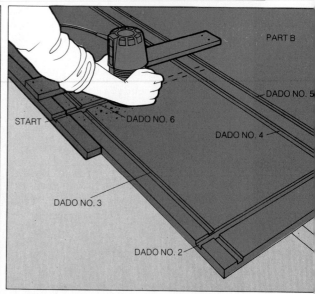

2 **Setting up a guide with a T square.** A piece of plywood about 6 inches wide and 80 inches long, left over from cutting the large parts of the bunk bed/room divider, makes an excellent guide for the longer dadoes. Place the guide on the wood to be routed so that the absolutely straight milled edge of the plywood faces the location of the dado to be cut. At one end, hold the T against the edge of the wood to be routed and butt the guide against the T's vertical piece (drawing). Clamp the guide to that end of the wood. Slide the T along the length of the guide, and nail down the center of the guide temporarily with several brads—extra-thin finishing nails—to keep it from moving while you are routing. Clamp the other end of the guide to keep it steady as well.

3 **Using a T square as a guide.** To rout dado No. 6 in the four bookshelf-closet sides (parts B and C), your longest T square can be used as a guide. Measuring each piece from the bottom edge, position the T by totaling all measurements given in Step 1 except the first. Using brads, tack the T square to the piece to be routed.

On parts B start the router at the edge of the T square's crosspiece; move the bit through the crosspiece and through part B (drawing) until the bit intersects dado No. 5—but be sure not to go through the far edge of dado No. 5. On parts C position the T square as above, but reverse the routing procedure: start at dado No. 5. Stand sideways to the work so you are not pulling the router directly toward your body. Continue the groove through the crosspiece of the T to avoid splintering the open end of the dado.

Notches for the Base Plates

Cutting the notches. To make space for the recessed base plates, measure and, using a saber saw or backsaw, cut 3-by-3-inch notches at the bottom corners of the bunk-bed ends (parts A) and the bookshelf-closet sides (parts B and C), as well as in the drawer-support panels (parts Q). The base plates will be screwed onto the bottoms of the units in the final assembly.

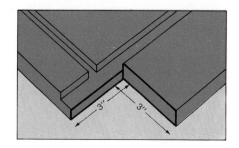

Ladder

1 Routing the ladder. For the ladder uprights, use the two 5-foot pieces of 5-by-¾-inch hardwood; for the treads, use the four pieces of 18-inch-long 3¼-by-¾-inch hardwood. Place the pieces for the uprights edge to edge on the work surface and clamp them to it with hand screws. Use scrap boards, nailed across the uprights, as guides for the router in making the dadoes.

Starting 2 inches from the bottom of the ladder uprights, rout four dadoes 12 inches apart in each board; make the dadoes ¼ inch deep, ¾ inch wide (the actual thickness of the tread material), and 3 inches long. Saw a notch ⅜ inch by ¼ inch deep at the back corners of each tread so that when the treads are assembled they will fit over the rounded ends of the dadoes, thus covering them. With a saber saw, round off the corners of the uprights at the top; sand them smooth.

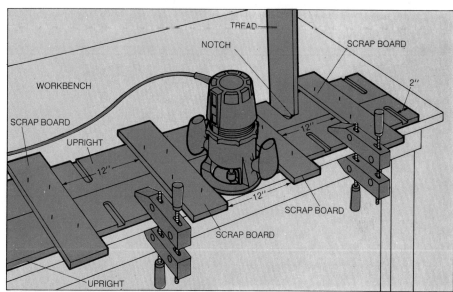

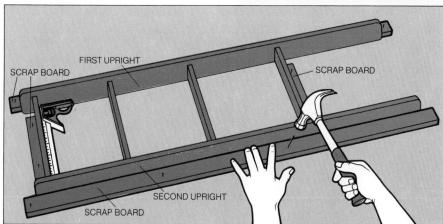

2 Assembling the ladder. To hold the ladder parts in place while you glue them, nail a straight scrap board as long as the uprights to the work surface. Stand one of the uprights on its edge with the open ends of the dadoes down, and butt the upright against the nailed board. Glue the treads into the dadoes. Place the second upright in position and glue the other ends of the treads into its dadoes. With a combination square, true the top and bottom treads, and nail short pieces of scrap board to the work surface to hold the treads and uprights square. Nail another long, straight piece of scrap board to the work surface so that it presses firmly against the second upright. Leave the assembled ladder in place until the glue dries; it is not necessary to use nails.

Drawers

Making the drawers. Rout a dado ¼ inch wide and ⁵⁄₁₆ inch deep ½ inch from the bottom edge of all drawer fronts and backs (parts T). Divide the drawer sides (parts U) into six left and six right sides and rout a dado in each, as above. At the front edge of each side (and on the same surface as the dado) rout a rabbet ¾ inch wide and ¼ inch deep; at the back of each side ¾ inch from the edge, rout a dado ¾ inch wide and ¼ inch deep. Assemble the drawers, following the procedure on pages 28 and 29. A false front will be added later when you assemble the bunk-bed section.

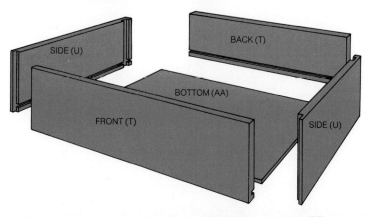

Trimming the Plywood Edges

All plywood edges that will be visible in the completed bunk bed/room divider should be covered with wood molding or veneer tape; besides giving your work a more professional appearance, such trim keeps the cut edges of plywood from splintering. Also, if you plan to paint the plywood, trim provides a ready base for the paint. If you do not use trim, the exposed edges of the plywood should be sealed with wood putty or spackling compound and then sanded smooth.

Because of the large size of many of the pieces in this project, it is easier to apply edge trim after all router cuts have been made and before the pieces are assembled. Two kinds of trim can be used:

☐ MOLDING. Strips of ¾-by-¾-inch molding, usually available in pine, will protect edges that get the most wear, such as the beds and the fronts and sides of the desks. The molding is attached with glue and finishing nails.

☐ VENEER TAPE. On edges that require no extra protection, use veneer tape. This thin, flexible wood trim generally comes in strips 8 feet long; for this project you will need almost 200 feet of tape. Veneer tape is available in a variety of woods to match the most commonly used plywoods, such as birch, oak, mahogany and walnut. The tape is best applied with contact cement *(page 61)*, but care must be taken to position it correctly since the cement bonds instantly when the two glued surfaces touch. Inexpensive paintbrushes 1 inch wide can be used to spread the contact cement. When the cement congeals on the brush, discard the brush and use a new one; cleaning brushes is difficult and time consuming. Keep handy a rag and lacquer thinner so you can quickly wipe off any accidental drips before they dry.

Veneer tape also comes with heat- and pressure-sensitive glue already on the back. Such tape is not readily available in retail outlets, but you may be able to order it through a large lumber-supply house. The tape is easy to apply: it is pressed on with an iron adjusted to the "cotton" setting, shaved with a razor blade to the correct width, as shown on the opposite page, and sanded.

Before applying trimming, refer to the chart below and mark with colored pencils the edges to be trimmed—one color for molding and one for veneer tape.

Edges to be Trimmed

Piece	Edge	Type of Trim
Lower-bunk side, part D	Top edge	¾" molding, 79⅜"
	Side and bottom edges	Tape
Lower-bunk wall, part E	Top edge	¾" molding, 79⅜"
	Side and bottom edges	Tape
Upper-bunk wall, part F	All four edges	Tape
Desks, part O	Front edge	¾" molding, 17⅜"
	Sides	¾" molding, 24⅜"
	Back edge (where hinge will be mounted)	Tape
Desk braces, part R	All four edges	Tape
Fixed shelves, part P	Front (17") edges	Tape
Adjustable shelves, part S	Front (16⅜") edge	Tape
Bookshelf/closet sides, parts B and C	Top of bookshelf edge to shorter horizontal dado;	¾" molding, 52⅞"
	top of shorter horizontal dado to bottom of bookshelf edge; edges of closet end	Tape Tape
Bookshelf/closet tops, part K	17" edge nearer dado	¾" molding, 18"
	17" edge farther from dado	Tape
Bookshelf/closet bottoms, part L	Both 17" edges	Tape
Cabinet sides, parts G and H	16" edge nearer dado	¾" molding, 17"
	16" edge farther from dado	Tape
Cabinet tops and bottoms, parts M and N	17" edge nearer dado	¾" molding, 18"
	17" edge farther from dado	Tape
Closet doors and cabinet doors, parts I and J	All edges	Tape
Base plates, part V and W	Short ends	Tape

Molding Trim

1 Attaching molding. Each small piece to which molding will be attached should be clamped in a woodworking vise, with the edge to be covered facing up. Large pieces can be clamped, edge up, to one side of the worktable with hand screws. Cut the molding about an inch longer than the edge it is to cover. For an especially strong bond use aliphatic resin glue (page 61); spread it liberally on the plywood edge and one face of the molding. Bring the two surfaces together. Every 6 to 8 inches drive in finishing nails, 1½ inches long, and countersink them with a nail set.

Wipe off excess glue with a wet rag. After the glue has dried, use a backsaw to trim excess molding flush with the ends of the piece, except on parts M, N and K. Fill the countersunk nail holes with wood putty and sand all surfaces.

2 Making cutaways for joints. To allow enough space for the joints, the molding on the storage-cabinet top (M) and bottom (N) and the bookshelf-closet tops (K) must be indented instead of being flush with the side edge of the plywood. Use a combination square and an awl to mark a line across the molding ¼ inch in from the plywood edge. With a saber saw or backsaw, cut along the line just to the glued edge of the plywood. Tap the excess molding from the rear with a hammer; it will break off cleanly at the saw cut.

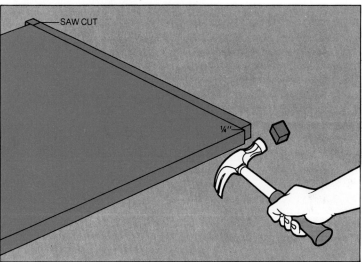

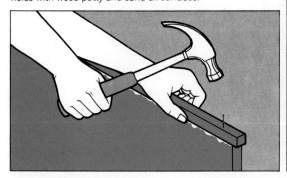

Veneer Trim

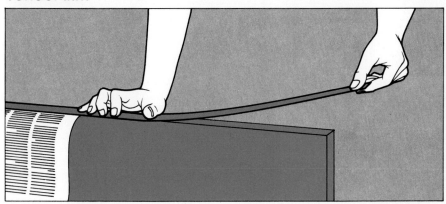

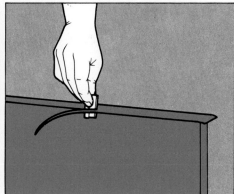

1 Applying veneer tape. Cut a strip of tape an inch longer than the edge to be covered. Brush contact cement onto both the plywood edge and the tape, moving the brush in only one direction to ensure an even coat; allow the cement to dry according to the manufacturer's directions. Add a second coat of cement to the plywood—the first coat will have soaked into the wood—and let it dry. On shorter edges lay the tape in one operation, from corner to corner. On longer edges it may be difficult to align the tape all at once. But because contact cement adheres only to itself when it is partially dry, you can use newspaper to cover approximately half of each long edge to prevent the tape from making accidental contact. Put the tape down about midway along the edge and work toward the uncovered corner; remove the paper and lay the tape to the other corner.

2 Trimming the tape. Press the veneer tape firmly into place by rolling it several times with a wooden dowel; continue rolling past the corners of the plywood edge to make a crease in the overhanging tape. With a single-edge razor blade slice off the overhanging tape and any excess tape along the edge. Using No. 120-grit abrasive paper, lightly sand the edges of the veneer tape to blend them into the surface of the plywood. Be careful not to sand the surface of the veneer tape. Contact cement that has dried on the plywood surface should be removed by careful sanding.

Assembling the Bunk Bed and Room Divider

Putting together the parts of the three largest sections of the bunk bed/room divider calls for no extraordinary skills. Even though the bunk-bed section is over 6 feet long and more than 3 feet wide, it is—like the bookshelf-closet and the cabinet sections—simply a box, and it is assembled with the same basic techniques used for other boxes: measuring and marking, drilling holes, gluing, and inserting screws.

Because the bunk-bed section is so large, assemble it in the room it is to occupy. The less bulky bookshelf-closet sections and the cabinet sections can be put together elsewhere and moved into the room, but first make sure there are no impossibly tight corners to turn.

As you assemble each section, you will occasionally need a helper to change the position of the piece you are working on

or to exert force against a part while you drill. A helper can also hold parts or wipe glue when you are joining a number of parts at the same time and must work fast before the glue sets.

After the five sections are assembled and in place, they can be attached to one another with screws to ensure greater strength and stability.

Assembling the various parts can be managed faster and with less effort by following certain practices throughout:

□ Because the many pieces must fit precisely, check often and carefully with a straightedge and combination square to make sure that the pieces are properly aligned before you secure them.

□ Drill countersunk pilot holes for all flathead screws; follow the instructions on page 29 for the size of drill bit in relation to screw size. (Pilot holes for oval-

head screws need not be countersunk; the washers used with them have a countersunk feature.) Do not drill pilot holes for continuous-hinge screws; use an awl to make starter holes for them.

□ Use a ⅜-inch variable-speed drill with a screwdriver bit to insert the Phillips-head screws speedily. (It is preferable to use Phillips-head screws with an electric drill: their cross slots keep the bit firmly in the screwhead. However, screws with standard slots, driven by drill or hand, will do just as well; they require more care and effort.)

□ For a project this size use aliphatic resin glue (page 61) because of its great bonding strength. Wipe off any excess glue immediately, or the affected area will not accept a stain or oil finish. Use wet sponges or rags for wiping (old towels are good) and rinse them out often.

Joining the Parts: Bunk-Bed Section

1 Bunk end supports. Saw the softwood 2-by-2s as follows: two pieces 76⅞ inches long, four pieces 38 inches long, and eight pieces 25⅛ inches long. The 38-inch lengths are horizontal supports for the ends of the bunk bottoms; set the other lengths aside for use in later steps.

Position the supports for the lower-bunk bottom 9⅞ inches from the bottom edges of the bunk-bed ends (parts A) and 1½ inches from the side edges. Position the supports for the upper-bunk bottom 51¾ inches from the bottom edges of the bunk-bed ends. Glue and screw the supports in place, using six No. 10 wood screws 2 inches long, placed at 7-inch intervals on each support.

2 Lower-bunk side. Cut a piece of scrap plywood 76⅞ inches long and approximately 3 inches wide to use as a spacer; clamp it to the back of the lower-bunk side (part D) so that the spacer is ¾ inch from each end of part D.

Set the bunk-bed ends on their long edges with the bunk end supports facing inward; use two sawhorses to keep the ends from falling. Position the lower-bunk side across the bunk-bed ends with its bottom edge 6⅞ inches above the base plate notches; butt the bunk-bed ends against the clamped-on spacer. Drill pilot holes and attach the lower-bunk side to one bunk-bed end with three countersunk washers and oval-head screws 1½ inches long. Attach the lower-bunk side to the other end in the same manner.

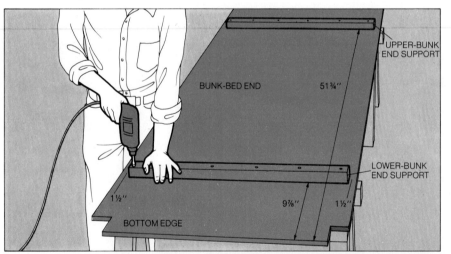

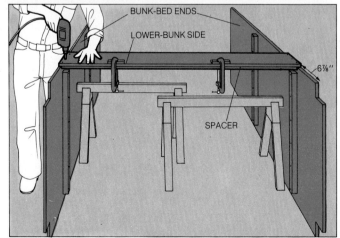

3 **Upper-bunk wall.** Clamp the spacer used in Step 2 to the back of the upper-bunk wall (part F) and along its bottom edge. Position the wall across the bunk-bed ends; butt the bunk-bed ends against the spacer. The top edge of the wall should be flush with the upper corners of the ends; use corner clamps to square the corners.

Attach the upper-bunk wall to the bunk-bed ends with countersunk washers and oval-head screws. Drill pilot holes and insert the screws first at the four corners of the wall; then add five more screws along each side of the wall, spacing them about 7 inches apart. With a helper, carefully stand the bunk-bed section upright.

4 **Lower-bunk wall.** Clamp the plywood spacer to the back of the lower-bunk wall (part E) and along its top edge. Clamp a pair of hand screws to the bunk-bed ends and against the undersides of the 2-by-2-inch supports for the lower-bunk bottom. Rest the lower-bunk wall on the hand screws with the clamped-on spacer butted against the bunk-bed ends. Hold the wall to the bunk-bed ends with bar clamps, and attach the wall to the ends with countersunk washers and oval-head screws, following the procedure in Step 3.

5 **Upper-bunk side supports.** The two pieces of 76⅞-inch-long 2-by-2s cut in Step 1 are side supports for the upper-bunk bottom. Hold them in position on the upper- and lower-bunk walls (parts F and E) with temporary rests made of scrap boards clamped to the undersides of the upper-bunk end supports already mounted on the bunk-bed ends (drawing). Attach the side supports to the upper- and lower-bunk walls with glue and wood screws that are 2 inches long.

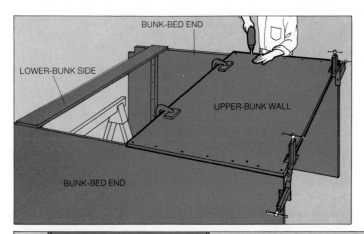

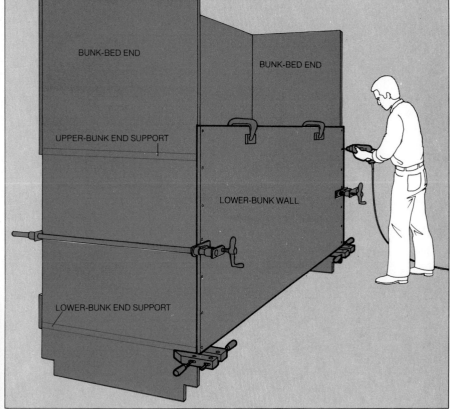

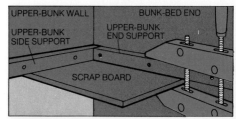

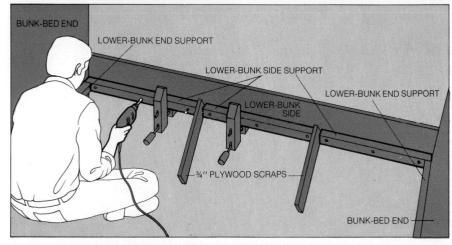

6 **Lower-bunk side supports.** Six of the 25⅛-inch-long 2-by-2s that you cut in Step 1 serve as side supports for the lower-bunk bottoms. Clamp three of these side supports on the lower-bunk side (part D) along the same plane as the end supports that are already attached to the bunk-bed ends. Keep them separated with ¾-inch plywood scraps (drawing) to allow spaces for inserting the drawer-support panels in a later step *(page 80)*. Glue and screw the side supports in place with wood screws that are 2 inches long and remove the scrap plywood spacers. Repeat all steps of the procedure in attaching the other three supports to the lower-bunk wall (part E) opposite the place where you have been working.

7 **First drawer-glide outer casing.** To position the first outer casing, use the junction of the bottom of the lower-bunk side and the bunk-bed end as a reference point (drawing) and measure down 6¾ inches (the 6⅝-inch depth of the drawer plus ⅛ inch). Mark that point, and from it extend a horizontal line across the bunk-bed end to indicate the position for the bottom of the outer casing. Screw the casing in place, following the instructions in Steps 2 and 3, pages 29 and 30. Since slight adjustments may have to be made later, do not tighten the screws for this or any of the other outer casings until you are ready to mount them permanently in Step 11.

8 **Remaining drawer outer casings.** To install the other casings, cut a plywood guide the length of the drawer casing you attached to the bunk-bed end in Step 7. The guide should be the same height as the space between the bottom of the casing and the floor. Be sure the edges of the guide are straight and the corners square. Using the guide (drawing), position and mount three more of the remaining 11 outer casings at the other three corners of the bunk-bed ends. Use the guide to position four outer casings on each of the two drawer-support panels (parts Q), placing them in the same relationship to the 3-inch notch as are the outer casings on the

bunk-bed ends. Still following the instructions in Steps 2 and 3 on pages 29 and 30, make pilot holes in the oblong-shaped screw locations of the casings. Slip the panels into the spaces between the 2-by-2 lower-bunk side supports; position the casings over the pilot holes, and screw them loosely in place. Install a pair of inner glides on each drawer, according to the instructions in Step 4 on page 30. Check all six drawers for fit before continuing with the assembly procedure.

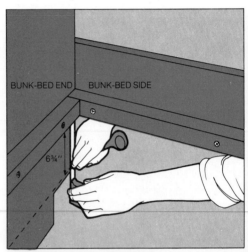

BUNK-BED END   BUNK-BED SIDE

6¾"

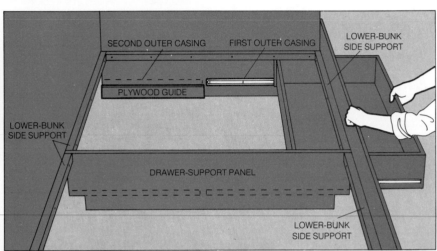

SECOND OUTER CASING   FIRST OUTER CASING   LOWER-BUNK SIDE SUPPORT

PLYWOOD GUIDE

LOWER-BUNK SIDE SUPPORT

DRAWER-SUPPORT PANEL

LOWER-BUNK SIDE SUPPORT

BASE PLATE

BASE PLATE (INSTALLED)

2 × 2 (INSTALLED)

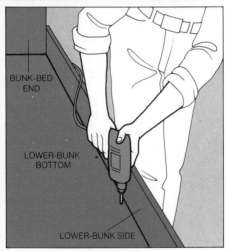

BUNK-BED END

LOWER-BUNK BOTTOM

LOWER-BUNK SIDE

9 **Base plates.** Before attaching the base plates, remove the drawers. Drill two pilot holes for oval-head screws with countersunk washers at each end of the two base plates (parts V); the centers of the holes should be ⅜ inch from the edges. Insert screws loosely to hold one base plate in position and, with an awl, mark a line on the back of the plate at the inner edges of the two drawer-support panels (drawing); repeat with the other base plate. Glue and screw the two remaining 25⅛-inch pieces of 2-by-2 between these marks flush with the bottom edges of the base plates. Screw the base plates to the bunk-bed ends.

10 **Bunk bottoms.** Both bunk bottoms (parts Z) are installed the same way. Place each bunk bottom on its supports. Make pilot holes for 2-inch screws 6 inches to the left and right of the middle of the long edges, drilling through the bunk bottoms and into the supports beneath (drawing). Have a helper push against the bunk walls while you are drilling to close any gap between the walls and the bottom. Screw the upper-bunk bottom in place; remove the lower-bunk bottom.

11 Drawer-support panels. To hold the panels in place temporarily, drive two nails at an angle through each drawer-support panel and into the lower-bunk side supports. Drill pilot holes for 2-inch screws (drawing) through the drawer-support panels and into the ends of the 2-by-2s attached to the back of the base plates. To wield the drill, you may have to make the holes at a slight angle. Insert the screws and pull out the nails. Put the drawers in place and check that the glides move freely in the outer casings. Make any necessary adjustments. Remove the drawers and tighten the screws in all the drawer casings and glides. Insert screws in the remaining holes.

12 False fronts for the drawers. With the drawers in place on both sides of the bunk-bed section, clamp to and across their fronts the 6⅞-inch-wide strips of lumber-core plywood that are left from cutting the bunk-bed ends. Insert wood shims 1⁄16 inch thick between these strips and both the lower-bunk side (part D) and the lower-bunk wall (part E). Using an awl, mark the lumber-core plywood strips with straight lines for cutting false-front pieces (drawing); mark at the midpoint of each drawer-support panel and also 1⁄16 inch in from the outer edges of the bunk-bed ends so that the drawers will clear the bookshelf-closet section after the final assembly is completed.

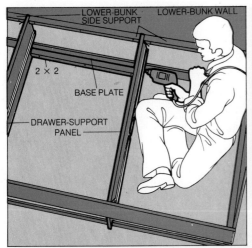

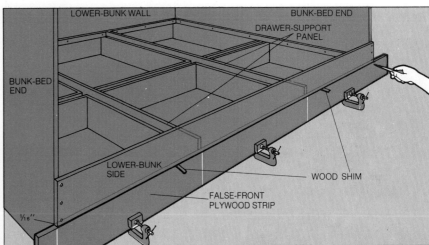

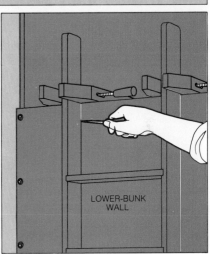

13 Final assembly. Pull the three drawers open simultaneously, taking care not to disturb the false-front plywood strip still clamped across them. Leave the C clamps in place and, for additional stability, use hand screws to hold the drawers and the plywood strip together. From the rear of each drawer front, drill four pilot holes for 1¼-inch screws (drawing) through the drawer and just into the false front. The marks will serve to position the false drawer fronts after they have been cut to size. Unclamp the strip and saw it into sections along the lines made in Step 12. Install drawer pulls on all three false-front pieces;

countersink the screws so that they are flush with the plywood surface. Line up the pilot holes in each drawer front with the pilot holes in the false-front pieces. Drive the screws all the way into the false-front pieces. Repeat this entire procedure for the drawers on the opposite side. Place the lower-bunk bottom in position and drive 2-inch screws through the pilot holes drilled in Step 9.

14 Ladder. After choosing a location for the ladder, attach hand screws to its uprights to suspend it against the lower-bunk wall (drawing). With an awl, mark each edge of both uprights; remove the ladder and, between each pair of lines that you have marked, drill five holes for each upright through the lower-bunk wall. Replace the ladder with the hand screws still on it. Have a helper hold it while, from the other side of the lower-bunk wall, you insert a slightly smaller drill bit through the holes; then drill pilot holes into the ladder uprights. Use countersunk washers and 1½-inch oval-head screws to attach the ladder.

Joining the Parts: Bookshelf-Closet Sections

1 Drop-leaf desk. To keep the drop leaf level and hold the braces in position when the desk is raised, mount two pieces of ¾-inch square molding—each 3 inches long and with a notch at one end measuring ½ inch by ¾ inch—on the underside of the drop leaf (part O), as shown. So that the molding can be swiveled aside when the drop leaf is down, make the pilot holes in the molding (but not in the drop leaf) slightly larger than the diameter of a No. 10 screw 1¼ inches long. Place the drop leaf and a fixed shelf (part P) flat, undersides up and butted together (drawing). Center a 15⅞-inch continuous hinge over the crack between the parts. With an awl, make starter holes and insert ⅜-inch screws. Repeat the procedure for the other desk.

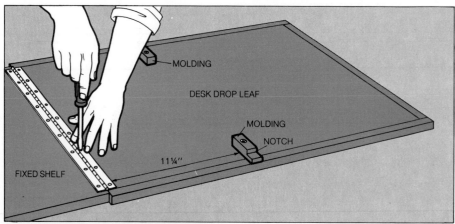

MOLDING
DESK DROP LEAF
MOLDING
NOTCH
11¼"
FIXED SHELF

2 Pilasters. Place one of the bookshelf-closet sides (part B or C) flat on the work surface or across two sawhorses and insert four pilaster strips (*page 48*) in the dadoes previously cut for them. Two 51⅜-inch pilasters go above the fixed-shelf dado and two 23¼-inch pilasters go below. Do not allow the pilasters to extend into the fixed-shelf dado; be sure to align the nail holes in the matching pilasters exactly, so that the shelves will be level when installed. With a hammer, drive in pilaster nails to secure the pilasters. Repeat the procedure for the other three bookshelf-closet sides.

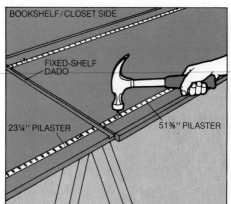

BOOKSHELF/CLOSET SIDE
FIXED-SHELF DADO
23¼" PILASTER
51⅜" PILASTER

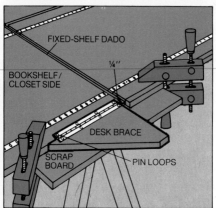

FIXED-SHELF DADO
BOOKSHELF/CLOSET SIDE
¼"
DESK BRACE
SCRAP BOARD
PIN LOOPS

3 Desk braces. Lay a bookshelf-closet side on the worktable or across two sawhorses. Clamp a piece of scrap board under the side to support the desk brace in its open position (drawing). Butt the desk brace (part R) against the bookshelf-closet side and ¼ inch below the fixed-shelf dado. Position a 10-inch continuous hinge with the pin loops of the hinge aligned on the edge of the bookshelf-closet side. Attach the hinge with screws according to the instructions given in Step 1. Mount the hinges for the other three desk braces in the same way. Fold the braces back against the bookshelf-closet sides and use masking tape to hold them there during the following steps.

4 Final assembly. From the grooved side of each bookshelf-closet side, drill pilot holes for 1½-inch screws in the horizontal dadoes and rabbets; start 1 inch from the ends of these grooves and space the holes about 6 inches apart. Drill only deep enough to break through the wood on the outside, then turn the pieces over and finish drilling; countersink the holes slightly on the outside.

Dry-fit the parts into one of the bookshelf-closet sides in the following order: bottom (part L), closet back (part X), fixed shelf with attached drop leaf, and top (part K). Disassemble, spread glue rapidly in the rabbet and all the dadoes in the side piece and on the edges of the parts to be joined to them, and reassemble. Glue the other side on. Drive screws into all the pilot holes. Quickly wipe off any excess glue before it dries. Using countersunk washers and oval-head screws, attach the base plates (parts W) in the 3-inch notches cut for them. Repeat the procedure for the other bookshelf-closet section.

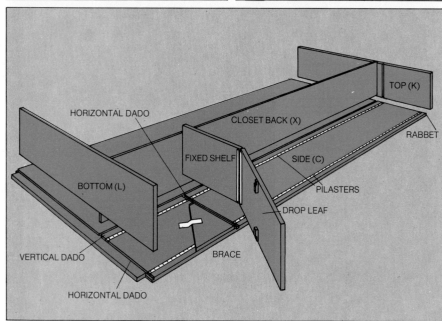

HORIZONTAL DADO
TOP (K)
CLOSET BACK (X)
RABBET
FIXED SHELF
SIDE (C)
BOTTOM (L)
PILASTERS
DROP LEAF
VERTICAL DADO
BRACE
HORIZONTAL DADO

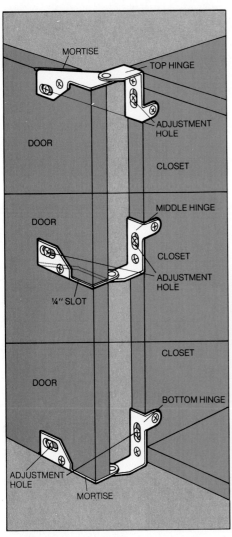

MORTISE
TOP HINGE
DOOR
ADJUSTMENT HOLE
CLOSET

MIDDLE HINGE
DOOR
CLOSET
ADJUSTMENT HOLE
¼" SLOT

CLOSET
DOOR
BOTTOM HINGE
ADJUSTMENT HOLE
MORTISE

5 **Closet door.** Tape the drop leaf to the sides of the bookshelf-closet and turn the entire unit so that the closet opening is facing up. To allow for hinges, the door (part I) is ⅛ inch narrower than the opening; the edge of the door where the catch will go should be flush with the side of the section. Install pivot hinges in mortises chiseled in the top and bottom edges of the door (upper and lower details in drawing).

To attach the middle hinge, chisel a horizontal slot ¼ inch wide in the edge of the door; shape the slot to fit the contour of the hinge (indicated by dash lines in the center detail of the drawing). Lay the door on top of the closet opening and screw the hinges in place, starting with the adjustment holes. Finally, install a door pull and a heavy-duty magnetic catch, following the directions on pages 32 and 91.

6 **Closet-bar supports.** For the clothes rod in each closet, use the two pieces of 1-inch dowel 16½ inches long. Drill holes for the rods in the four closet-bar supports (parts BB); make the holes 5 inches from the front edge of each support and 2 inches from the bottom edge. Insert the rods in the holes and mount the supports on the sides of each closet, butted against the closet back; the bottom edges of the supports are 53½ inches from the closet floor. Use two 1¼-inch screws in each support (drawing). Rest an adjustable shelf (part S) atop each pair of closet-bar supports.

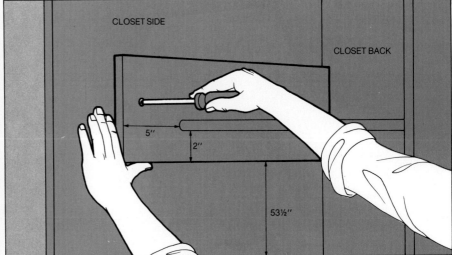

CLOSET SIDE
CLOSET BACK
5"
2"
53½"

Joining the Parts: Cabinet Sections

Assembling the cabinets. Following the procedures described in Step 4 for assembling the bookshelf-closet, drill pilot holes in the rabbets in the four cabinet sides (parts G and H). Place a cabinet side flat on the work surface and dry-fit the parts in the following order: cabinet partition (part Y), cabinet top (part M), cabinet bottom (part N) and the second cabinet side (part H). Disassemble the parts and apply glue to all grooves and edges; then reassemble and insert 1½-inch screws in all pilot holes. Mount the cabinet door (part J) with two pivot hinges as in Step 5, and attach a door pull and magnetic catch. Repeat for the other cabinet.

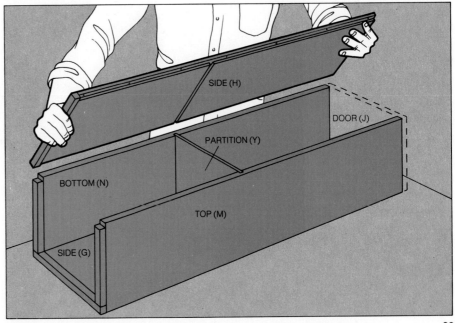

SIDE (H)
DOOR (J)
PARTITION (Y)
BOTTOM (N)
TOP (M)
SIDE (G)

Organizing Space with Modular Units

The four interchangeable units on these pages demonstrate the concept of modular storage. Each unit is 7 feet high, 30 inches wide and 15⅞ inches deep, and all together they provide more than 80 cubic feet of vertical storage space. Because the units are freestanding, they can be built in any number needed, and they can be set up in any combination desired —in the center of a room as a divider,

around a corner in an L configuration, back to back or, as shown in the photograph on page 6, along a wall. If you plan to use several units in combination, be sure the floor is level so that all units will be in proper alignment; if the floor is uneven, place wood shims beneath the units to position them correctly.

The units share a basic design but each has been adapted for different storage requirements. The first unit *(below, left)* has movable bookshelves, space for a stereo speaker at the top, and, at the bottom, a cabinet with a movable shelf. The second unit, in addition to shelves and a cabinet with drawers, has a drop-leaf desk with a laminated-plastic surface and a set of compartments inside (without

the compartments, the space could serve as a bar). The third unit has a display case behind glass doors, with optional glass shelves inside; four roomy drawers below provide storage space for linens, silverware, place mats or anything else. The fourth unit matches the first, with a roll-out shelf to hold a record player.

The complete four-unit project needs all the wood, hardware and accessories detailed in the shopping list on page 86. But you can easily alter the size of the units or add to them as you choose by following the instructions on pages 54 through 57 for revising or making new plans. The number of doors, drawers and shelves can be reduced or increased at will. You may also choose materials oth-

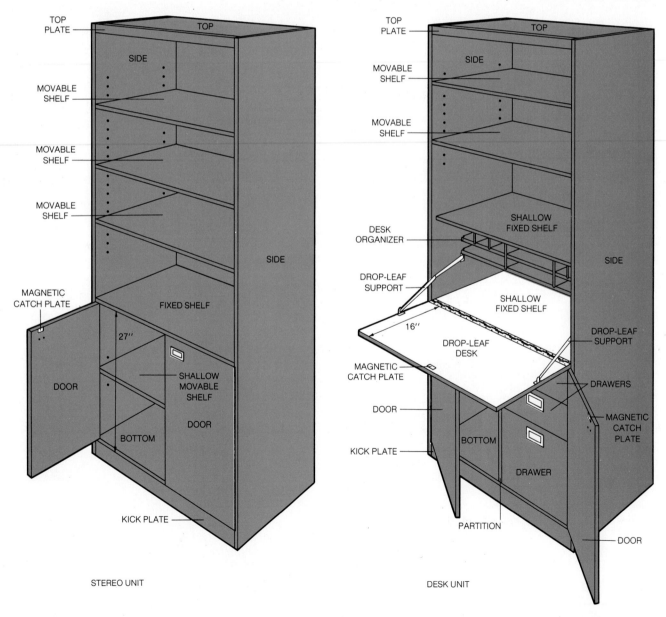

STEREO UNIT

DESK UNIT

er than those specified in the shopping list. See pages 58 and 59 for a description of types and grades of wood.

After gathering together the necessary wood and hardware called for in the shopping list, cut the sheets of plywood and the lumber into the required pieces indicated in the cutting diagrams. The joints should then be cut according to the routing diagrams on page 88. Before starting to assemble the pieces, use 150-grit sandpaper to smooth all of the surfaces that will be visible.

Since the shells of the four units have the same structure—they are all, essentially, oblong boxes—the instructions for assembling one of them (pages 89-90) serve for all. As soon as these shells are

assembled and all of the fixed shelves are installed, apply veneer tape to the visible edges of the plywood (page 77) before installing the doors, drawers, roll-out shelf or the drop-leaf desk.

Instructions beginning on page 91 explain in detail how to install the special features of each unit. (All the drawers are sized to accept drawer-glide assemblies ½ inch thick; be sure to buy assemblies of this thickness.)

Veneer should be applied to the edges of drawers and doors only after they have been installed. Before gluing the veneer, slip a piece of scrap veneer between closed doors and drawers and the cabinet walls to make sure there is sufficient clearance. Sand down the edges

if necessary. When the assembling and veneering are done, go over the entire unit with 220-grit sandpaper to prepare the surfaces for wax or oil, or another finish of your choice.

Planning the project. The perspective drawings that appear below will serve as an indispensable guide for building the wall-storage units. If you should not want to make all four units, or if you want to change dimensions or eliminate or add certain features, revise the plans accordingly and alter the cutting diagrams (pages 86-87) to reflect the changes. Each piece of the units is labeled for easy cross-reference to the cutting diagrams. The inside and outside dimensions marked on the stereo unit at the right apply to all of the units. Measurements for special interior features are located within each unit.

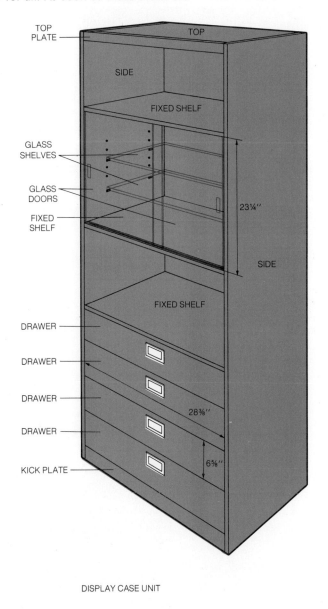

DISPLAY CASE UNIT

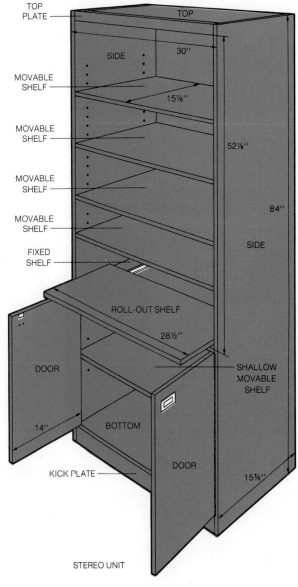

STEREO UNIT

Shopping List

7 sheets A-A hardwood plywood, ¾″ × 4′ × 8′
4 sheets A-2 hardwood plywood, ¼″ × 4′ × 8′
3 pieces scrap plywood, ⅛″ × 1½″ × 12″
3 lengths hardwood, ½″ × 10″ × 28⅜″
1 length clear softwood, 1″ × 8″ × 12′
1 length clear softwood, 1″ × 8″ × 14′
2 glass doors, 23¾″ × 15″
2 glass shelves, 28⅜″ × 10″
6 continuous hinges, 26¾″
1 continuous hinge, 28⅜″
6 door pulls
7 drawer pulls
7 magnetic door catches
4 pairs drawer-glide assemblies, 14″
3 pairs drawer-glide assemblies, 12″
1 pair shelf-glide assemblies, 15″
2 desk supports
25 rolls veneer tape, 1″ × 8′
2 quarts contact cement
1 quart lacquer thinner
1 quart white glue
10 inexpensive paintbrushes, 1″
1 length wood dowel, ¼″ × 6′
1 pound finishing nails, 1½″
200 flathead wood screws, ¾″
8 clear plastic shelf-support pegs
2 pieces plastic-laminate sheet,
   15⅞″ × 28⅞″, 13½″ × 28⅜″

Cutting Diagrams

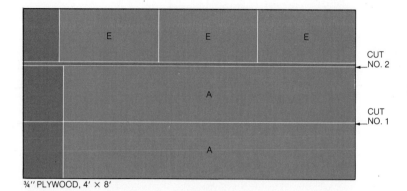

¾″ PLYWOOD, 4′ × 8′

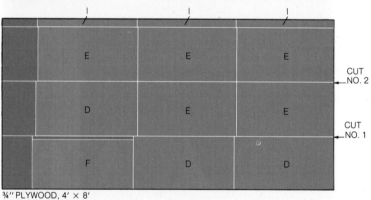

¾″ PLYWOOD, 4′ × 8′

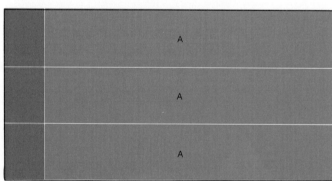

¾″ PLYWOOD, 4′ × 8′

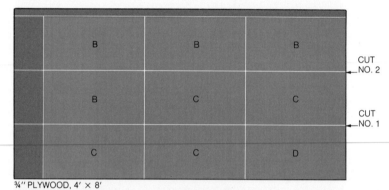

¾″ PLYWOOD, 4′ × 8′

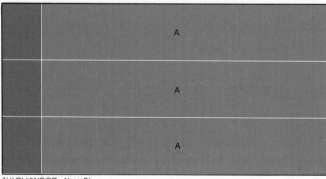

¾″ PLYWOOD, 4′ × 8′

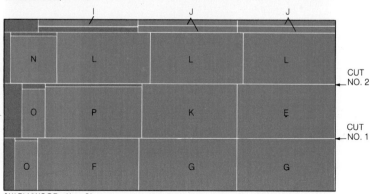

¾″ PLYWOOD, 4′ × 8′

Making the basic cuts. To build all four units cut the plywood sheets and lengths of lumber into the pieces shown in these diagrams. Do not, however, cut the kick plate (parts I) or the top plate (parts J) until each basic unit has been assembled (*Step 4, page 90*). The cuts identified as Nos. 1 and 2 should be done in order, to minimize waste and avoid errors. The diagrams have been laid out so that lengthwise cuts precede crosscuts; exceptions have been indicated. Re-measure each piece before cutting to allow for the saw kerf. Dark-shaded pieces are scrap; save them for additional shelves or other features you may want to install. Make masking-tape labels for each part to indicate its name, key letter and, where appropriate, the side that will be more visible. Designate the top with an arrow. The name and dimensions of each piece, identified by letter in the diagrams, are given in the key below:

A| side, 84″ × 15⅞″
B| top, 29″ × 15⅛″
C| bottom, 29″ × 15⅛″
D| fixed shelf, 29″ × 15⅛″
E| movable shelf, 28⅜″ × 15⅛″
F| shallow fixed shelf, 29″ × 14¼″
G| shallow movable shelf, 28⅜″ × 14¼″
H| narrow movable shelf, 14¼″ × 13⅞″
I| kick plate, 28½″ × 2¼″
J| top plate, 28½″ × 1⅞″
K| roll-out shelf, 28¼″ × 15⅛″
L| door, 26¾″ × 14″
M| wide-drawer front, 28⅜″ × 6⅝″
N| desk-drawer front, 13½″ × 13½″
O| desk-drawer front, 13½″ × 6½″
P| desk-cabinet partition, 27¾″ × 14¼″
Q| drawer side, 13¾″ × 13″
R| drawer back, 13″ × 11⅞″
S| desk drop leaf, 28⅜″ × 16″
T| cabinet back, 81¾″ × 29″
U| wide-drawer bottom, 26⅜″ × 13⅞″
V| desk-drawer bottom, 12⅞″ × 11⅝″
W| desk-organizer upright, 9½″ × 7¾″
X| organizer dividers, 9½″ × 5⅛″
AA| desk-organizer shelf, 28⅜″ × 9½″
BB| wide-drawer back, 26½″ × 6″
CC| desk-drawer back, 11⅞″ × 6″
DD| wide-drawer side, 14¼″ × 6″
EE| desk-drawer side, 13¾″ × 6″

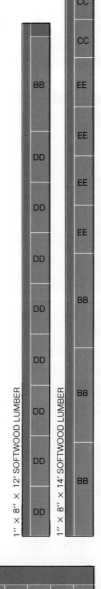

1″ × 8″ × 12′ SOFTWOOD LUMBER

1″ × 8″ × 14′ SOFTWOOD LUMBER

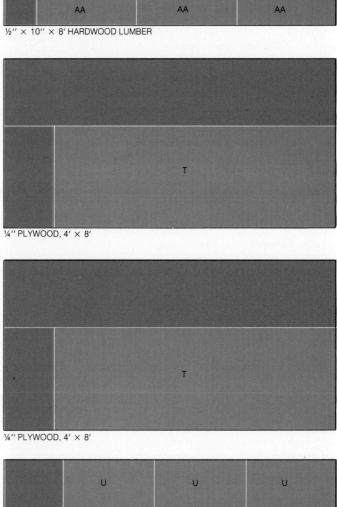

½″ × 10″ × 8′ HARDWOOD LUMBER

¼″ PLYWOOD, 4′ × 8′

¼″ PLYWOOD, 4′ × 8′

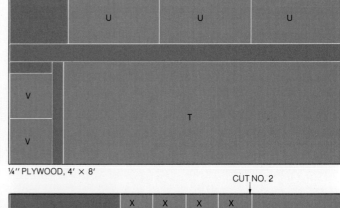

¼″ PLYWOOD, 4′ × 8′

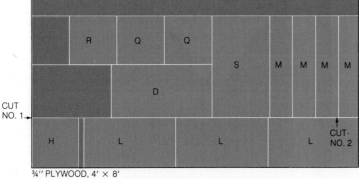

¾″ PLYWOOD, 4′ × 8′

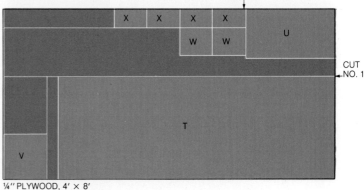

¼″ PLYWOOD, 4′ × 8′

Cutting Joints and Peg Holes

Grooves and peg holes for side pieces. The left side pieces for all four wall-storage units are represented in the three diagrams at the right (the sides of the two stereo units are identical). The right side pieces must be cut to make mirror images of the left sides—with one exception: do not drill any peg holes near the bottom of the right side of the desk unit; instead, drill them in the desk partition (diagram A, below) to match the peg holes in the left side piece. All the peg holes are ½ inch deep and ¼ inch wide. The number and location of the peg holes can be changed to suit your particular storage needs. Cut the ¼-inch dowel into 1-inch lengths to make the pegs.

The dadoes at the bottoms and the rabbets at the tops of each side piece are all ¾ inch wide and ¼ inch deep. Start routing these cuts from the back edge, and stop ½ inch from the front edge. The bottom line of the dadoes is 1¼ inches from the bottom edge; the ends of the dadoes and rabbets need not be squared off.

Exact positions of the middle dadoes, which are also ¾ inch wide and ¼ inch deep, are indicated by the figures in the diagrams. The middle dadoes in the desk unit must be squared off ⅞ inch from the front edge. All dadoes along the back edges are ¼ inch wide and ¼ inch deep; their outside edges are ½ inch from the back edge.

Dadoes for smaller pieces. All top and bottom pieces have a dado ¼ inch wide, ¼ inch deep and ½ inch from the back edge, as in diagram B. Cut them on the underside of the top pieces and on the top surface of the bottom pieces. The bottom of the desk unit (diagram C) has an additional dado, ¾ inch wide and ¼ inch deep, 14 inches from the right edge.

Cut a dado in the desk unit's shallow fixed shelf (diagram D) ¼ inch wide and ¼ inch deep, 14 inches from the right edge. On the underside of the top shelf in the display-case unit (diagram E), cut two dadoes ¼ inch wide and ½ inch deep. One dado is ¼ inch from the front edge and the other is ¾ inch from the same edge. On the top surface of the bottom shelf for the display case (diagram F), cut two dadoes ¼ inch wide and ¼ inch deep. One dado is ¼ inch from the front edge and the other is ¾ inch from the same edge.

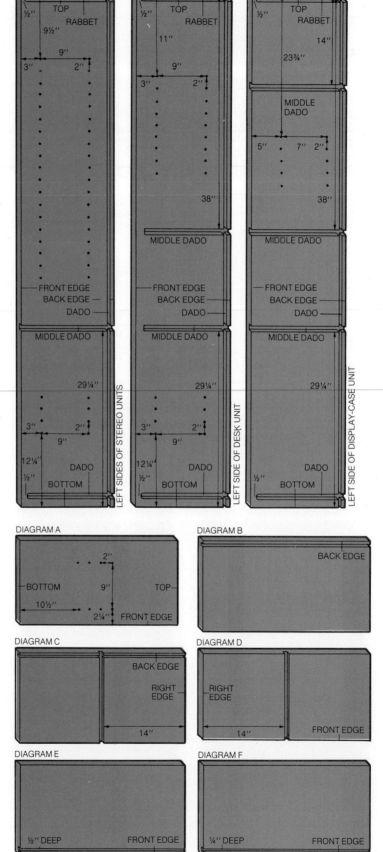

Assembling the Basic Pieces of the Wall Storage Units

The basic structural components. The three different wall-storage units appear in exploded diagrams below, with dadoes cut according to the diagrams opposite. Two essentially similar stereo-speaker units were built for the complete four-unit installation shown on page 6. Instructions for installing doors, drawers and desk compartments begin on page 91.

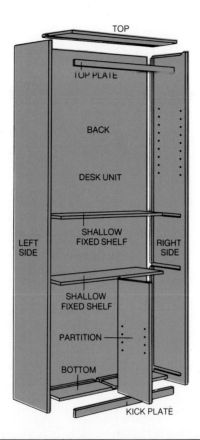

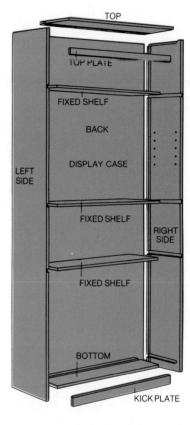

Stereo-speaker unit labels: TOP, TOP PLATE, BACK, STEREO-SPEAKER UNIT, LEFT SIDE, RIGHT SIDE, FIXED SHELF, BOTTOM, KICK PLATE

Desk unit labels: TOP, TOP PLATE, BACK, DESK UNIT, SHALLOW FIXED SHELF, LEFT SIDE, RIGHT SIDE, SHALLOW FIXED SHELF, PARTITION, BOTTOM, KICK PLATE

Display-case unit labels: TOP, TOP PLATE, FIXED SHELF, BACK, DISPLAY CASE, LEFT SIDE, FIXED SHELF, RIGHT SIDE, FIXED SHELF, BOTTOM, KICK PLATE

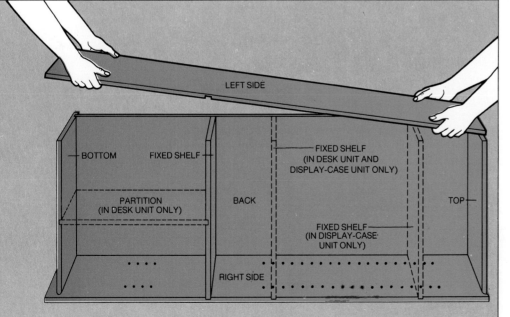

Labels: LEFT SIDE, BOTTOM, FIXED SHELF, FIXED SHELF (IN DESK UNIT AND DISPLAY-CASE UNIT ONLY), PARTITION (IN DESK UNIT ONLY), BACK, TOP, FIXED SHELF (IN DISPLAY-CASE UNIT ONLY), RIGHT SIDE

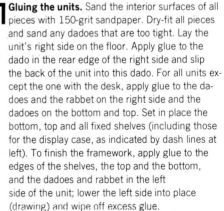

1 Gluing the units. Sand the interior surfaces of all pieces with 150-grit sandpaper. Dry-fit all pieces and sand any dadoes that are too tight. Lay the unit's right side on the floor. Apply glue to the dado in the rear edge of the right side and slip the back of the unit into this dado. For all units except the one with the desk, apply glue to the dadoes and the rabbet on the right side and the dadoes on the bottom and top. Set in place the bottom, top and all fixed shelves (including those for the display case, as indicated by dash lines at left). To finish the framework, apply glue to the edges of the shelves, the top and the bottom, and the dadoes and rabbet in the left side of the unit; lower the left side into place (drawing) and wipe off excess glue.

To assemble the desk unit, install the back in the right side, glue the edges of the partition (indicated by dash lines) and the dadoes in the middle of the bottom and in the fixed shelf; join these pieces and install them in the right side. Then assemble the top, the remaining fixed shelf and the left side, as in the instructions above.

2 **Nailing the pieces.** Use an awl to mark guidelines lightly on both of the side pieces to indicate the centers of the top, bottom, and shelf pieces. Drive three 1½-inch finishing nails along each of these lines through the sides into the top, bottom, and shelves. Nails are not required in the back panel. Countersink all nails.

3 **Squaring the units.** Check the corners of all units with a steel square before the glue has had time to set. If a unit is not square, clamp a steel square tightly into one corner with hand screws (drawing). Leave the hand screws in place until the glue has dried. Squaring one corner should bring all of the other corners into alignment.

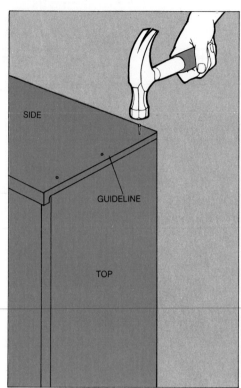

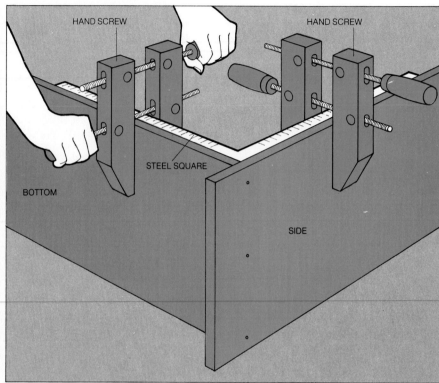

4 **Installing kick plate and top plate.** Measure the inside distance between the two sides of the unit at the top and at the bottom. Using these measurements for the lengths, cut the top plate 1⅞ inches wide and the kick plate 2¼ inches wide from ¾-inch plywood. Apply glue to all the surfaces that touch. As you slip the plates into position, insert behind them two pieces of cardboard ⅟₃₂ inch thick (drawing). These shims will hold the plates out far enough so that their surfaces will be flush with the veneer that will be applied later to the raw edges of the sides. Drive two finishing nails through each side into the plates, and three nails through the fronts of the plates into the top and bottom pieces.

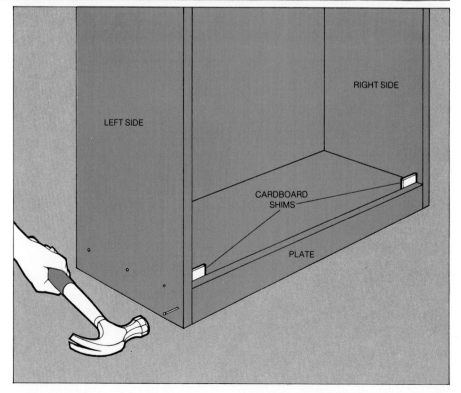

Hanging the Cabinet Doors

1 **Attaching hinges to doors.** Before hanging the doors, install veneer stripping on the front edges of the cabinet walls, following the method described on page 77. Place the door in a woodworking vise with the edge to be hinged facing up. Measure this edge and, with a hacksaw, cut a piece of continuous hinge to fit. Make the cuts at least ¼ inch away from screw holes. Lay the open hinge on the door edge with the flat side of the hinge down and the round pin loops just beyond the front edge (drawing, below). The unattached leaf of the hinge should extend over the front side of the door. Start the screw holes with an awl. Screw the hinge down, beginning with the end and middle screws, then working from each end toward the middle. Repeat the procedure to attach a hinge to the other door.

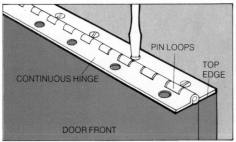

PIN LOOPS
CONTINUOUS HINGE
TOP EDGE
DOOR FRONT

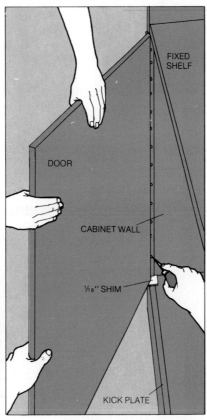

FIXED SHELF
DOOR
CABINET WALL
1/16″ SHIM
KICK PLATE

2 **Attaching hinges to the cabinet.** Place a 1/16-inch-thick shim on top of the kick plate, and against the cabinet wall. Rest the door on the shim, and put the door in place. Hold the unattached leaf of the hinge firmly against the cabinet wall, and have a helper adjust the position of the door so that the pin loops protrude just beyond the edge of the cabinet wall (drawing). Properly positioned, the door should close flush with the unit's front and open completely.

Mark the centers of the top and bottom screw holes with an awl and drive in these two screws first. Test the swing; if the door does not open and close properly, take the screws out, readjust the position of the door and attach the door to the cabinet again—this time inserting screws in the second holes from each end. When the door is hung correctly, put in all of the screws. Repeat the procedure for the other door.

Installing Door Catches

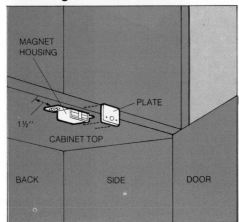

MAGNET HOUSING
PLATE
1½″
CABINET TOP
BACK
SIDE
DOOR

CABINET TOP
PLATE
DOOR

1 **Positioning the magnet.** Magnetic catches that hold cabinet doors closed consist of two parts: a magnet in a plastic or metal housing that is screwed to the cabinet, and a metal plate that is screwed to the inside of the door.

Place the magnet housing on the underside of the cabinet top about ⅝ inch from the front edge and about 1½ inches away from the point where the side edge of the door meets the cabinet top. Install screws in the centers of the housing slots, leaving the screws just loose enough to permit the magnet to move back and forth freely. Place the separate metal plate in position on the magnet (drawing), with the screw hole down.

2 **Attaching the plate.** With the metal plate in position against the magnet housing, use a combination square to measure the distance from the edge of the plate to the point where the cabinet door meets the cabinet top (drawing). Transfer the measurement to the inside of the cabinet door to mark a guideline for mounting the plate on the door. This procedure will work even if the cabinet includes a wall or partition at the edge of the door, as in the desk-unit cabinet.

For this unit, which has no such divider, simply close the door on the plate, reach inside with a pencil and mark a guideline on the door at the edge of the plate. Install the plate on the door. To

set the magnet housing at its proper depth, close the door flush with the edge of the cabinet top, reach inside and slide the magnet housing forward so that it is against the plate. Holding the magnet housing in position, open the door and tighten the magnet-housing screws.

Assembling the Desk Organizer

1 **Cutting the joints.** The three shelves and the two uprights required for the desk organizer are diagramed below. All of the dadoes are ⅛ inch deep and ¼ inch wide. The dimensions of the lap-joint slots are given on the diagrams. The dadoes can most easily be made with a router and a ¼-inch straight bit. The lap-joint slots can be cut with multiple passes of a circular saw, as in Step 2. To mark the location of all cuts on the three shelves, begin measuring at the center of each board—that is, 14³⁄₁₆ inches from the ends. This ensures that the grooves will be in correct alignment and the compartments will be square —in case you should find later that the shelves must be trimmed for snug fit. To allow both desk-lid supports to close completely, cut out pieces ⅜ inch wide and ½ inch deep at the front corners of the middle and bottom shelves.

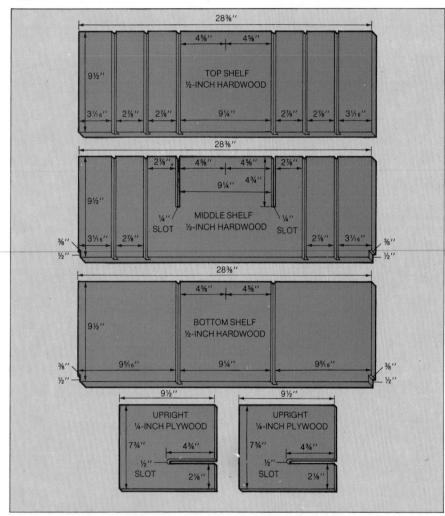

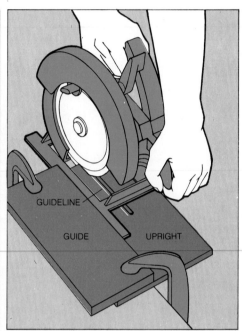

2 **Cutting the lap-joint slots.** Use a circular saw with the blade depth set at ¾ inch (drawing) to cut the lap-joint slots in the uprights and in the middle shelf. Instructions for setting up a circular-saw guide, like the one shown here, are given on page 27. After marking the location of both sides of the slots with an awl, make as many passes with the saw as needed to cut them out, but take care to stay within the awl lines.

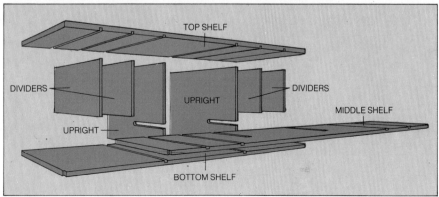

3 **Dry-fitting all the pieces.** This exploded diagram shows how the three shelves of ½-inch hardwood fit together with the two uprights and four dividers of ¼-inch plywood to form a set of compartments that will be installed above the desk. After making the cuts described in Steps 1 and 2, dry-fit each piece into its grooves; sand down any dado or slot that is not wide enough. All the pieces will be glued together (no nails or screws are used) following the assembly procedure that begins on the opposite page.

4 **Assembling uprights and middle shelf.** Apply glue to the sides of the two slots in the middle shelf and to the slot in each upright, and slip the uprights down over the shelf as shown in the drawing below. With a mallet, tap the uprights all the way down into the shelf slots until the edges are flush. Check the joints with a square. If the uprights are not at right angles to the shelf, attach corner clamps and leave them in place until the glue has set.

5 **Assembling dividers and top shelf.** When the joints of the uprights and the middle shelf have dried, set the assembly on a table with the dadoes facing up. Apply glue to the four dadoes in the shelf, and slip the dividers into these grooves. Next, apply glue to the tops of the dividers and the tops of the uprights, and to the dadoes on the top shelf. Carefully lower the top shelf onto the dividers and uprights so that each vertical piece slips into the proper dado on the shelf.

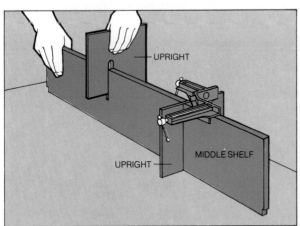

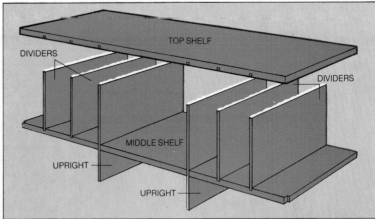

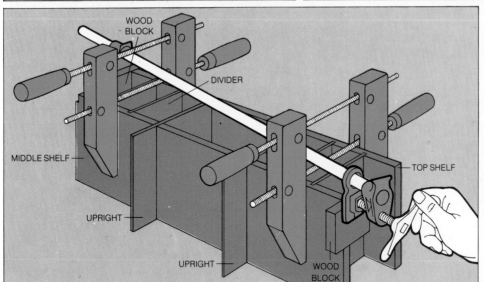

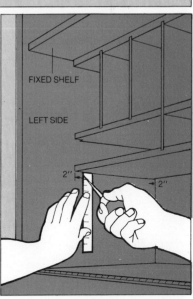

6 **Clamping dividers and shelves.** After the dividers, uprights and top shelf have been glued and assembled, but before the glue has dried, place hand screws across the shelves, outside the uprights. Check the joints with a square. The likelihood is that the unit will be askew and that you will have to use a bar clamp to straighten it. If the top shelf twists to the left, place the screw end of the bar clamp on the middle shelf and the other end on the top shelf (drawing). If the top shelf twists to the right, put the screw end of the bar clamp on the top shelf. Place blocks of scrap wood between the clamp faces and the shelf ends to protect the shelves. Tight-

en the clamp until the joints are square. When the glue has dried, remove all the clamps. To complete the assembly of the compartments, apply glue to the bottoms of the uprights and the dadoes of the bottom shelf; slip the shelf onto the uprights and place hand screws across the shelves directly over the uprights; tighten the hand screws and allow to dry.

7 **Drilling peg holes.** Position the desk organizer firmly under the fixed shelf above the desk, and against the back panel, either by means of pieces of scrap wood wedged underneath, or with the aid of a helper. With an awl, mark the locations for four peg holes—two underneath the compartments on the left side and two on the right side. The center of all four holes should be $\frac{5}{32}$ inch below the organizer. The centers of two of the peg holes should be located 2 inches from the front edge of the organizer and the other two holes should be centered 2 inches from the back edge. Remove the organizer and drill ½-inch-deep holes with a ¼-inch bit.

Installing the Drop-Leaf Desk

1 Laminating the shelf. Using a circular saw with a plywood-cutting blade, cut a piece of plastic laminate with the good side down, 13½ inches deep and 28⅜ inches wide, to cover the shelf of the drop-leaf desk. These dimensions leave ¾ inch uncovered at the front of the shelf to accommodate the continuous hinge. Cover the top surface of the shelf and the back of the laminate with contact cement. Place the back edge of the laminate above the back edge of the shelf, taking care to keep the cemented surfaces apart until the pieces are in the correct position. Let the back edge of the laminate drop into place; lower the laminate onto the shelf, and press the whole surface firmly with the heel of your hand.

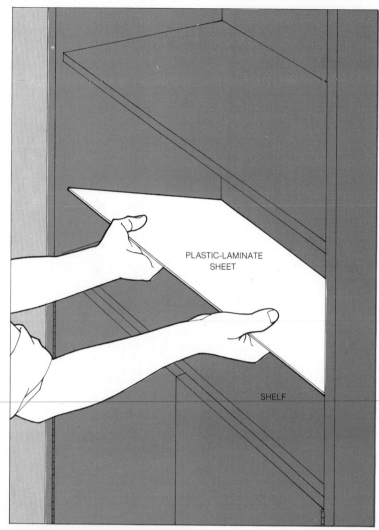

PLASTIC-LAMINATE SHEET

SHELF

2 Preparing edges for the hinge. To bevel the edges of the pieces that will be joined by the continuous hinge, draw guidelines ³⁄₁₆ inch along the top back edge of the drop leaf (drawing); draw the same guidelines along the top front edge of the shelf. If the round bulge of your hinge is wider than the standard ³⁄₁₆ inch, mark the guidelines that much deeper. Clamp the drop leaf to a worktable for support. Hold a block plane at a 45° angle to the top of the shelf and cut away the triangle of wood marked by the guidelines; repeat for the shelf. Use a wood chisel, beveled side up, to finish beveling the corner of the shelf.

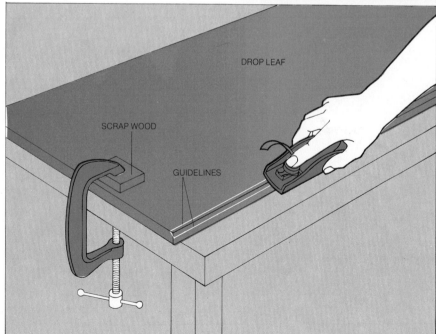

DROP LEAF

SCRAP WOOD

GUIDELINES

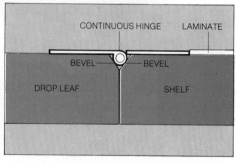

CONTINUOUS HINGE   LAMINATE

BEVEL   BEVEL

DROP LEAF   SHELF

3 Attaching the hinge to the drop leaf. With a hacksaw, cut a piece of continuous hinge 28⅜ inches long. Hold the drop leaf in position against the shelf and place the round bulge of the hinge into the beveled groove between the two pieces. If the hinge does not lie perfectly flat, as shown above, chisel or sand the bevels until it does. With the drop leaf and hinge in position against the shelf, mark the centers of the end screw holes on the drop leaf with an awl. Clamp the drop leaf to the worktable. Screw the hinge down, starting with the end and middle screws, then working in from each end toward the middle.

4 Laminating and attaching the drop leaf. Cut a sheet of plastic laminate 15⅞ inches by 28⅞ inches to cover the drop leaf. Lay the drop leaf on a worktable for support, and apply contact cement to the top of the drop leaf and the back of the laminate. Place the back edge of the laminate against the edge of the hinge and lower the laminate onto the drop leaf so that the laminate overhangs the drop leaf about ¼ inch all around. Press the laminate firmly onto the drop leaf. Trim the excess laminate from the edges with a router and flush-trimming bit (drawing, right).

Apply veneer tape to the three sides of the drop leaf that will be visible (see page 77 for directions on edge stripping). While a helper holds the drop leaf and hinge in position against the shelf, use an awl to mark on the shelf the centers of the screw holes at the ends. Then screw the continuous hinge to the shelf, starting with the end screws and working toward the middle.

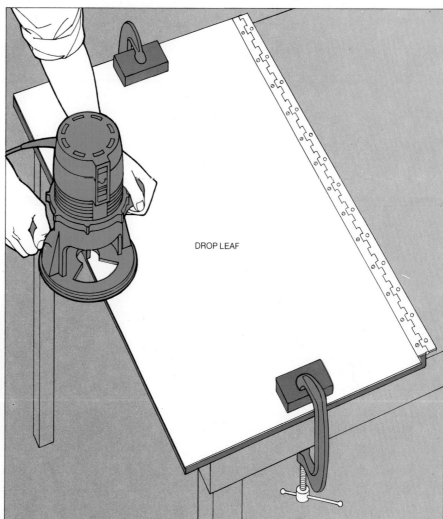

DROP LEAF

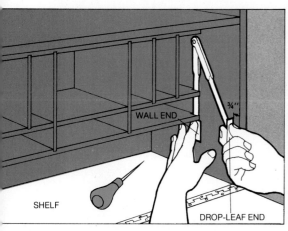

WALL END

¾"

SHELF

DROP-LEAF END

5 Attaching the drop-leaf supports. Put the desk organizer in place on its pegs. Place the drop-leaf end of a fully extended 15-inch desk support about 7 inches from the back edge of the drop leaf, and the opposite end on the side of the cabinet, about 5 inches above the shelf. The final position may change slightly, depending on the make of support purchased. To ensure that the joint of the support clears the upper shelf when folded, hold the wall end of the support firmly in place and move the drop-leaf end so that its base is ¾ inch inside the cabinet (drawing, above).

Still holding the wall end of the support in place, use an awl to mark the centers of the screw holes on the cabinet wall, and install the screws. Repeat this entire procedure for the second support. Extend both supports fully, with the bases resting on the drop leaf. Place a level half on the drop leaf and half on the shelf. Once the drop leaf is level, mark on the laminate the centers of the screw holes for both support bases. Drill holes the same diameter as the support screws through the laminate but not into the wood. Mark the centers for all the screws and install them.

ROUTER BASE

CATCH PLATE OUTLINE

6 Attaching the catch plate. Place the catch plate at the midpoint of the front edge of the drop leaf, ⅞ inch from the edge, and trace its outline on the laminate with an awl. Mount a ¼-inch straight bit in a router and adjust the bit depth to equal the thickness of the plate. Hold the router at an angle over the plate outline on the laminate, with the router base pressed against the edge of the drop leaf to steady it (drawing, left). Then lower the rotating bit gently but firmly into the laminate and rout out the area within the outline. Screw the catch plate into the routed area. Remove the desk organizer, then apply wood finish to the unit. After the finish has dried, replace the organizer and attach the magnetic catch for the drop leaf under the cabinet shelf.

Constructing the Drawers

Cutting the joints. Dadoes and rabbets for the drawers *(right)* may be cut with a router or a circular saw *(pages 26-27)*. All dadoes on the sides of the front pieces are ¾ inch wide and ⅜ inch deep, and end ¼ inch from the top. Note, however, that on the desk-unit drawers one dado is ½ inch from the right side of the front piece, and the other is ¼ inch from the left side. All other dadoes are ¼ inch wide, ¼ inch deep and ¼ inch from the bottom of each piece. All of the rabbets are ¾ inch wide and ⅜ inch deep.

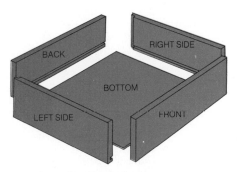

Assembling the pieces. Although the drawers come in three different sizes, their parts fit together in the same manner, as shown in the exploded diagram above. Before applying glue, dry-fit all the pieces to make sure the joints have been properly cut. Begin by placing the front piece on the worktable with the outside face down. Place the two sides in the dadoes on the front, slip the bottom into the dadoes on the sides and front and lower the back into position on the sides and bottom. Sand down any joints that are too tight. Assemble the pieces again in the same order, this time applying glue to all joints. Place bar clamps along the sides and along the back. Nails are not necessary.

Adding the Finishing Touches

Installing glass shelves and doors. Before you install the sliding glass doors, put the shelves into the display case. For support, use clear plastic pegs, which are less noticeable than wooden ones under the glass shelves.

With a cotton-tipped swab, apply paste wax to the grooves on the bottom shelf of the display case, so that the glass doors will slide easily. Hold the rear door almost vertical, with the pull indentation toward the side of the cabinet, as shown in the drawing at right. Slip the top of the door into the rear groove on the underside of the top shelf, then swing the bottom of the door in and lower it into the rear groove on the bottom shelf. Install the other door in the front grooves, following the same sequence.

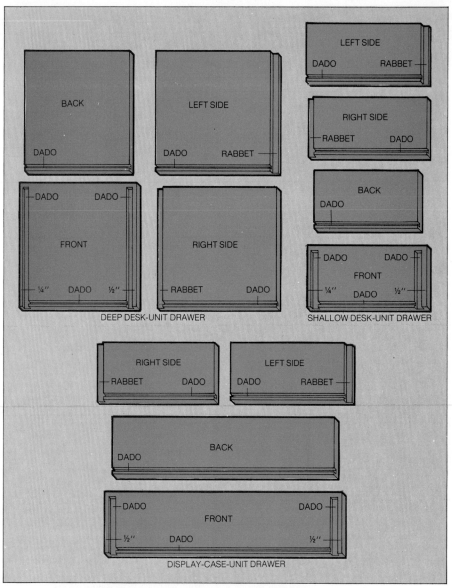

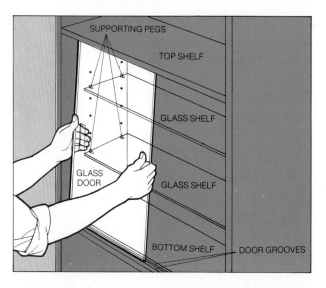

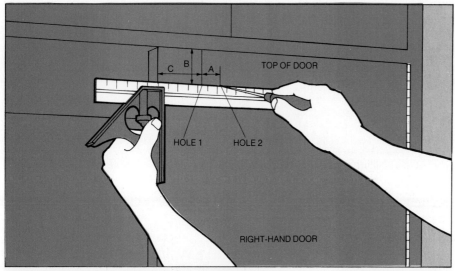

Attaching door and drawer pulls. Most pulls, like the ones used here, are installed by drilling holes through the door or drawer and attaching the pull with screws. The procedure varies with other types of pulls, but no matter what type you use, be sure to install it parallel to the edge of the door or drawer. To position the pulls properly on the cabinet doors, mark the position of the first screw hole about 2 inches from both edges of the door (hole 1 in the diagram, left). For hole 2, measure the distance between the centers of the screw holes on the pull and, with a combination square, transfer this measurement (A) to the door. Drill holes at these points and install the first pull. Then measure the distance from hole 1 to the top of the door (B) and to the side of the door (C), and transfer measurements A, B and C to the second door to position the screw holes there.

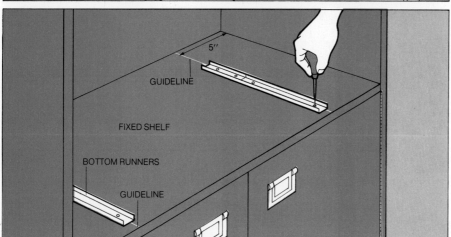

Installing shelf glides. To install the glides that support the roll-out shelf in the stereo unit, use a steel square to mark guidelines on the fixed shelf, perpendicular to the front edge of the shelf and 5 inches from the sides. Center the roll-out shelf on top and transfer the guidelines to the front edge of the roll-out shelf. Remove the roll-out shelf and attach the bottom runners of the glides to the fixed shelf, with the centers of the screw holes on the guidelines, and the glides 1 inch from the front edge. Start the screw holes with an awl (drawing). Begin at the guidelines on the front edge of the roll-out shelf and mark parallel guidelines on the underside. Attach the upper runners the same way.

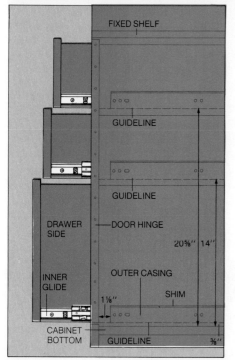

Installing drawer-glide assemblies. To install the three drawers of the desk-unit cabinet, attach the inner glides to both sides of each drawer, following the instructions on page 30. Locations of the outer casings on the right side of the desk-unit cabinet appear in the diagram at left. Using an awl and a steel square, mark three guidelines, one for each outer casing, on the inner cabinet side; mark three matching guidelines on the right side of the cabinet partition. The lines are respectively ⅜ inch, 14 inches and 20⅝ inches above the bottom of the cabinet.

Cut three shims of ⅛-inch-thick plywood 1½ inches wide and 12 inches long. Hold each outer casing on one of the shims and place the shim against the inner side of the cabinet with the bottom edges of both the casing and the shim precisely on the guideline. The front edges of both the casing and the shim should be 1⅛ inches from the rear edge of the cabinet-door hinge. (The shim is necessary so that the glide assembly will clear the hinge.) With an awl, mark the centers of the casing screw holes on the shim; drill pilot holes through the shim and just into the cabinet side. Screw the casing and shim

in place. Following the same procedure, mount three other casings on the partition, but without using shims. The front edges of the casings are 1⅛ inches from the front edge of the partition. Install glide assemblies for the four drawers in the display-case unit following the same procedures as above. Mark the outer-casing guidelines on the cabinet sides ⁷⁄₁₆ inch, 7⅛ inches, 13⁹⁄₁₆ inches and 20½ inches above the cabinet bottom.

Finding Space within Walls

The interior walls of most houses are supported by wood studs—posts located at regular intervals within the walls. The cavities between the studs are usually 14½ inches wide and vary in depth, depending on the kind of wall construction, from about 3½ inches to 6 inches. This is ample space for recessing a clothes hamper—as explained in the instructions given here—or for other bathroom storage units, most of which are made to standard dimensions so they fit between studs. These same instructions also apply to installing shelves between existing studs in any room.

The first step is to determine that the part of the wall you have chosen does not contain pipes or electrical wires. And do not forget to inspect the corresponding area on the wall in the next room. If neither side holds electrical or plumbing fixtures, it is still a good idea to check underlying and overlying locations. If you are now reasonably certain the space is clear, determine the exact spacing of the studs by following the directions on page 42. Then cut an exploratory opening just large enough for you to see or probe for unsuspected pipes or wires. Obviously, in a bathroom the test hole should be made above the tiles.

If, in spite of having reduced the odds, you still encounter pipes or wires, seal the opening and try again—either to the left or right of the original position.

Cutting an exploratory opening and breaking through the wall later is no problem if the wall is thin plasterboard or wood paneling, both of which can be sliced through easily with a saber saw. Many walls are thicker, however, consisting of hard plaster attached to wood or metal lath. In this case you may have to remove some of the plaster with a cold chisel to determine the kind of lath behind it. Use the special saw blades that cut either plaster and metal or plaster and wood. If tiles cover a section of the wall, you will have to remove them before you can cut into the wall itself.

Finally, in cutting into any wall, remember to avoid the baseboard, which conceals the horizontal plate that supports the studs.

Installing a Hamper

1 Marking the position. With a grease pencil, indicate on the tiled wall the inside edges of the two studs you have located and between which you wish to place the hamper. Prop the hamper between the stud lines, raising it on scraps of wood so that the bottom of the hamper frame is just above the baseboard. Outline the top and sides of the recessed hamper frame on the tiles (drawing) with the grease pencil. Extend each line several inches beyond the hamper to provide reference points when the tiles are removed.

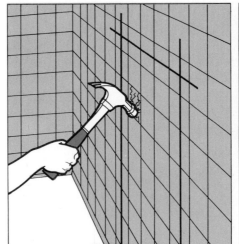

2 Removing the tiles. Smash one central tile with a hammer (drawing) and pry off the pieces. If the top and sides of the hamper's outline enclose an area of whole tiles, remove all tiles within the outline. If, however, the marks outlining the hamper bisect tiles at the top and sides, remove the whole tiles within the outline, but be very careful in removing the tiles with the grease-pencil marks on them. Indicate on each its sequence on the plaster just exposed. These marked tiles will be cut to the proper size later and replaced on the wall in that sequence before the hamper is installed.

3 Breaking through the plaster. Onto the newly exposed plaster, extend the vertical grease-pencil lines marking the position of the two studs. Connect the horizontal lines that indicate the top of the hamper frame. Use a cold chisel and hammer to clear out a thin strip of plaster at one corner of the outline to see if the inner wall is of wood or metal lath. (The drawing above shows metal lath.)

4 **Sawing through the wall.** Attach the appropriate blade for wood or metal lath to the saber saw and cut away the wall, following the grease-pencil marks on the plaster. Then clear away the debris from the exposed space.

5 **Scoring tiles for re-use.** Place one of the tiles bisected by the hamper outline on a flat surface. With a straight-edged piece of wood as a guide, use a glass cutter to score the tile along the mark made for the hamper outline. Press firmly on the glass cutter and pull it along the guide in one smooth motion. Score all the marked tiles in the same manner except the two from the top corners of the hamper outline; do not score these all the way across their surface but only along the pencil marks outlining the corner area to be removed from each of the tiles.

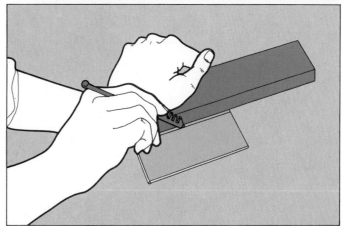

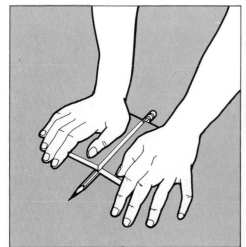

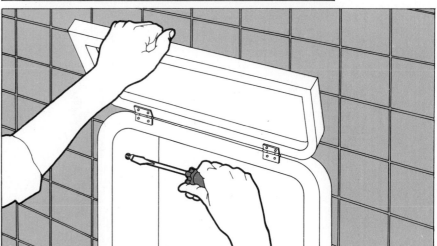

6 **Breaking the tiles.** Break all the scored tiles except the two from the top corners of the hamper outline as follows: Place a pencil on a flat surface and position the tile on the pencil so that the scored line is directly over it. Press down on each side of the line simultaneously until the tile snaps (drawing). If necessary, true uneven edges of the tiles with pliers. To remove the unwanted area from the two corner tiles, use the pliers to break off small bits at a time up to the scored lines. Apply tile adhesive to the back of each tile section and return it to its original marked position on the plaster.

7 **Installing the hamper.** Insert the hamper into the recess and use an awl to mark on the studs the positions of the screw holes. Remove the hamper, drill pilot holes in the studs, replace the hamper and secure it with screws (drawing). Use silicone caulking compound to seal the edges of the hamper frame where they meet the tiles.

Building Shelves Between Studs

1. Locating the shelves. With an awl, indicate on the wall the inside edges of the two studs you have located and between which you wish to place shelves. Also mark the top and bottom limits of the desired shelf area (drawing); connect the marks to form a rectangle, as indicated by dash lines. Use a combination square to check that the top and bottom lines of the rectangle are perfectly horizontal. Cut out the wall within the rectangle, following the directions in Steps 3 and 4 for installing the hamper (pages 98-99).

2. Putting in cleats. Measure the depth of the two exposed studs and cut two strips of 1-by-2 wood to the same dimension to serve as cleats. Hammer two or three 1½-inch-long finishing nails through each cleat so that the points of the nails just appear on the opposite side; apply glue to the surface through which the nails protrude. Position the two cleats horizontally against the studs so the top of each cleat is flush with the bottom edge of the wall opening (drawing). Use a level to make sure that the cleats are horizontal. Then drive the nails into the studs.

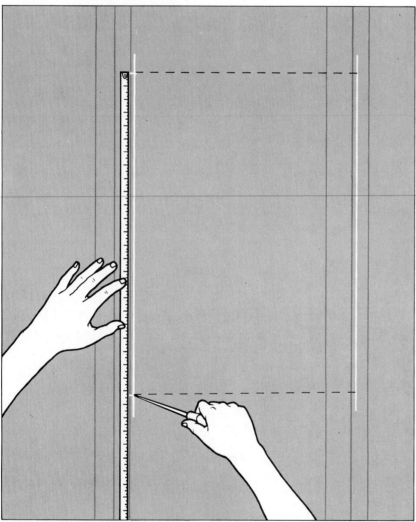

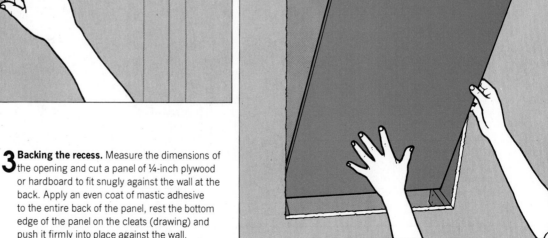

3. Backing the recess. Measure the dimensions of the opening and cut a panel of ¼-inch plywood or hardboard to fit snugly against the wall at the back. Apply an even coat of mastic adhesive to the entire back of the panel, rest the bottom edge of the panel on the cleats (drawing) and push it firmly into place against the wall.

4 **Putting in the shelves.** Cut the desired number of shelves from ½-inch-thick wood; make them as deep as the wall opening. From the same wood cut two supports for each shelf, equal in length to the height wanted between shelves. Attach the bottom shelf to the cleats with nails, place a pair of supports on the bottom shelf (drawing) and nail each support to a stud. Nail the second shelf to the tops of the supports. Install the remaining shelves in the same manner. To close off the top of the wall opening, attach a piece of wood the same size and thickness as the shelves to the uppermost supports before installing them. Secure the unit thus formed to the studs.

5 **Trimming the opening.** From molding wide enough to cover the edges of the plaster and the exposed edges of wood at the top, bottom and sides of the wall opening, cut two strips as long as the height of the opening. Glue and nail the strips along the sides of the opening, aligning the inner edges with the inside edges of the shelf supports. Cut two more strips of molding as long as the width of the opening plus the width of the two side strips; attach them to the top and bottom of the opening in the same manner.

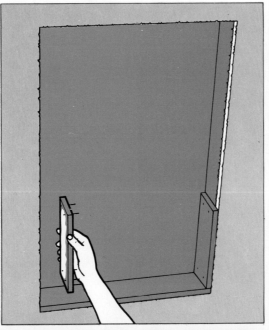

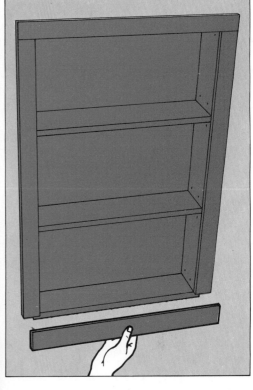

6 **Expanding the opening.** For more shelf room, several units like those completed in Steps 1 through 4 can be installed between adjacent studs. Add strips of molding as in Step 5 to cover the top, bottom and sides of the extended opening. Add molding strips wide enough to cover the intermediate studs and the edges of the shelf supports attached to them (drawing).

Building Extra Space into Kitchen Cabinets

A ready-made kitchen cabinet that provides only one drawer and a shelf is wasteful of space and frustrating to find things in. But it can be turned into an efficient storage unit by adding custom-built, roll-out bins like the ones shown on these pages.

The plans and instructions for building these bins were designed to fit a standard wood or hardboard counter cabinet with a depth of 23 inches and a door opening 14¾ inches wide and 21 inches high; if your cabinet differs from this standard, adapt dimensions to fit. Perhaps one large bin instead of two would serve you better. And by tailoring shelf locations and dimensions to the kitchen appliances and utensils you need space for, you can make bins to solve many storage problems.

Before starting to build the bins, you may have to remove an existing shelf. If the shelf is fixed in dadoes, you can do this by cutting a wide V into the shelf with a saber saw so that the point of the V is at the back. When the V drops out, the other pieces can be pulled from the dadoes. It may be necessary to remove the cabinet door if it does not open wide enough to give full access to the inside.

The dadoed and rabbeted joints specified here give the bins extra rigidity and strength, both desirable qualities if the bins are used for storing heavy utensils or canned goods, as these were designed to do. Such joints are more time consuming to make, however, and require the use of a router (page 26) or a power saw. If the bins will be used only for lightweight items, they can be built with simple butt joints reinforced with glued wood blocks (page 23).

Dual bins for convenient storage. The left-hand roll-out bin in the drawing below is designed to hold long-handled skillets in its rear compartment and saucepans in the top front shelf, with space below for lids. The right-hand bin in the drawing below at right has a front compartment for tall items that never seem to fit anywhere, such as a two-quart insulated bottle or large containers. The tray on top holds large cutlery, spatulas, wooden spoons and other flatware, while the shelves that are toward the back are for nested baking pans and mixing bowls.

Shopping List

2 lengths clear pine, ½″ × 10″ × 8′
1 length clear pine, ½″ × 8″ × 8′
1 piece hardboard or 2-2 hardwood plywood, ¼″ × 22½″ × 20¾″
4 pieces wood for glide mounts (for instructions on size, see page 106, Step 6)
4 ounces white wood glue
8 dozen finishing nails, 1″
6 finishing nails for ledge strips, ¾″
2 pairs drawer-glide assemblies, 22″

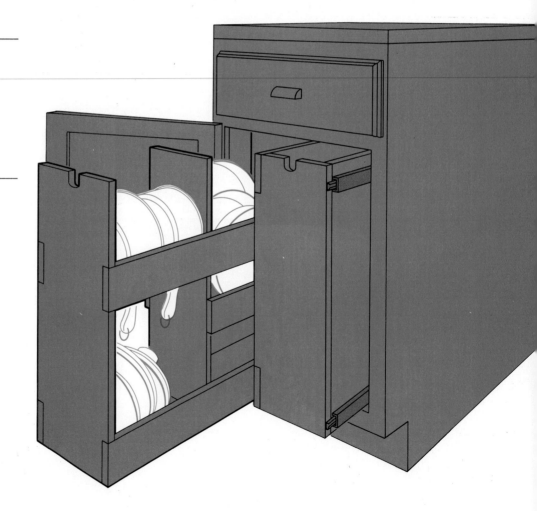

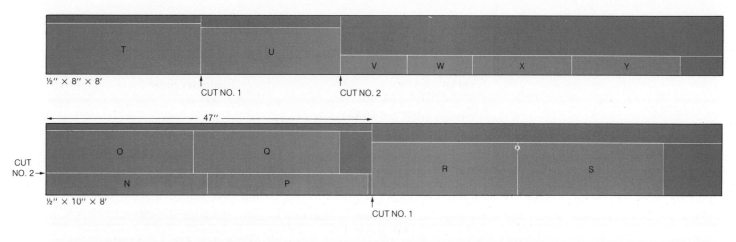

T
U
V
W
X
Y
½″ × 8″ × 8′
CUT NO. 1
CUT NO. 2
47″
O
Q
CUT NO. 2
N
P
R
S
½″ × 10″ × 8′
CUT NO. 1
CUT NO. 2
L
M
B
D
F
H
J
K
I
CUT NO. 1
A
C
E
G
½″ × 10″ × 8′

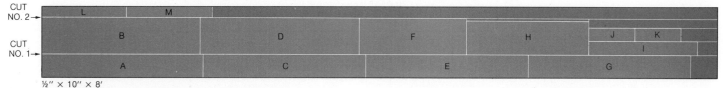

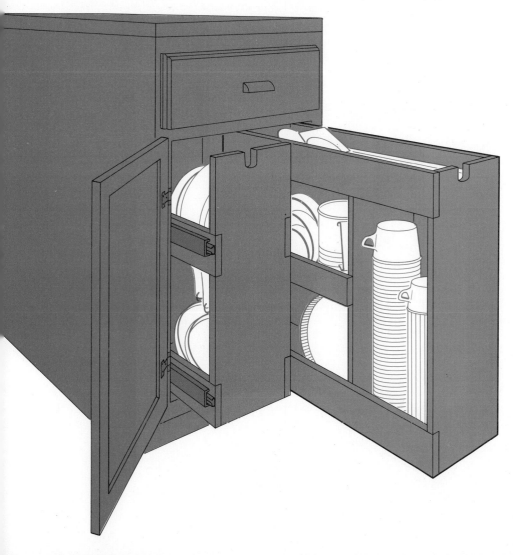

Making the basic cuts. To build both bins, cut three lengths of lumber into pieces as shown in the diagrams above. As with any cutting diagram, the initial cuts are critical in minimizing waste and eliminating errors. The remaining cuts may be made in any sequence, but be sure to remeasure each piece before cutting, and allow for the saw kerf. The dark-shaded portions are not needed for the bins; save the larger scrap pieces for other projects. Identify each piece with its name written on masking-tape labels. The name and dimensions of each piece, identified by letter in the diagrams, are given in the following key.

A | left bin rail, 3″ × 23″
B | right bin top, 5½″ × 22½″
C | left bin rail, 3″ × 23″
D | right bin bottom, 5½″ × 22½″
E | left bin rail, 3″ × 23″
F | right bin shelf, 5½″ × 15″
G | left bin rail, 3″ × 23″
H | right bin partition, 5¼″ × 17¾″
I | right bin middle rail, 2″ × 15½″
J | left bin short support, 2″ × 6½″
K | left bin short support, 2″ × 6½″
L | left bin ledge strip, ¾″ × 12½″
M | left bin ledge strip, ¾″ × 12½″
N | right bin rail, 3″ × 23″
O | right bin front, 6″ × 20¾″
P | right bin rail, 3″ × 23″
Q | right bin back, 6″ × 20¾″
R | left bin front, 7½″ × 20¾″
S | left bin back, 7½″ × 20¾″
T | left bin bottom, 7″ × 22″
U | left bin partition, 6½″ × 20″
V | left bin support, 2½″ × 9½″
W | left bin support, 2½″ × 9½″
X | left bin middle rail, 2½″ × 13½″
Y | left bin middle rail, 2½″ × 13½″

Cutting Grooves and Notches

Right-hand bin. Dadoes and corner cutouts are most easily made with a router and a ½-inch straight bit, but multiple cuts with a hand-held circular saw *(page 27)* accomplish the job also. All dadoes are ½ inch wide (the thickness of the lumber used) and ¼ inch deep. Cutouts at the corners are ½ inch deep by 3 inches long. Rabbets on the front and back pieces are ¼ inch wide and ¼ inch deep. They can be cut with a router and a ¼-inch rabbet bit or with a circular saw. Also make a cutout in the top edge of the front piece 1 inch wide and ¾ inch deep, using the router or a saber saw. The cutout will provide a fingerhold so that the finished bin can be pulled open.

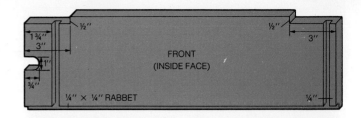

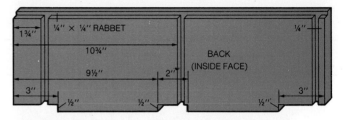

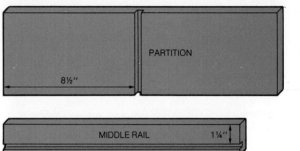

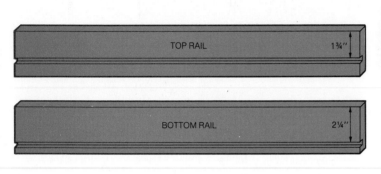

Left-hand bin. Make dadoes and cutouts for the left-hand bin, as shown in the diagrams at right and below, following the procedures described above. But take special care in positioning the middle dadoes on the front and back pieces of this bin precisely; otherwise the middle and top rails may not fit properly.

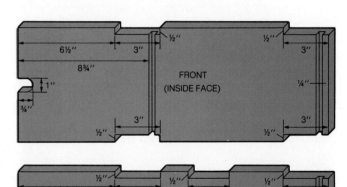

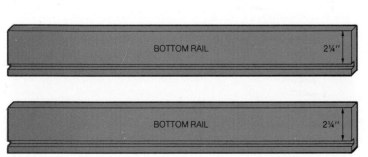

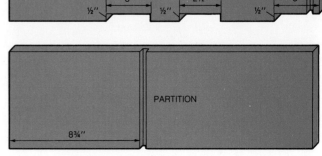

104

How to Put the Bins Together

1 **Assembling the right-hand bin.** Apply glue to both ends of the top and bottom, and slip them into the dadoes on the front and back. Position the top and bottom so that one edge of each piece extends ¼ inch into the cutouts for the rails, and the other edge is flush with the rabbets. Clamp all four pieces together with corner clamps and drive finishing nails through the front and back into the top and bottom. When the glue has set, remove the clamps. Lay the bin on the side that will be next to the cabinet wall, and apply glue along the edges of the top and bottom, and to the corner cutouts on the front and back. Nail the top and bottom rails in place.

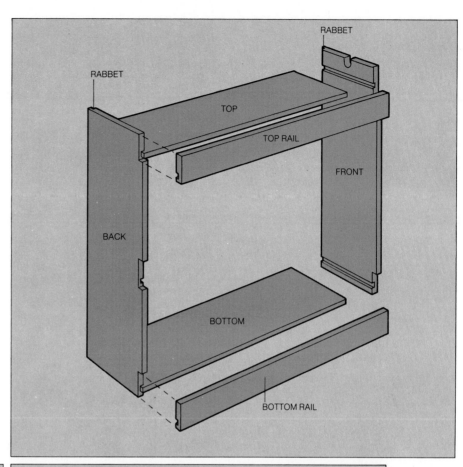

2 **Assembling the shelf and partition.** Apply glue to one end of the shelf and slip it into the dado in the vertical partition. Keep the shelf edge flush with the edge of the partition that will be next to the cabinet wall; the other shelf edge extends ¼ inch beyond the partition. Clamp the two pieces together with corner clamps and drive nails through the partition into the shelf. Allow the glue to set, and remove the clamps.

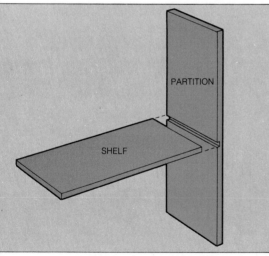

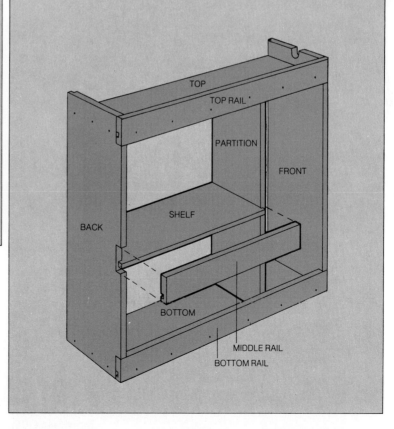

3 **Installing the shelf.** Apply glue to the free end of the shelf and to the top and bottom edges of the partition. Set the assembly into the bin so that the shelf edge that extends beyond the edge of the partition extends ¼ inch into the cutout for the middle rail, and the other shelf edge is flush with the rabbet. Drive nails through the back into the shelf, and through the top and bottom into the partition. Apply glue to the protruding edge of the shelf and nail the middle rail in place.

4 **Attaching the side panel.** Place the bin so that the side that will fit against the wall of the cabinet faces up. Position the side panel over the bin. Lift the panel as necessary so that you can see the edges of the pieces underneath. Using an awl, mark lines on the panel to indicate the centers of the pieces and to locate where the nails are to be driven. Remove the panel, apply glue to all of the edges and reposition the panel on the bin. Drive nails through the panel along the lines. Countersink all nails.

5 **Positioning the glides.** Place both inner glide sections on the side panel, one at the top and the other at the bottom, so that the screw holes in the glides align precisely with the lines made in Step 4 and both glides are flush with the front of the bin. Drill pilot holes where the top glide's screw holes fall, and attach the glide to the side panel. With a steel square, measure from the top glide to the bottom glide at both ends (drawing) to make sure the glides are parallel. Drill pilot holes and attach the bottom glide.

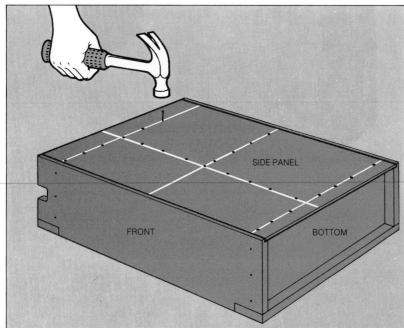

SIDE PANEL

FRONT

BOTTOM

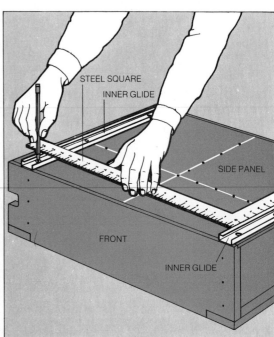

STEEL SQUARE

INNER GLIDE

SIDE PANEL

FRONT

INNER GLIDE

6 **Attaching the outer casings.** For use as mounts, cut two pieces of wood 23 inches long and the same thickness as the space between the inside cabinet wall and the inside edge of the cabinet frame. Place the outer casings on the mounts, drill pilot holes through the casing screw holes and screw the casings to the mounts.

If the cabinet you are modifying is a free-standing one, slip the mounted casings over the glides that were attached to the bins in Step 5 above. If the cabinet is not freestanding, do not insert the glides in the casings at this time.

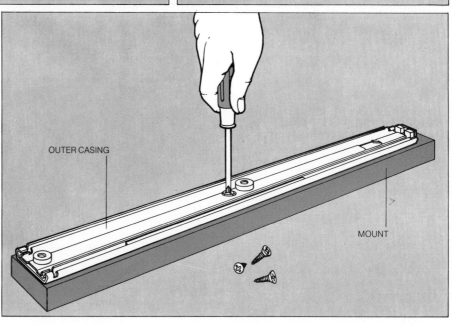

OUTER CASING

MOUNT

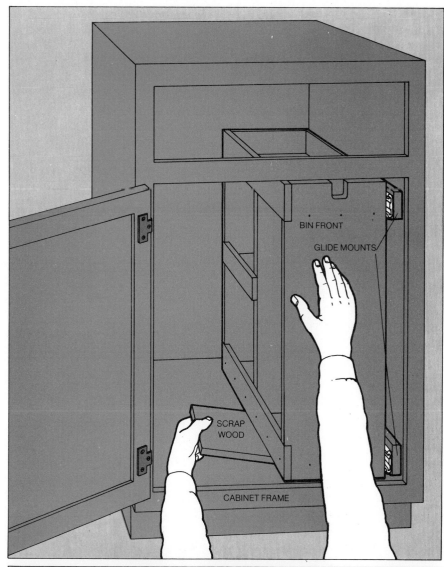

7 **Positioning the right-hand bin.** Place the bin, with the completed drawer-glides attached, inside the cabinet so that the glide mounts are against the inside of the cabinet frame. Slip a piece of scrap wood under the bin to raise it temporarily, adjusting the height so that the bin clears the bottom of the cabinet frame when extended.

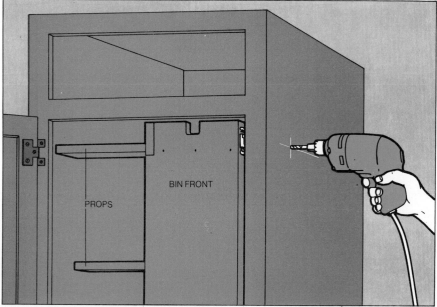

8 **Installing the bin.** Wedge two or three pieces of scrap wood between the bin and the opposite side of the cabinet to prop the bin firmly so that the glide mounts are flush against the inside of the cabinet. Using a steel square, mark lines on the outside of the cabinet wall to indicate the location of the centers of the glide mounts. Drill pilot holes on these lines through the cabinet wall and into the glide mounts. Screw the mounts securely to the cabinet. Remove the wood props, then remove the bin from the cabinet by lifting the glides out of their casings.

If the cabinet you are modifying is not free-standing, you will have to install the glides from the inside. Position the bin as shown and mark locations for the glides on the front edge of the cabinet frame. Remove the bin, then extend the lines along the inside cabinet wall. Center the wood mounts on these lines and screw them to the cabinet wall from the inside.

9 **Assembling the left-hand bin.** Apply glue to the ends of the bottom piece and slip them into the dadoes in the front and back pieces. Position the bottom so its edges extend ¼ inch into the cutouts on both sides of the front and back. Clamp the pieces together with corner clamps and drive nails through the front and back into the bottom. After the glue has dried, remove the clamps and apply glue to the edges of the bottom piece and to the bottom cutouts on the front and back pieces. Position the bottom rails and nail them to the front, back and bottom.

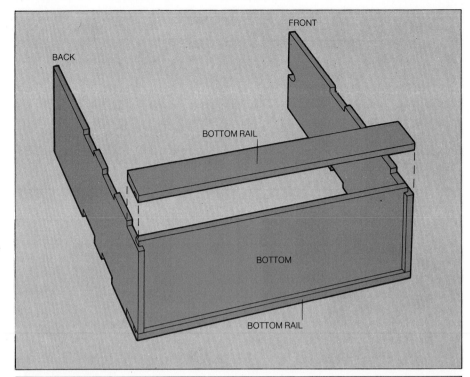

10 **Installing partition and supports.** Apply glue to one end of each long support and slip them into the dado in the vertical partition. Position the supports so their outer edges are flush with the edges of the partition. Clamp the pieces together with corner clamps and drive nails through the partition into the supports. Apply glue to the other ends of the supports and the bottom edge of the partition. Set the support-and-partition assembly into the bin so that the supports fit firmly in the dado on the front, and the edges are flush with the edges of the cutouts. Then drive nails through the front into the supports, and through the bottom into the partition.

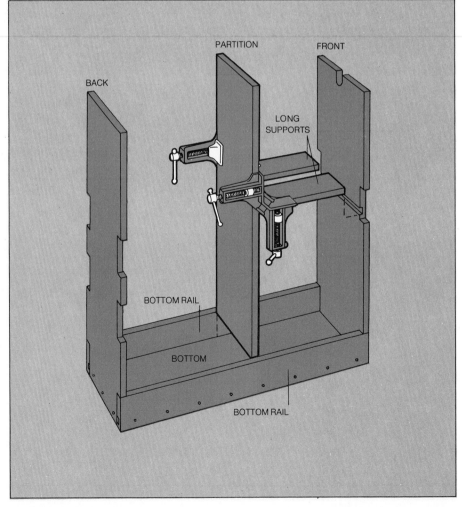

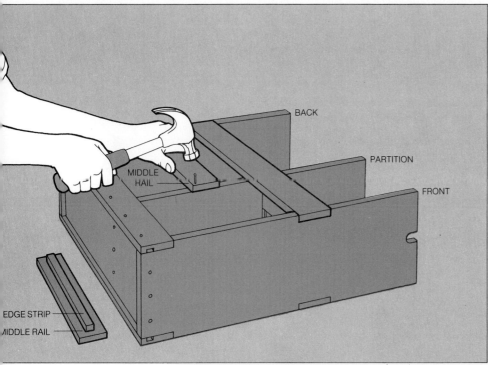

BACK

PARTITION

FRONT

MIDDLE
RAIL

EDGE STRIP

MIDDLE RAIL

11 **Installing the top and middle rails.** Glue and nail the top rails to the top cutouts on the front and back pieces. Glue and nail the ledge strips to the short middle rails, positioning the strips in the center of the rails and parallel to the sides (drawing). Use ¾-inch nails. Apply glue to the middle cutouts on the back and set the middle rails into the cutouts with the ledge strips facing inward. Nail the rails to the partition and the back.

12 **Completing the left-hand bin.** Slip the short supports down inside the bin so they rest on the ledge strips. (They may be glued in place or left loose to accommodate different-sized utensils.) Attach drawer-glide assemblies to the bottom and top rails of the bin and the cabinet wall, and install the bin following the instructions for the right-hand bin (Steps 5 through 8).

If the cabinet that you are modifying is not a freestanding one, follow the alternate procedure for mounting the glides given in Step 8.

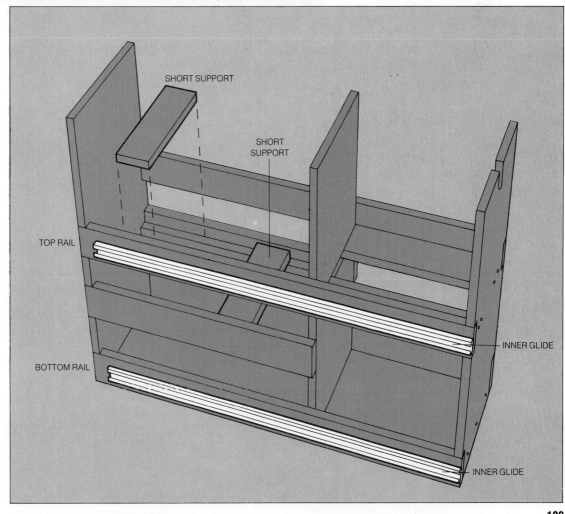

SHORT SUPPORT

SHORT
SUPPORT

TOP RAIL

INNER GLIDE

BOTTOM RAIL

INNER GLIDE

Traveling Platforms for Unfinished Attics

An attic is far too valuable as storage space to be left unused merely because it has an unfinished floor or a roof so low as to make it little more than crawl space. Putting in flooring is an expensive, time-consuming, uncomfortable job that will solve your storage problem only if your attic is high enough for you to stand in. You can also lay down plywood panels around the trap door to provide a make-shift storage area.

But a more efficient solution may be to put together trains of movable platforms, such as the ones shown below, that can give you access even to the space at the ends of the attic. Once you have installed the train tracks, you need never crawl along the attic again. The trains are ideal for use in long, low-roofed attics where the location of the trap-door opening permits them to be several cars long. They may be less effective where space is limited—or where all the available space is within easy reach of the trap-door opening without the use of trains.

Each plywood platform is really a miniature flatcar that runs back and forth on casters along 2-by-4-inch wooden tracks laid at right angles across the joists—the horizontal structural beams in the attic. When you nail the tracks to the joists be sure that they are parallel so the platforms will move smoothly. A clothesline pulley draws each platform past the trap door for loading and unloading. The cars are hitched together with heavy-duty hooks and eyes. Rails around the platform edges keep the cargo in place.

The width of the platform units will be largely determined by the spacing between the tracks. Do not set the tracks so wide apart that you will have difficulty in reaching the far side of a platform (a 15-to-20-inch spacing is generally advisable). Before building the platforms, measure the attic trap-door opening to be sure that the finished platforms will fit through it. The amount of wood you need depends on the size and number of platforms you build; your only limitation is the size and shape of your attic.

Providing for maximum storage. Usable attic space can be maximized by building two trains of storage platforms, one on each side of the trap door. For easy loading and unloading, you must be able to pull the cars to within reach of the trap-door opening; therefore, each train should be not much longer than half the length of the attic.

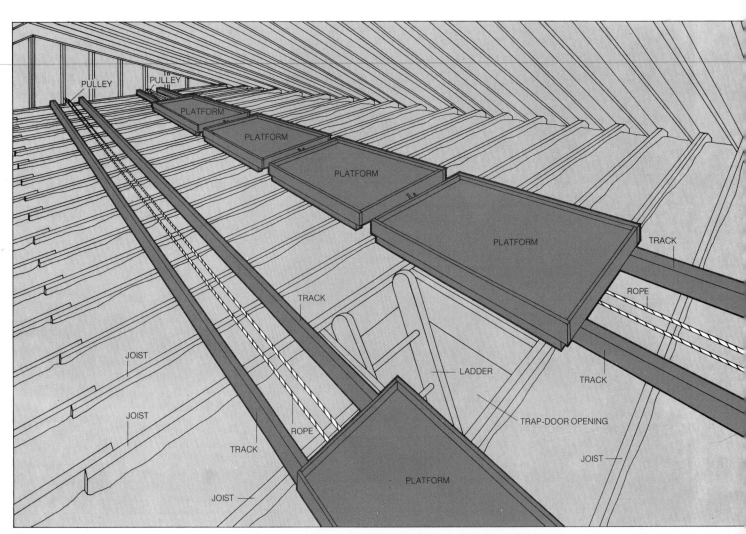

Constructing the platforms. The positions of the parts that make up a platform and the sizes of wood recommended are shown in a head-on view *(below)* and from underneath *(right)*. Fixed casters—not the swiveling type—are used for both the weight-bearing wheels attached to each platform bottom and for the rollers attached to the guide rails that stabilize the platform on the tracks. Remember to allow for the height of the casters you have selected when calculating measurements for the platforms. The pulley rope should be anchored securely to the platform bases of both the front and rear cars of each train.

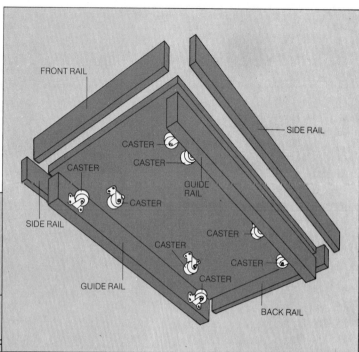

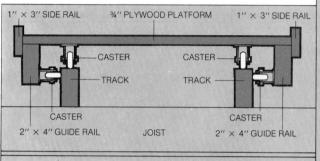

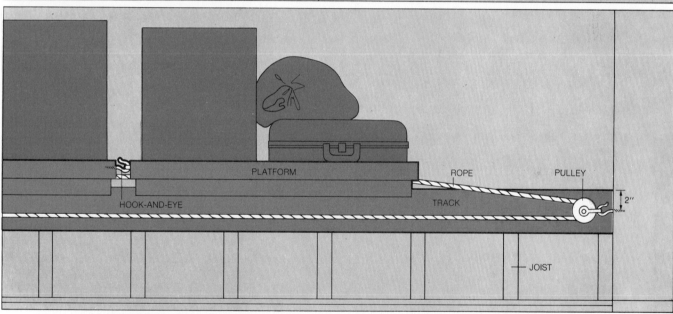

Installing the pulleys. For each storage train, clothesline pulleys should be screwed into beams at opposite ends of the attic, about 2 inches below the top level of the tracks. If there are no beams to which the pulleys can be conveniently attached, nail lengths of 2-by-4-inch beams between the track ends and screw the pulleys into them. Run a single length of clothesline through one of the pulleys and then through the other pulley; tie the ends together to form a loop and leave the knot in the center of the attic where it will be concealed under one of the platforms. If the knotted part of the rope is left too close to a pulley it could become jammed when the train is moved. Put the first, fully assembled platform on the tracks and fasten the looped rope directly to the bottom of the platform with a heavy-duty fencing staple or nail. Link the middle cars together with hooks and eyes; they need not be attached to the rope. Finish by fastening a second point on the pulley to the car at the other end of the train.

Roll-Out Storage Bins to Fit under the Stairs

The awkward triangular space beneath cellar stairs or other open stairways does not lend itself readily to convenient use. But if storage space is at a premium in your home, three roll-out units like the ones shown below can turn the below-stairs area into an efficient repository for many things that clutter up your home.

The tallest unit slides into a framework of 2-by-4-inch lumber beneath the high end of the stairs; the unit is designed to store cleaning equipment such as brooms, mops and floor polishers. The middle unit is shorter but wider and provides shelves to hold cans, bottles, tools, linens or whatever. A small bin, handy for holding kindling, foot gear, toys or sports equipment, completes the trio. All three pieces roll on 3½-inch-high fixed casters. A strong handle of your choice should be attached to each one to help in pulling it out and maneuvering it.

The units are made entirely of ¾-inch plywood. The side pieces and the back are dadoed to hold the bottom; the side pieces are also rabbeted to hold the back. All of the shelves are held in place with wood cleats (page 48) cut from scrap pieces of plywood.

After assembly, the units can be faced with wood paneling to give them a well-finished look. If paneling is added, it should also be attached to the exposed areas of the frame that positions the tall storage unit. A small triangular panel at the lowest end of the understairs space will mask the remaining open section, which is too low to be of use.

The project was designed to utilize the space in a typical understairs area, where the stringers—the long beams supporting the stair treads—rise at a 35° angle. But since cellar stairs come in a great variety of heights, widths, lengths and angles of ascent, you will have to measure the space available under your stairs before deciding how many units you can accommodate and what size they should be. In making your calculations, follow the steps on pages 52 through 57. To duplicate the angle of ascent of your stairs, stand a plywood sheet on its end flush against the stringer and draw a line on the plywood, using the stringer's bottom edge as a guide.

If your basement stairs have treads but no risers (the vertical boards behind the treads), you will have to seal the back of the staircase to keep dust and dirt from falling through into the storage units. The easiest way is to cover the back of the staircase with a sheet of ½-inch plywood; nail it to the underside of the stringers.

Three types of roll-outs. The amount of space beneath the stairs usually is large enough to accommodate versions of the three units pictured below. The units should be designed to leave about 3 inches of lateral clearance between them, so they can be moved from under the stairs without scraping against one another. If the stairs rest on vertical supports, build your units to fit between them. The framework into which the tallest unit slides should include a pair of 2-by-4-inch beams and a pair of 2-by-4-inch guide rails running along the floor to the wall at the back of the understairs space. One of these rails also helps steer the middle unit into position. A third 2-by-4 should be added as a guide for the small bin.

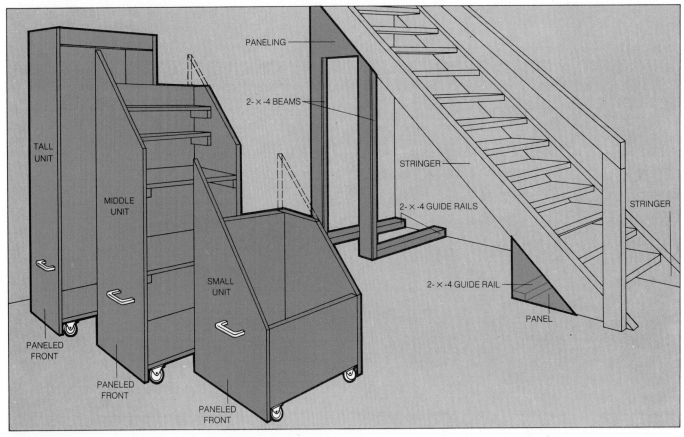

PANELING

2- × -4 BEAMS

TALL UNIT

MIDDLE UNIT

SMALL UNIT

PANELED FRONT

PANELED FRONT

PANELED FRONT

STRINGER

2- × -4 GUIDE RAILS

2- × -4 GUIDE RAIL

PANEL

STRINGER

Assembling the Units

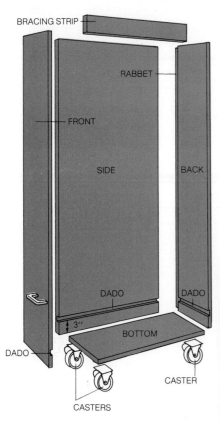

The tall unit. This storage unit is merely an oblong box with one side left open. Dadoes into which the unit's bottom is glued are ¼ inch deep and ¾ inch wide and are cut into the front, back and side pieces 3 inches above the bottom edges. This allows for ½-inch clearance between the unit and the floor when 3½-inch-high casters are attached to the bottom. Rabbets ¼ inch deep and ¾ inch wide are cut along the inside edges of the front and back to hold the side more securely. The parts are then glued together. A strip of wood across the top of the open side braces the structure at that point. Metal hooks or clips can be added to hold a variety of tall objects neatly.

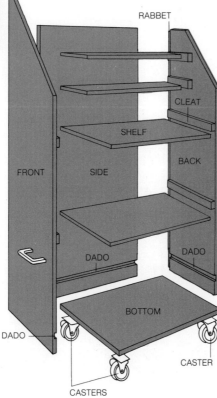

The middle unit. The front, side, back and bottom of this unit are joined with dadoes and rabbets positioned in exactly the same way as those in the tall unit and they are cut to the same depth and width. All shelves are supported by ¾-inch-by-1⅞-inch wood cleats cut from scrap plywood. (A more complicated alternative would be to install adjustable shelves, as shown on pages 46 through 48.) To place shelves at an efficient level, measure the height of items you plan to store before nailing in the cleats.

The small unit. This unit is essentially a smaller version of the middle unit, but with a closed side and no shelves. It is dadoed and rabbeted in the same way as the other units. If you require additional shelf space, the bin can be modified to take shelves like those in the middle unit.

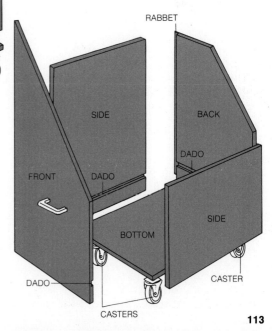

Reorganizing Closets

Closet clutter is often due less to an actual shortage of space than to wasteful design. The project on the following pages shows one way to reorganize a typical wide and shallow closet to make the most of space that now goes unused or is utilized inadequately. The interior may be sufficiently spacious: the usual sliding-door closet is 2 feet deep, 8 feet high and often 6 or more feet wide; but the standard clothes pole, 65 inches high, seems designed only for full-length coats and dresses, and 2 feet or more of valuable room under the shorter garments is left empty. The one shelf usually found above the pole is often narrow and hard to reach, so that significant space is also wasted at the top of the closet. These unused areas can be put to work; by reorganizing facilities for hanging clothes and by installing a unit consisting of drawers and a set of movable shelves, you can increase the storage capacity of the closet by as much as 50 per cent.

The first step in remodeling a clothes closet is to group your garments according to length. The longer ones should still be hung on a 65-inch-high pole. The shorter garments—such as blouses, folded slacks and sport coats—can be hung on two poles, one above the other. The space saved can be converted into a central drawer-and-shelf section for folded clothing, linens or shoes. Shelves for luggage or other seldom-used items can also be added to take advantage of the space above the clothes poles.

A more efficient clothes closet. The completed project shows how a wide, 2-foot-deep closet can be efficiently redesigned by eliminating the typical long clothes pole and shelf fixtures, and adding new storage elements. The pole has been replaced with three shorter poles: one, at right, is at the standard height for dresses and other long clothing; and two, at left, are for shorter garments, such as jackets and folded slacks.

A 24-inch-wide central storage area, combining drawers and a series of shelves, extends from floor to door height and provides 26 cubic feet of additional storage. The lower unit, 36 inches high, has two shallow and two deep drawers. The upper unit, also 36 inches high, consists of six shelves; the entire shelf unit is mounted on full-extension glides so that it can be rolled out for easy access from the sides. Additional shelving for bulky or less frequently used items is provided on top of the central structure and over the right-hand clothes pole. To allow full access, sliding doors have been replaced with bifold doors.

Many closets are fitted with sliding doors that overlap when opened, so that only half the closet is accessible at one time. By removing such doors and replacing them with accordion-type folding doors or with plain or louvered bifold doors, the interior can be made completely accessible. The new doors, which are available to fit all standard-sized closet openings, should be added before a drawer-and-shelf unit is built; otherwise it may be difficult to install the overhead track necessary for folding doors.

The project described here can be varied to suit either a smaller closet or a smaller budget. The storage unit illustrated, 24 inches wide, is designed for closets 6 feet or more in width, but smaller closets can be reorganized by building a narrower stack of drawers and shelves. Or you can simply divide the closet with a central panel, placing a 65-inch-high clothes pole on one side of the panel and two poles for short clothes, one above the other, on the other side.

The parts of the drawer-and-shelf unit that will be exposed to view can be built of hardwood plywood (such as birch) if you plan to apply a stain or oil finish, but a less expensive softwood plywood can be used throughout if you plan to paint the completed unit.

Using the techniques explained here and elsewhere in this volume, you can imaginatively redesign other closets for specialized uses. The office/hobby center below is just one alternative suggestion. However, by adding pegboard, and shelves and other fittings, any utility, linen or pantry closet can be modified to accommodate more items in a more convenient and easily accessible manner.

Shopping List for the Clothes Closet

1 sheet A-B softwood veneer-core plywood, ¾" × 4' × 8'
1 sheet A-2 hardwood veneer-core plywood, ¾" × 4' × 8'
1 sheet A-2 hardwood veneer-core plywood, ⅜" × 4' × 8'
1 sheet A-2 hardwood veneer-core plywood, ¼" × 4' × 8'
1 length select A softwood, 1" × 2" × 6'
1 length select A softwood, 1" × 2" × 8'
2 lengths select A softwood, ½" × 6" × 8'
2 lengths select A softwood, ½" × 10" × 8'
4 pairs 22" full-extension drawer-glide assemblies, 50-pound capacity
1 pair 22" full-extension drawer-glide assemblies, 100-pound capacity
8 drawer pulls

3 pairs pole sockets, 1" diameter
3 lengths chrome-steel tubing, cut to appropriate closet width
¼ pound finishing nails, 1½"
½ pound finishing nails, 1"
50 No. 6 flathead wood screws, 1¼"
12 ounces white glue
4 ounces contact cement
4 ounces powdered wood putty
2 rolls 1" × 8' veneer tape to match ¾" softwood plywood
2 rolls 1" × 8' veneer tape to match ¾" hardwood plywood
5 sheets 120-grit abrasive paper
2 sheets 280-grit abrasive paper
1 pair bifold doors and matching door track (only to replace sliding doors)

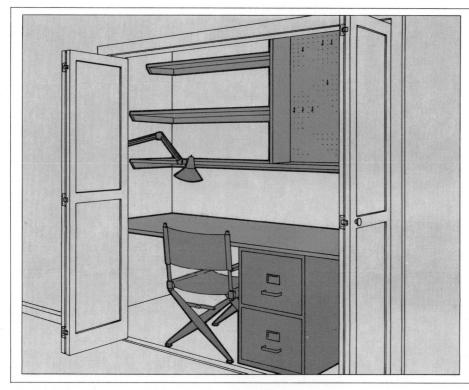

An Alternate Design

A spare closet whose dimensions are similar to the one at left can be readily converted into a home study, office or hobby center. The desk, which is a standard 29 inches high, is made by cutting a sheet of plywood to size, covering the surface with plastic laminate (page 94) and mounting the plywood top on 1-by-6-inch wood cleats attached to the closet's back and side walls. A ready-made filing cabinet serves both for storage and as a brace for the desk top. Deep overhead shelves are mounted on 1-by-2-inch wood cleats (as shown) or with adjustable standards and brackets (pages 46-47); the highest shelf is less deep to afford access. Pegboard, spaced away from the back of the closet by a frame of ¾-inch-square molding, provides additional room to hang miscellaneous items. An adjustable reading lamp is mounted on the side wall.

Cutting Diagrams

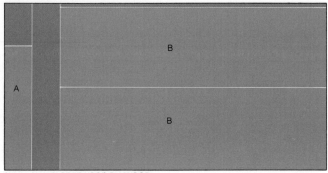

¾″ × 4′ × 8′ SOFTWOOD PLYWOOD

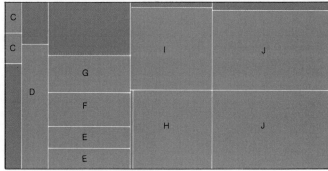

¾″ × 4′ × 8′ HARDWOOD PLYWOOD

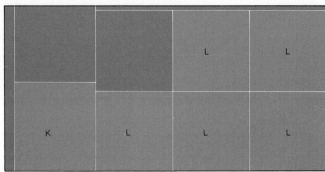

⅜″ × 4′ × 8′ HARDWOOD PLYWOOD

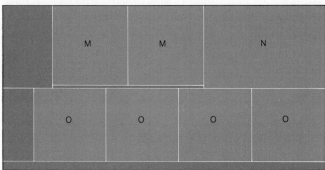

¼″ × 4′ × 8′ HARDWOOD PLYWOOD

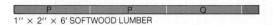

1″ × 2″ × 6′ SOFTWOOD LUMBER

1″ × 2″ × 8′ SOFTWOOD LUMBER

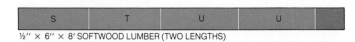

½″ × 6″ × 8′ SOFTWOOD LUMBER (TWO LENGTHS)

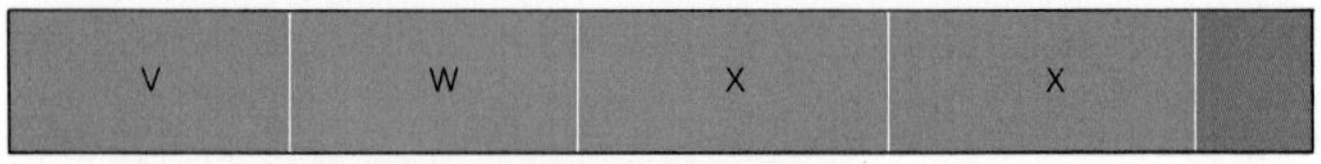

½″ × 10″ × 8′ SOFTWOOD LUMBER (TWO LENGTHS)

Making the basic cuts. Names and dimensions of all the plywood and lumber parts are given in the key below, and are identified by corresponding letters on the cutting diagrams. As each piece is cut, attach masking tape to it and mark the tape with the letter designation of the piece. The scrap pieces, identified by dark shading in the cutting diagrams, can be used for extra shelving, and as guides for the circular saw and router.

A| back shelf support, 8″ × 36″
B| side panels (two pieces), 23¼″ × 80″
C| shelf-unit false front (two pieces), 4″ × 8¾″
D| front shelf support, 8″ × 36″
E| false drawer front (two pieces), 6⅛″ × 24″
F| false drawer front, 9⅞″ × 24″
G| false drawer front, 10⅝″ × 24″
H| drawer-unit bottom, 23¼″ × 23″
I| drawer-unit top, 24″ × 23¾″
J| drawer-unit sides (two pieces), 23″ × 35¼″
K| central-structure top, 25½″ × 23¼″
L| shelf-unit shelves (five pieces), 23″ × 23¼″
M| top and bottom of shelf-unit base (two pieces),
    23″ × 22½″
N| drawer-unit back, 24″ × 36″
O| drawer bottoms (four pieces),
    21″ × 21¾″
P| side pieces for shelf-unit base (two pieces),
    1″ × 2″ × 22½″
Q| brace for shelf supports, 1″ × 2″ × 22½″
R| cross pieces for shelf-unit base (four pieces),
    1″ × 2″ × 21½″
S| shallow-drawer fronts (two pieces),
    ½″ × 6″ × 21″
T| shallow-drawer backs (two pieces),
    ½″ × 6″ × 21″
U| shallow-drawer sides (four pieces),
    ½″ × 6″ × 22¾″
V| deep-drawer fronts (two pieces), ½″ × 10″ × 21″
W| deep-drawer backs (two pieces), ½″ × 10″ × 21″
X| deep-drawer sides (four pieces),
    ½″ × 10″ × 22¾″

Routing Diagrams

1 Routing the drawer parts. Sort the drawer parts into fronts, backs and sides, and then separate the sides into left and right pieces. To avoid confusion while cutting, mark the inner surface of each part to indicate the top and bottom edge, and also mark the sides to indicate the front and back edges. A half inch from the bottom edge of each front, back and side piece, rout a horizontal dado ¼ inch wide and ¼ inch deep. (For routing techniques, see pages 26 and 27.) A half inch from the back edge of each side piece, rout a vertical dado ½ inch wide and ¼ inch deep. At the front edge of each side piece, rout a vertical rabbet ½ inch wide and ¼ inch deep.

2 Routing the shelf supports. Place the two shelf supports on the work surface, butted together side by side, with their inner surfaces up. Carefully align their top and bottom edges, and fix them to the work surface with C clamps. To indicate where the dadoes will be cut, locate five points on the surface of each support; the distance of each point from the bottom edge is indicated in the drawing (below). At each point, use a combination square and an awl to scratch lines across each shelf support. Rout a dado ⅜ inch wide and ⅜ inch deep, positioning the router so that the bottom edge of each dado is flush with each scratch line.

3 Routing the drawer-unit sides. The bottom of the drawer-unit should be positioned 2 inches above floor level so that the bottom drawer will clear the closet door sill when the drawer is opened. To mark positions for dadoes in the drawer-unit bottom, place both drawer-unit sides on a flat surface, measure 2 inches from the bottom edge of each and make awl marks across each side. Then rout a dado ¾ inch wide and ⅜ inch deep along each mark.

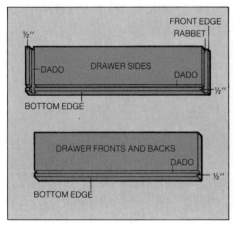

FRONT EDGE
RABBET
½″
DADO   DRAWER SIDES   DADO
½″
BOTTOM EDGE

DRAWER FRONTS AND BACKS
DADO
½″
BOTTOM EDGE

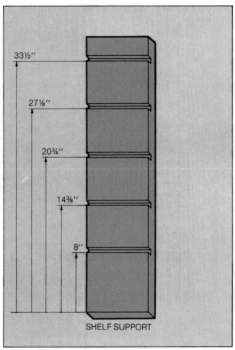

33½″
27⅛″
20¾″
14⅜″
8″
SHELF SUPPORT

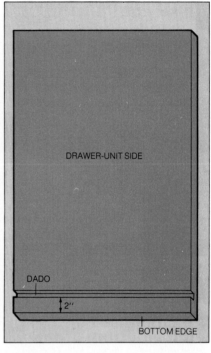

DRAWER-UNIT SIDE
DADO
2″
BOTTOM EDGE

Building the Drawer Unit

1 Assembling the drawers. Sort the drawer parts into two identical sets for the smaller two 6-inch-deep drawers (left and right sides, fronts, backs and bottoms), and into two other sets for the two 10-inch-deep drawers. Assemble the drawers, following the instructions in Steps 1 through 3 on pages 28 and 29. Glue the drawer bottoms in the horizontal dadoes and use glue and 1-inch finishing nails to strengthen the vertical dado and rabbet joints. Finally, attach a set of 50-pound-capacity inner glides to the sides of each drawer, as shown in Step 3 on page 30.

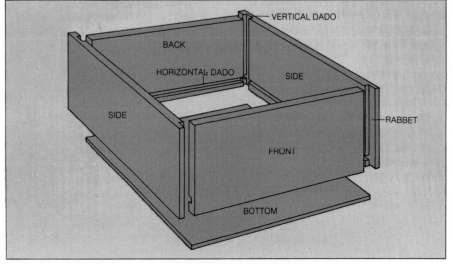

VERTICAL DADO
BACK
HORIZONTAL DADO
SIDE
SIDE
RABBET
FRONT
BOTTOM

2 **Measuring for glide assemblies.** Place the two drawer-unit sides on a flat surface with their inside surfaces up and their front edges butting. Align both sides exactly at the top and bottom and at the dado. Hook a measuring tape in the dado and extend the tape along the butted edges. To locate the positions of the glide-assembly outer casings, scratch awl marks across both butted edges (drawing) at the following measurements, starting from the dado: ¼ inch, 10¼ inches, 20¼ inches and 26½ inches. Lift one side piece and reposition it so that the back edges butt. Repeat the marking procedure. Finally, join all scratch marks across the sides.

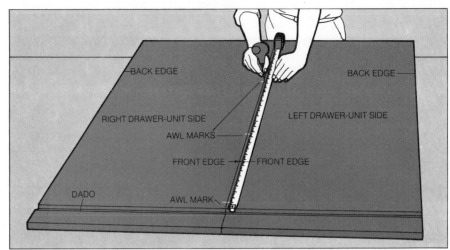

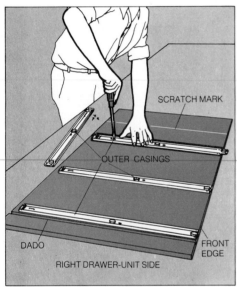

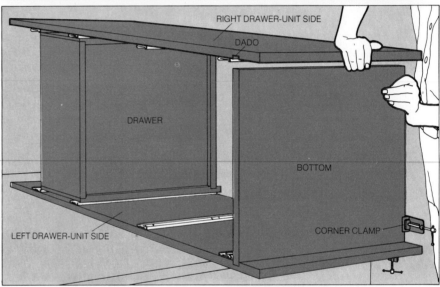

3 **Attaching the outer casings.** Sort the outer casings of the 50-pound-capacity drawer-glide assemblies into left- and right-hand units. Place a right-hand casing on the right side piece; the bottom edge of the casing should be flush with the ¼-inch mark made in Step 2, and the front end of the casing should be flush with the front edge of the side piece. Make awl marks for the mounting screws; remove the casing and drill shallow pilot holes. Place the casing in position and secure it with the screws. Repeat this procedure for the three other right-hand casings, installing them at the locations previously marked (drawing). Attach the four left-hand casings to the left side piece in the same manner.

4 **Assembling the sides and bottom.** After dry-fitting, apply glue to the dadoes in both side pieces and to the side edges of the drawer-unit bottom. Insert the bottom into the dado in the left side piece and place a corner clamp on the lower rear joint. Put the second drawer from the top in position by inserting the drawer's inner glide into the corresponding outer casing on the left side piece. With a helper to align the right-hand glide assembly, slide the right side piece into position on the corresponding inner glide. Using the drawer as a support, position the dado in the right side piece over the bottom and press the side into position (drawing). Place another corner clamp on the upper rear joint.

5 **Fastening the sides.** With the corner clamps and drawer still in place, make three awl marks for screw holes on the right side piece centered over the dado. Using a No. 6 counterbore bit, drill pilot holes through the side and into the bottom; fasten the side with three 1¼-inch flathead screws. Turn the drawer unit over, taking care that the drawer does not slide out. Mark, drill and fasten the left side piece in the same manner.

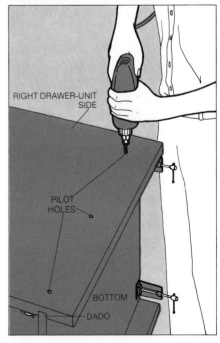

6 Attaching the top. Stand the drawer unit upright and apply glue to the top edges of the side pieces. Place the top in position by aligning its back edge flush with the rear corners, but leaving a ¾-inch overhang in front. Place clamps in the top rear corners. Mark and drill four evenly spaced pilot holes through the top and into the side pieces. Fasten the top with 1¼-inch countersunk screws. Fill all screw holes on the sides and top with wood putty and sand smooth, following instructions on page 16 (*Steps 11 and 12*).

7 Adding the back. Remove the drawer and all corner clamps. Place the drawer unit face down on the worktable as shown. Measure 2⅜ inches from the bottom edge of the back piece and make a scratch mark across the width of the back to locate the center line of the bottom piece. Apply glue to the inner edges of the back piece and to the rear edges of the side, top and bottom pieces. Place the back in position and fasten it with 1-inch finishing nails; nail the corners first, then add nails 5½ inches apart around the edges.

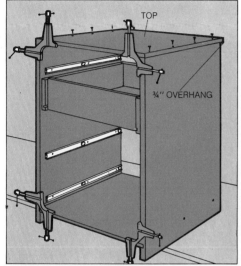

TOP

¾" OVERHANG

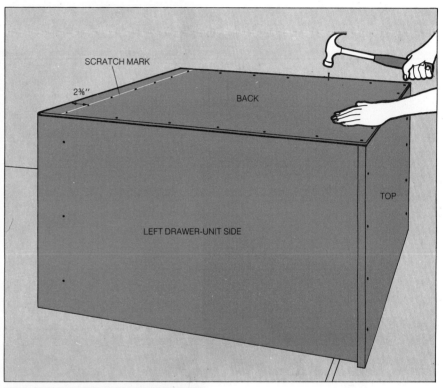

SCRATCH MARK

2⅜"

BACK

LEFT DRAWER-UNIT SIDE

TOP

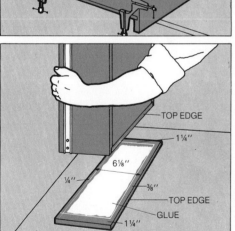

TOP EDGE

1¼"

6⅛"

¼"

⅜"

TOP EDGE

GLUE

1¼"

8 Gluing the false fronts. Place a 6⅛-inch-wide false drawer front face down and outline a rectangle on its back as follows: mark a line 1¼ inches in from each side edge, a line ⅜ inch in from the top edge and another line ¼ inch in from the bottom edge. Mark the other three false fronts in the same manner but, for the line at the bottom edge of the 10⅝-inch-wide front piece, measure in 1 inch instead of ¼ inch, so that when this front is attached to the lowest drawer it will extend down over the front edge of the cabinet bottom. Apply glue to the front of the top drawer and also to the area within the rectangle marked on the 6⅛-inch-wide false front. Place the drawer on the false front as shown in the drawing above, aligning it with all sides of the rectangle formed by the scratch marks. (Make sure that the top edge of the drawer is on the ⅜-inch line.)

9 Securing the false fronts. When the glue has become just tacky enough to hold the false front in place on the top drawer, slide the drawer into the outer-glide casings previously attached to the side pieces. Make sure that the overlapping side edges of the false front are flush with the sides of the drawer unit and that there is a ⅛-inch clearance between the false front and the top of the drawer unit. If necessary, adjust the alignment by carefully sliding the false front on its film of glue (drawing). Remove the drawer and fasten the front to it with screws (*page 32, Step 2*).

Position and fasten the other false fronts as follows: the remaining 6⅛-inch front on the second drawer from the top, the 9⅞-inch front on the third drawer, and the 10⅝-inch front on the bottom drawer. Check for a ⅛-inch clearance between the top and bottom of each front before fastening it. Attach drawer pulls to all drawers (*page 32*). Using contact cement, apply veneer tape (*page 77*) to the front edge of the cabinet top and to the side edges of the false fronts.

Building the Shelf Unit

1 **Assembling the base.** To make the 22½-by-23-inch frame for the base, butt the four 21½-inch crosspieces against the 22½-inch side pieces of the base at 6½-inch intervals. Use glue, 1½-inch finishing nails and corner clamps to secure the joints, as shown in Steps 1-7 on pages 12 through 14. Next, position the 23-by-22½-inch plywood bottom and top pieces (drawing) and attach them to the frame with glue and 1-inch finishing nails. Then attach the inner glides of the 100-pound-capacity assemblies to the 22½-inch side pieces, as explained in Step 3 on page 30.

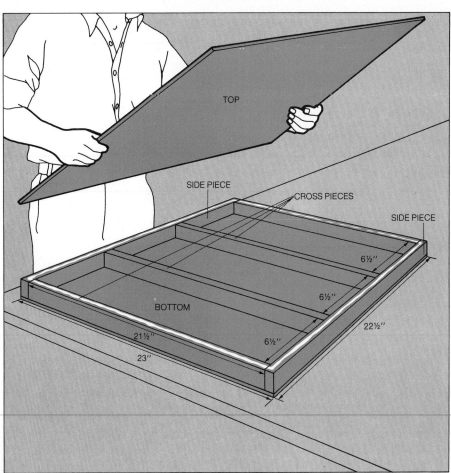

2 **Positioning the first shelf support.** In the lower front corners of the front shelf support make awl marks for four screw holes at the locations shown. To center the support on the base, measure in 7½ inches from each corner of the base and mark with the awl. Apply glue between these marks, and to the corresponding area on the grooved side of the support. Place the support between the marks. To be sure the shelves will be level when installed in the dadoes in both supports, the supports must be perfectly square with the base; while the glue is still tacky, check the front support with a combination square (drawing, below). If necessary, realign the support and keep it true with cardboard shims between the worktable and the bottom edge of the support.

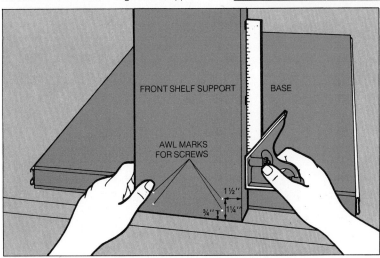

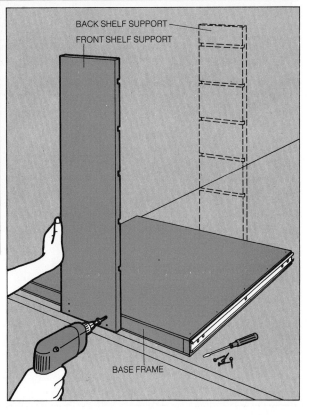

3 **Attaching the two supports.** Hold the front shelf support firmly in the squared position. With a No. 6 counterbore bit, drill pilot holes through the four marks in the support and into the base frame. Use 1¼-inch flathead screws to fasten the support to the base. Turn the base around. Position, square up and attach the back shelf support, following the same procedure as for the front support. Fill all countersunk screw holes with wood putty, and sand them smooth.

4 **Installing the shelves.** Stack together the five 23-by-23¼-inch shelves. On both of the 23-inch edges of the uppermost shelf, make an awl mark 7½ inches in from each corner. Extend these marks down the edges of the other shelves. Starting with the bottom shelf, apply glue between the marks on both edges and slide each shelf into the dadoes in the shelf supports (do not apply glue to the dadoes themselves; the glue would be pushed out and smeared as the shelves are inserted). In the same manner, install the other shelves in ascending order.

Before you insert the fourth shelf, attach the 22½-inch-long 1-by-2 cut previously (page 116) to the underside of the shelf to act as a brace for the unit. Center the brace between the awl marks, and ⅜ inch in from the edges. Glue and nail the shelf to the brace with 1-inch finishing nails. Slide the shelf into its dadoes, then mark both supports 3¾ inches from each side edge and ⅜ inch below the bottom edges of the dadoes. Drill countersunk pilot holes at these points into the brace. Then fasten the supports to the brace with 1¼-inch-long No. 6 screws.

If a shelf does not slide freely into place, use a piece of scrap wood and a hammer to tap it gently into position (drawing).

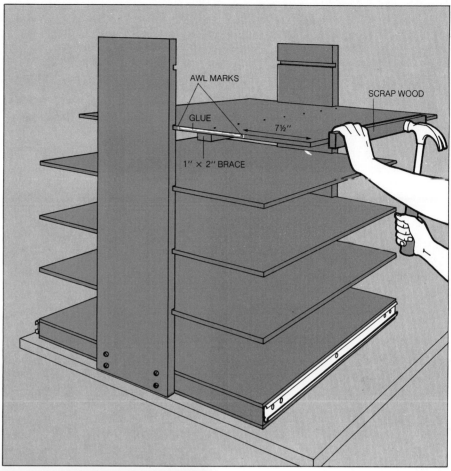

AWL MARKS

GLUE

7½"

SCRAP WOOD

1" × 2" BRACE

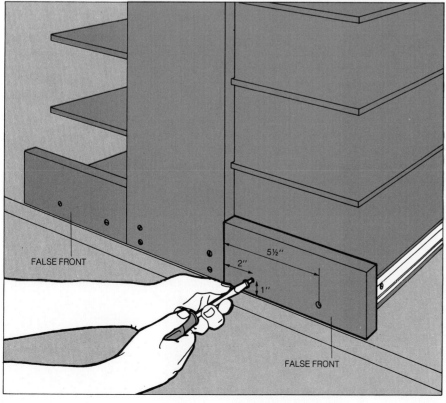

FALSE FRONT

5½"

2"

1"

FALSE FRONT

5 **Adding false fronts.** The two false-front pieces for the shelf unit serve as handles for pulling out the unit and as stops when it is pushed back in. With an awl, mark each false-front piece for two screw holes at the points indicated. Butt the pieces against the front shelf support, with the bottom of each false front flush with the bottom of the base; check for a tight, even fit. Apply glue to the false fronts and base; let the glue get tacky so it will help hold the fronts in place. Drill the marked pilot holes through the front pieces and into the base, using a No. 6 counterbore bit. Attach each false front with two 1¼-inch flathead screws. Fill the countersunk screw holes with wood putty, and sand smooth.

Installing the Storage Unit

1 Preparing the side panels. Apply veneer tape to the front edges of both side panels with contact cement. Place both panels flat with their inner surfaces facing up. Measure up 36½ inches from the bottom edge of each panel and at that point scratch an awl line across each panel. Position the 100-pound-capacity outer-glide casings on the panels, with the bottom edges of the casings flush with the scratch lines, and their front edges flush with the front edges of the panels (drawing), then screw the casings in place.

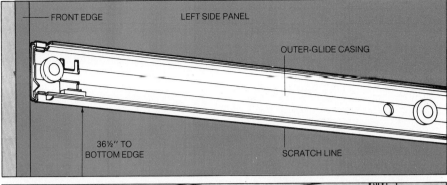

FRONT EDGE — LEFT SIDE PANEL

OUTER-GLIDE CASING

36½" TO BOTTOM EDGE

SCRATCH LINE

2 Fastening the panels. On the outer surfaces of both side panels mark positions for screws as follows: two screws 9 inches from the bottom of each panel and 6 inches from each edge; one screw 18 inches from the bottom and centered in each panel; two screws 27 inches from the bottom of each panel and 6 inches from each edge.

Since it would be difficult to get the bulky panels into the closet after the cabinet is positioned, move the panels into the closet now, leaning them against the end walls. Install the drawer unit, centering it on the closet floor. Place the right panel against the right side of the drawer unit, aligning the front edge flush with the front edge of the unit's side. Clamp the two together with hand screws. Drill countersunk pilot holes at the points previously marked, and fasten the panel with five 1¼-inch screws (drawing). Position and attach the left panel in the same manner.

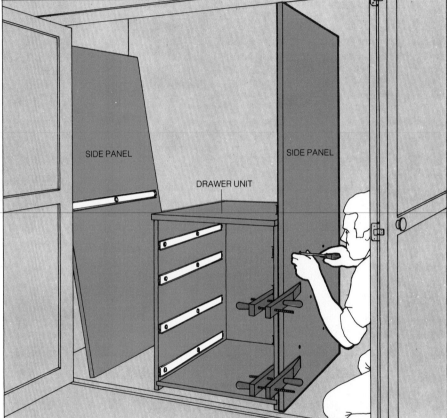

SIDE PANEL

SIDE PANEL

DRAWER UNIT

3 Attaching the top. Standing on a chair or stepladder, apply glue to the top edges of the side panels of the storage section, and to the corresponding edges of the top. Place the top in position and fasten it with four 1½-inch finishing nails on each side (drawing). Slide the drawers onto their outer casings. With a helper, complete the storage section by sliding the entire shelf unit onto its outer casings on the side panels.

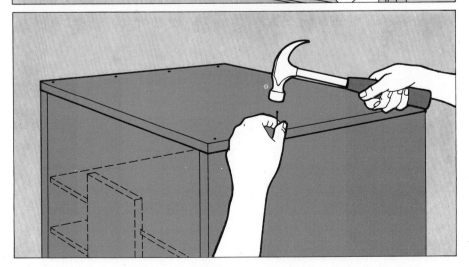

OPEN-END
SOCKET

75"

OPEN-END
SOCKET

39"

SIDE
PANEL

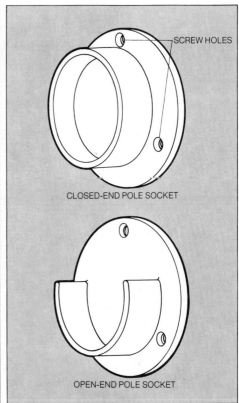

SCREW HOLES

CLOSED-END POLE SOCKET

OPEN-END POLE SOCKET

4 **Installing clothes poles.** With an awl, mark two points in the center of the left side panel: make one mark 39 inches and the other 75 inches from the floor. Mark the closet wall facing the panel the same way. Screw two closed-end pole sockets to the wall at the points marked, and two open-end sockets to the panel (drawing). Measure the distance between wall and panel, and cut two clothes poles of chrome-steel tubing, each ¼ inch shorter than that measurement. Insert an end of each pole into a closed-end socket and drop the other end into the opposite open-end socket. Follow the same procedure to install the single clothes pole in the right side of the closet, but position it at a height of 65 inches.

1" × 2" × 12"
CLEAT

12"-DEEP
SHELF

5 **Additional shelving.** An extra shelf mounted on cleats goes over the single clothes pole at the right of the central storage section. Remove the pole from its sockets and attach a 1-by-2-inch wood cleat 12 inches long to the closet wall (refer to the charts on pages 42 and 43 for the correct wall fastener), and about 2 inches above the sockets. Attach another cleat at the same height on the facing side panel. Cut the shelf from ¾-inch plywood scrap; make it the same length as the clothes pole and 12 inches deep. Another shelf can be installed the same way over the top pole on the left side of the central section.

Picture Credits

The sources for the illustrations in this book are shown below. Credits from left to right are separated by semicolons, from top to bottom by dashes.
Cover—Ken Kay. 6, 10, 11—Henry Groskinsky. 12 through 16—Drawings by Ron Jones. 17, 18—Drawing by Fred Wolff. 19 through 24—Drawings by Peter Trojan. 25—Drawings by Gerry Contreras. 26, 27—Drawings by Dale Gustafson. 28 through 32—Drawings by Ron Jones. 33 through 39—Drawings by Adolph E. Brotman. 40, 41—Drawings by Vantage Art, Inc. 42 through 49—Drawings by Dana Rasmussen. 50—Henry Groskinsky. 52—Drawings by Dana Rasmussen. 55 through 57—Drawings by Vantage Art, Inc. 60—Drawings by Vantage Art, Inc. 62 through 65—Drawings by Dale Gustafson. 66—Ken Kay. 68 through 73—Drawings by Lennart Johnson Designs. 74, 75—Drawings by Dale Gustafson. 77 through 83—Drawings by Dale Gustafson. 84 through 89—Drawings by Vantage Art, Inc. 90 through 97—Drawings by Adolph E. Brotman. 98, 99—Drawings by Kurt Ortell. 100, 101—Drawings by Peter McGinn. 102, 103—Drawings by Vantage Art, Inc. 104, 105—Drawings by Dale Gustafson. 106, 107—Drawings by Whitman Studio, Inc. 108, 109—Drawings by Dale Gustafson. 110 through 113—Drawings by Kurt Ortell. 114 through 123—Drawings by Whitman Studio, Inc.

Acknowledgments

For their help in the preparation of this book the editors thank the following individuals: Merlin Blais, Manager, Product Publicity, Western Wood Products Association, Portland, Ore.; Christine Donovan, Design Research, Inc., New York City; Durand Harootunian and Sons, Inc., New York City; Ronnie Jaffe, Tech Hi Fi, New York City; Michael Kallman, Skiltech, New York City; Clark McDonald, Managing Director, Hardwood Plywood Manufacturers Association, Arlington, Va., Benjamin Boyd, Allen Fletcher, Arnold S. Silver, Barney Silver, W. H. Silver's Hardware, Inc., New York City; American Plywood Association, Tacoma, Wash.; National Forest Products Association, Washington, D.C.

Index/Glossary